SHAKESPEARE'S BIBLICAL KNOWLEDGE

SHAKESPEARE'S
BIBLICAL KNOWLEDGE

AND

USE OF THE BOOK OF COMMON PRAYER

AS EXEMPLIFIED IN THE PLAYS OF THE FIRST FOLIO

BY

RICHMOND NOBLE

AUTHOR OF "SHAKESPEARE'S USE OF SONG"

1970

OCTAGON BOOKS

New York

First published in 1935
by the Society for Promoting Christian Knowledge

Reprinted 1970
by special arrangement with the Society for Promoting Christian Knowledge

Second Octagon printing 1977

OCTAGON BOOKS
A DIVISION OF FARRAR, STRAUS & GIROUX, INC.
19 Union Square West
New York, N.Y. 10003

LIBRARY OF CONGRESS CATALOG CARD NUMBER: 78-111329
ISBN 0-374-96115-8

Manufactured by Braun-Brumfield, Inc.
Ann Arbor, Michigan
Printed in the United States of America

PREFACE

THE object of the study represented in these pages has been the collection of evidence to enable an estimate to be formed of the extent of Shakespeare's acquaintance with the English Bible and the Book of Common Prayer. Principally it differs from previous studies of the kind in that an exhaustive search of Tudor printed versions of Scripture has been made. All Tudor versions have been examined, but attention has been concentrated most on those in active circulation in Shakespeare's lifetime. It is hoped that by this means the versions actually used by Shakespeare have been distinguished.

The project to make the inquiry took its first definite shape at the urgent request of Mr. Peter Alexander. He had been annoyed by confident assumptions made by several who had relied on inspiration rather than on knowledge for their generalizations. I was encouraged by the generosity of the University of Liverpool. The Senate of that University decided to recognize the subject as important and awarded me the William Noble Fellowship for 1933-4. Apart from the financial benefit accruing to me, which enabled me to purchase expensive Bibles more freely than I otherwise should have done, the action of the University had other advantages for me. By its association with the work, its seal was set on the purely academic character of the research and I was relieved from the suspicion which almost inevitably attaches to undertakings of the kind.

For the information of those unfamiliar with the use of the Church of England, references to the Book of Common Prayer have been made with greater amplitude than some may think necessary.

As no authentic text exists for *Pericles*, it was deemed inadvisable to include that play.

I have made free use of the Shakespearian Variorum editions. Although I have rejected most of the examples advanced by Bishop Wordsworth and Dr. Carter, I am

under deep obligation to them both. Dr. Carter added
to my obligation by his generous permission to make any
use I liked of his material in spite of my frank avowal that
I was in sharp disagreement with many of his conclusions.
At one time and another, so many have interested themselves
in detecting Scriptural reminiscences in Shakespeare's
plays, that it may seem surprising that it has been possible
to add anything new. To the best of my belief about a
quarter of the instances recorded in these pages appear in
print for the first time.

Canon Henry Todd, formerly Chancellor of Armagh
Cathedral and now a Canon of St. Patrick's, Dublin—whose
knowledge of words and phrases in Shakespeare's Plays and
in the Authorised Version is probably unsurpassed by that
of any man living—Dr. Lowther Clarke and Mr. Peter
Alexander were kind enough to read through my manuscript.
I am indebted to them for many valuable suggestions.

I should like also to acknowledge assistance given me by
Dr. W. R. Cunningham, the genial and learned Librarian
of Glasgow University; Dr. G. A. Michell, Principal of St.
Stephen's House, Oxford; Mr. K. G. Rendall, British Museum;
the Librarian of the British and Foreign Bible Society;
Dr. Arthur Ryan, Lecturer in Scholastic Philosophy,
Queen's University; Professor F. W. Baxter, Queen's University; Professor L. C. Martin, Liverpool University; the Dean
of Belfast; and Professor Stevenson, Glasgow University.
Dr. Dover Wilson, with characteristic generosity, sent me
advance proofs of his *Hamlet*.

From this catalogue of benefactors I must not exclude
my daughter. She prepared my MS. for the press and
accompanied me on expeditions to various libraries.
Throughout I have had the benefit of her criticism and
several times she noted instances of Scriptural and Liturgical
influence which had escaped me. Great care has been
exercised to make the quotations from Elizabethan Bibles
minutely accurate and in so far as the effort has been successful her aid has been invaluable.

EXPLANATION OF TEXTS AND ABBREVIATIONS USED

THE Shakespearian text has been constituted from the reputed *editio princeps* of each play, collated in cases of difficulty with such other editions, published not later than 1623, as afford evidence of having been in whole or in part independently derived. The spelling has been modernized and it has not been possible to retain the original punctuation, although its dramatic significance has not been overlooked. Acts, Scenes and lines are as in the Oxford Edition.

Unless otherwise stated, the text, numbering and verses of the Psalms are as in the present Book of Common Prayer. Similarly, in the absence of any mention to the contrary, the text of the other Biblical Books is as in the 1585 folio edition of the Bishops' Bible, as are also the chapter and verse numberings (the earlier editions of the Bishops' Bible are not in all cases divided in the same way). Of the other versions, unless otherwise indicated, the texts followed are: Genevan, 1596 quarto black letter; Genevan-Tomson, 1590 quarto roman letter (the Tomson text is not quoted unless specifically named); Rheims, 1841 English Hexapla reprint of 1582 text compared with the 1582 edition in the Glasgow University Collection; Great Bible, 1569 quarto in the Glasgow University Collection. Titles of Biblical Books are as in the Authorised Version.

The portions of the Book of Common Prayer unchanged since Shakespeare's time are as in the present book of the English Church. For other portions the quotations made are from a modern reprint of the Second Book of Edward VI., from the Parker Society edition of the Elizabethan Liturgies, and from the 1871 Ordnance Survey facsimile of the 1636 Book (with the manuscript alterations and additions made in 1661), all corrected by the exact reprints of the books of 1559 and 1604 in the possession of Glasgow University.

References to the Vulgate are to the ninth edition of the text edited by Dr. Valentinus Loch, Ratisbon, 1902.

Any reference to metrical versions of the Psalms is to the edition of 1587, printed by John Wolfe for the assignees of Richard Day and bound up with the Genevan-Tomson roman letter quarto of 1590. The text of the Homilies is according to the edition of 1833, published by The Prayer Book and Homily Society.

In the reproduction of sixteenth-century Biblical texts the following conventions have been pursued: With the exception of " & " for " and," abbreviating signs have been dropped in favour of writing the words in full; it has been assumed that all initial u's are v's (that they were so, in fact, in the Bishops' Bible is not always certain) and internal v's are u's; while the brackets of the Bishops' Bible have been reproduced, the italics of the Rheims, which were used to indicate quotations, and of the Genevan have been written in ordinary roman.

The following abbreviations are used to denote versions:

B=Bishops' Bible.
*B*1=Bishops' New Testament of 1568 and 1569.
*B*2=Bishops' Revised New Testament of 1572 *et seq.*
C=Great Bible (sometimes called Cranmer's).
G=Genevan Bible of 1560 *et seq.*
L=Book of Common Prayer.
R=Rheims' New Testament.
T=Tomson Revised Genevan New Testament.

CHRONOLOGY OF THE PLAYS ASSUMED

The plays have been arranged according to the following assumed order of production:

1588-9
The Comedy of Errors.

1589-90
1 King Henry VI.
King John.

1590-1
The Taming of the Shrew.
2 King Henry VI.

1591-2
3 King Henry VI.
King Richard III.

1592-3
Titus Andronicus.
Two Gentlemen of Verona.

1593-4
Love's Labour's Lost.
Romeo and Juliet

1594-5
King Richard II.
A Midsummer-Night's Dream.

1595-6
The Merchant of Venice.
1 King Henry IV.

1596-7
2 King Henry IV.
The Merry Wives of Windsor.

1597-8
King Henry V.
Much Ado About Nothing.

1598-9
Julius Cæsar.
As You Like It.

1599-1600
All's Well That Ends Well.

1600-1
Hamlet.

1601-2
Twelfth Night.

1602-3
Troilus and Cressida.

1603-4
Othello.

1604-5
Measure for Measure.

1605-6
King Lear.
Macbeth.

1606-7
Timon of Athens.

1607-8
Antony and Cleopatra.

1608-9
Coriolanus.

1609-10	1611-12
Cymbeline.	The Tempest.
1610-11	1612-13
The Winter's Tale.	King Henry VIII.

Note.—The legal and official Year commenced on March 25th, and that of the Golden Number on January 1st.   Calendars were displayed according to the latter.

TABLE OF CONTENTS

xi

CHAPTER I

TUDOR PRINTED VERSIONS OF SCRIPTURE

WILLIAM TINDALE, 1526.

In Shakespeare's time the printed Bible in English was comparatively a modern innovation; when he was born, Tindale had not been dead thirty years and Coverdale was still alive. It was as late as 1526 that William Tindale had brought out his New Testament in English. For many years Bibles had been printed abroad in vernacular translations, but none in English other than in extracts. With Tindale's New Testament commenced the history of the English Bible as we know it, and as Shakespeare knew it. We may leave on one side the Wicliffite translation of the Vulgate, and *The Golden Legend* printed by Caxton and containing considerable portions of Scriptural narrative. Perhaps the Wicliffite may have suggested to Tindale a word here and a word there, such as " hallowed " in the Lord's Prayer, but it does not appear to have exercised any perceptible influence on him and there is no evidence that Shakespeare ever saw either it or *The Golden Legend*. The first page of the story of our English Bible opens with Tindale and he predominates even in the Revised New Testament of to-day.

Tindale translated from the second and third editions of Erasmus's Greek Testament, with the brilliant German of Martin Luther in front of him and the Latin Vulgate beside him for consultation. This would be a true statement of the case. Notwithstanding his neglect of the Greek connecting participles, it is abundantly evident that he translated from Erasmus's Greek. He translated very freely and in some instances Luther's influence is apparent. Thus, in Luke iv. 5, Tindale has " and shewed hym all the kyngdoms of the erth euen in the twyncklynge of an eye "; where from the Greek or the Latin we should have expected " in an instant of time " but where Tindale has translated the German " Augenblick " that stands in Luther's text. More

important, in that it has been copied by all Anglican and
Genevan versions, including even the Revised, was his
acceptance of " natural man " from Luther in 1 Cor. ii. 14
and his rejection of the Vulgate's " animalis." Thus we
have in our English Bible the antithesis of " natural " and
" spiritual," implying a belief in human depravity. In
many places Tindale rejected both Luther and the Vulgate.

Tindale's English is rich, terse and expressive. As a
translator he had many faults, some of them more or less
to be expected since he lacked the academic training requisite in critical scholarship. But he had other faults.
He paraphrased, he introduced interpolations, and he
evinced an anti-ecclesiastical bias in an unreasonable rejection of ecclesiastical terms. Worse still, he used the text
to annoy his enemies, as when in Matt. xxviii. 11 he translated " arch-priests " as " prelates " because of the odious
way the Jewish hierarchy had acted. To be just, he modified
his anti-ecclesiastical bias in subsequent editions and he
substituted " hie priests " for prelates. The incident throws
a light on the fury he aroused in some quarters and shows
that he was not entirely blameless.

Occasionally he imitated the Religious Plays of the Middle
Ages by using terms familiar to his own time, as for instance
where he employed the English Calendar in Matt. xxvii. 62:
" The nexte daye, that foloweth good frydaye "; or in
Rev. i. 10 : " I was in the sprete on a sondaye."

In 1530, Tindale issued his Pentateuch—*Genesis* and
Numbers in black letter, and *Exodus*, *Leviticus* and *Deuteronomy* in roman. *Jonah* appeared in 1531 (a book that, like
the 1st Quarto of *Hamlet*, was long lost until discovered by
Lord Arthur Hervey, Bishop of Bath and Wells, in the
library at Irkworth). Numbers of Hebrew scholars have
expressed themselves as satisfied that Tindale's claim to
have translated from the Hebrew is true, while also admitting
the influence on him of Luther and the Vulgate. Tindale
revised his *Genesis* and issued it in 1534 in roman letter
along with the other books of the Pentateuch unrevised.

Tindale's final New Testament was that of 1535-4, known
as " G.H." (the trade mark of the publisher, Godfried van
der Haghen). This edition is the ancestor of our present
New Testament. In 1536, almost about the time Tindale
was suffering death by being strangled and burnt, his Testament was being printed in folio size in England. The New

Testament was reprinted in Edward VI.'s reign and again in Elizabeth's.

MYLES COVERDALE, 1535.

The first complete English Bible printed was that of Myles Coverdale in 1535. Coverdale shares with Tindale the paternity of the English Bible. He did not profess to translate from the Hebrew and Greek ; he frankly acknowledged that his translation was from the German and Latin. Apparently his Bible was derived from five "interpreters." His New Testament was a revision of Tindale's and he certainly consulted Tindale's Pentateuch. As for the rest, he chiefly relied upon the Zurich Bible (the German-Swiss revision of Luther), Luther, the Latin Vulgate, and the Latin version of Pagninus. Dr. Ginsburg proved conclusively that Coverdale's *Ecclesiastes* was a direct translation from the Zurich Bible.

Coverdale was the first in England to separate the Hebrew Canonical Books from those Old Testament books found in the Vulgate and the Greek Bible but not in the Hebrew. These books, accepted by the Council of Trent as canonical (with the exception of *The Prayer of Manasses* and *3rd and 4th Esdras*), are called the Apocrypha by English-speaking Protestants and are so named in all Anglican Bibles. For the sake of convenience that name is used throughout this volume. In the official Bibles of the English Church (*i.e.*, Matthew's, Great Bible, Bishops', Authorised and Revised) these books are arranged in the order found in the 1529 Zurich Bible.

Coverdale gave the first expression to that prejudice which English-speaking Reformers have developed against the books of the Apocrypha and which is the cause of their being almost unknown in Britain to-day except among students, although portions of the books are read in the English Church services. While this is so, it is important to remember that the books were well known to Shakespeare and his contemporaries, for they were included in all complete Bibles of his time. It is true that there are some Genevan-Tomson Bibles dated 1599 from which the books (with the exception of *The Prayer of Manasses*) are omitted, but such date in any ostensibly complete Bible omitting the books is fraudulent. Numbers of Bibles printed abroad in Charles I.'s reign were smuggled into the country with the date 1599 affixed to them.

Coverdale was one of the most golden-tongued of the preachers of his day and, while his version has not the rich idiomatic English of Tindale, it is full of wonderful cadences. Much of the marvellous melody of the English Bible is due to him and there is a delight in his *Proverbs* which his more accurate successors have failed to maintain. Coverdale's version is essentially one to be spoken, and that is one reason why his *Psalms* (as found in the Great Bible) have so much endeared themselves to members of the Church of England. See Clapton's *Our Prayer Book Psalter* (S.P.C.K.) for the variations in the *Psalms* as between Coverdale's 1535 Bible and the present Psalter as well as for information showing the melodious turn Coverdale imparted to his sources.

THOMAS MATTHEW, 1537.

Coverdale was less provocative than Tindale and much more conciliatory and self-effacing. His second edition was set forth with the King's most gracious licence, and so it is strange that his was not the first official version. That was a privilege reserved for Matthew's Bible of 1537, and when we realize how largely Tindale looms in that Bible, the more surprising it becomes.

We have never had a completely satisfactory explanation of the association of the name of Thomas Matthew with the version; no one of the name has yet been discovered in definite connection with the issue. The real man behind the version was John Rogers, the first of the Marian martyrs, who was stigmatized by the prosecution as " alias Thomas Matthew."

The Bible was made up of Tindale's Pentateuch, his G.H. 1535-4 New Testament, and Coverdale's version from the end of *2nd Chronicles* to the end of *2nd Maccabees*, with the exception of the *Prayer of Manasses* (excluded from Coverdale's Bible presumably because it was not found in some MSS. of the Septuagint) contributed by Rogers from the French of Olivetan. The portion from *Joshua* to the end of *2nd Chronicles* was new, never before published, and the consensus of competent opinion is that it is Tindale's work, done in prison while awaiting execution. His *Jonah* was not used nor were his " Lessons " from the Old Testament and Apocrypha which he had supplied for the Mass according to the Use of Sarum.

Matthew's Bible is the ancestor of the Revised Bible of

1881-5. All official Bibles of the Church of England have been revisions of it or of its descendants—Matthew, Great Bible, Bishops', Authorised, Revised.

RICHARD TAVERNER, 1539.

In the evolution of the English Bible, the Bible of Richard Taverner, a revision of Matthew's, is of little importance. Richard is not to be confused with John Taverner, the great composer and likewise a reformer. It was Taverner who introduced the word " parable " for " similitude."

In Edward VI.'s reign a Bible made up of Tindale and Taverner was published in five instalments to enable poor people to buy it.

GREAT BIBLE (COMMONLY·CALLED CRANMER'S), 1539-41.

There were seven folio editions of the Great Bible, all differing from one another, issued between April 1539 and December 1541: sometimes a reading appeared in an early edition, and was amended in a later, only to be restored again in a still later. It was obligatory on every cathedral and church to display a copy. The total number of copies printed is said by some to have amounted to 20,000 and by others to 11,000.

The Great Bible was a revision of Matthew's largely in the light of the Vulgate and Münster's Latin Bible, and the task was entrusted to Coverdale assisted by others. Nothing is known as to the identity of the others. The fourth and sixth editions were stated to have been " ouérseene and perused " by Bishop Tunstall of Durham and Bishop Heath of Rochester, but it is obvious that any supervision can only have been of the most perfunctory character. The name of Cranmer is associated with the revision, though it is unlikely that he took any greater part than writing the Prologue, which appeared in the second and subsequent editions and was reproduced in Genevan and Bishops' Bibles.

It cannot be said that the revision was an improvement on Matthew's—the Bible was being forced on an unwilling clergy and contrary influences were at work. It had been designed to incorporate explanatory notes, but in the event all notes were jettisoned and the Great Bible appeared without notes.

It was reprinted in Edward's and Elizabeth's reigns in quarto as well as in folio. The last edition, as far as known, was the quarto of 1569 (there are said to have been three issues that year), a most corrupt edition with sometimes as much as a half-chapter missing.

No fresh version appeared in Edward's reign, but there were numerous issues of all versions from Tindale to the Great Bible. There were over thirty such issues, so that there must have been many copies of the Bible in circulation up and down the country.

Although the Princess Mary had translated into English part of Erasmus's Latin Paraphrase of *St. John*, no Bibles were printed in England in her reign. Numbers of Bibles were destroyed, and to read a Bible in the vernacular was to invite suspicion.

WILLIAM WHITTINGHAM, 1557.

With the publication of the Great Bible, the first chapter in the evolution of the English Bible may be said to have been concluded. No man could honestly say that the translation had been well done. A notable reformer such as Hugh Latimer preferred to use the Vulgate and to make his own translations therefrom for the texts in his sermons. The position of the Bible in English received attention among the exiles in Geneva and with their effort began the second chapter.

A preliminary to that effort was Whittingham's single-handed revision of the New Testament issued in 1557. For his purpose he used Tindale compared with the Great Bible. He also used the Latin version of Beza, who was ranked in authority with Stephanus.

GENEVAN, 1560.

Whittingham's New Testament possessed many faults, but it had the great effect of suggesting to his more competent fellow-refugees the need for a combined effort to put the English Bible into better shape. A number set to work and the result of their labours was the Genevan Bible of 1560. Its publication marks a most important milestone in the history of the English Bible. It was the first corporate revision (the Great Bible cannot seriously be regarded as such), the kind of revision not yet enjoyed by the Shakespearian text. Numbers of scholars have been named as associated with it, but the only ones with any degree of certainty are

Anthony Gilby, Thomas Sampson (reputed as a great Hebrew scholar), and William Whittingham.

The Genevan is popularly called "The Breeches Bible" from its treatment of Gen. iii. 7, but "Breeches Bible" is not really a distinctive title any more than "Treacle Bible" is of the Bishops'. Both the Wicliffite and *The Golden Legend* used the term "breeches" in Gen. iii. 7 and the Bishops' "Is there not tryacle at Gilead?" (Jer. viii. 22) was inherited from the Great Bible. Such labels do not indicate knowledge and are only tolerable when they have some witty point, as for instance in the case of the Genevan of 1562, nicknamed later the "Whig Bible" because of the misprint, "Blessed are the placemakers."

The Great Bible Old Testament was conflated with the Hebrew, and guidance in interpretation was sought in the Latin versions of Pagninus, Münster, and Leo Juda. All the earlier English versions of the Apocrypha had rested on the Latin text, the Genevans rendered the Greek. Whittingham's New Testament was revised to such an extent as virtually to supersede it, and the influence of Beza's text is evident. The Greek connecting participles, neglected by Tindale and Whittingham, were rendered. The New Testament would have been stronger had more of Whittingham been discarded and had the translation been less free; as it is, its text is less interesting than the Revised New Testament of the Bishops'.

The Genevan Bible enjoyed a large circulation in Shakespeare's day and the reasons for its popularity are easy to understand. First, its sale was enthusiastically pushed. Secondly, it was available in handy size at a low price. A good many editions were in roman letter, though numbers were in black. Like Whittingham's, it was divided into verses, and however objectionable this division may be in principle, its practical advantages must be admitted. The margin was full of explanatory notes, some of them, it is true, questionable and bitter, but many of them really illuminating and scholarly. It abounded in striking words and phrases, *e.g.*, "Teach a childe in the trade of his way" (Prov. xxii. 6); "whose marchants are princes, whose chapmen are the nobles of the world?" (Isaiah xxiii. 8); "sides of the earth" (Jer. vi. 22); "and layde him in a cratch" (Luke ii. 7); "wee trussed vp our fardels" (Acts xxi. 15). It is the least archaic of the versions; it favours direct statement frequently at the expense of rhythm and it has not the full sonorous ring of the Bishops', as a comparison of the first chapter of *Hebrews* in the two versions will show.

With many Genevan Bibles were bound up metrical versions of the *Psalms*, the *Athanasian Creed* and the *Ten Commandments*. These served as hymns, a function they no longer perform in the Church of England, though the type is preserved in the Church of Scotland. These metrical psalms were also bound up with numbers of Bishops' Bibles and Prayer Books. Prayer Book *Psalms* appeared in many Genevan Bibles, usually prefixed, though in the 1578 Genevan folio they were exhibited in black letter alongside the Genevan in roman letter. Garbled forms of Common Prayer were issued with many Genevan Bibles. From 1578 onwards, a concordance, based on a French original, was added to Genevan Bibles; and, from 1579, to ordinary Genevan New Testaments, but not to Tomson's, there was prefixed a kind of catechism dealing with Predestination.

All sorts of men possessed Genevan Bibles. King James confessed to a copy presented to him by an English lady. Hooker quoted Genevan readings, as did Archbishop Whitgift. Preachers, whether of the Puritan party or not, on account of its convenient size for use in the pulpit often took their texts from it. It was the Bible for family and private use and its possession was no badge of party.

One curious feature of the Genevan Bible may be remarked. Alone of English Bibles, it placed *The Prayer of Manasses* among the canonical books, between *2nd Chronicles* and *Ezra*. By neither the Latin nor the English Church is the *Prayer of Manasses* accepted as canonical.

LAWRENCE TOMSON'S REVISED GENEVAN NEW TESTAMENT, 1576.

In 1576 Tomson, a follower of Walsingham's, issued a revised Genevan Testament. From our point of view Tomson's Testament is most important as there is good reason to believe that Shakespeare owned or otherwise had access to a quarto Tomson New Testament bound up with a Genevan Old Testament of 1595 or subsequent date.

As far as Tomson's revision of the Genevan text was concerned there was very little in it and that little was not very good. Sometimes it is not easy to say from where he derived his readings; certainly not from Beza by whose

Latin text he was supposed to correct his predecessors. He borrowed from Beza the habit of exaggerating the Greek definite article. A good example would be in Rev. xx. 10, quoted under *Titus Andronicus*. Where the Geneva reads " where the beast and the false prophet shall be tormented," Tomson has " where that beast and that false prophet are, and shall be tormented." Notice the " that " for " the." Specially interesting in this connection is its " Syr, we would see that Iesus " (John xii. 21).

In his New Testament, Tomson discarded the Genevan notes altogether and inserted instead notes by Beza. Some of Beza's notes were really very useful and disclosed great learning, but many of them were needlessly bitter. Beza attached few notes to *Revelation*. The defect was remedied. A translation of Franciscus Junius's *Revelation*, differing widely from other versions, was published in 1594, printed by Richard Field, the printer of Shakespeare's *Venus and Adonis*. Its notes were absorbed by Tomson Testaments, making of each page of the *Apocalypse* more notes than text; some of these notes were extremely virulent. In some editions Junius's text displaced Tomson's.

Tomson's version acquired great popularity and, to a certain extent, ousted the genuine Genevan text. In 1587 it was issued bound up with the Genevan Old Testament and Apocrypha, and from thenceforth for a long while all quarto roman letter Genevan Bibles contained its version and not the genuine Genevan. Genevan Bibles, with the Genevan New Testament in octavo roman letter and in quarto black letter, continued to be printed, but none in quarto roman letter as far as can be ascertained.

BISHOPS', 1568.

The policy of Queen Elizabeth as to English Bibles was one of non-interference. Bibles were to be allowed to circulate, but it was none of the Queen's concern to promote the circulation, beyond providing that every parish church was to own a copy and every Master of Arts a New Testament. Otherwise everybody could do as he pleased. Bibles began to be printed again: editions of Tindale, Coverdale, the Great Bible and Genevan issued from the presses, and, if quantity is a criterion, then Tindale and the Genevan were the most popular.

Obviously the Church of England had to adopt as official

some version or other, the difficulty was which. Now that
the Genevan had appeared, the Great Bible was out of date,
and its position as the official Bible of the Church was no
longer possible. At one time Archbishop Parker contemplated the adoption of the Genevan, but its association
with Calvin and the bitter anti-ecclesiastical tone of some of
its notes made such a course inexpedient. There was no
option but to provide a new version for the official use of the
Church. The Archbishop, himself a scholar of distinction,
in want of Royal co-operation and with no adequate machin-
ery at his disposal, decided to enlist the aid of a number
of prelates and other dignitaries in bringing out a new
revision of the Great Bible.

The work of revising the Great Bible, with the restriction
to keep to that text as much as the sense would allow, was
entrusted to a number of busy diocesans and others, who
held no consultation with each other, with the Primate
nominally as general editor. This method, of a sort not
unfamiliar to Shakespearian students, produced the kind
of revision that might have been expected. Unequal quality
is its marked feature; criticism that would apply to one book
would not necessarily apply to another.

Especially is this true of the Old Testament. The Bishops'
revision of the Old Testament consists in the greater part of
a casual and superficial touching up and trimming of the
Great Bible with here and there a borrowing from the
Genevan. The *Psalms* cannot be taken seriously. In
Psalm vii. 14, where the Genevan reads, " Beholde, he shall
trauaile with wickednesse: for hee hath conceiued mischiefe,
but he shall bring forth a lye," the Bishops' has this rather
startling rendering, " Beholde, he will be in trauayle of a
mischiefe, for he hath conceaued a labour: but yet he shalbe
brought to bed of a falsehood." The version of the *Psalms*
could not have been very highly esteemed by the authorities,
seeing that it was only printed three times—in 1568, 1572
(alongside the Prayer Book *Psalms*), and 1585. In all other
editions, of which there were some score, the Prayer Book
Psalms were printed.

BISHOPS' REVISED NEW TESTAMENT, 1572.

The New Testament was on a very different footing. The
Bishops' New Testament is full of interest, and frequently
exhibits a high standard of scholarship. Its great feature

was the literalness of numbers of its renderings. Thus Luke iv. 5, " in a moment of time " (accepted by all succeeding versions); Luke i. 37, " no worde " (rejected by the Authorised in favour of the Genevan, adopted by the Revised); Matt. xv. 26 and 27, " litle dogs " (not accepted by succeeding versions).

Unfortunately the 1568 edition was carelessly printed and was laden with mistakes. A corrected edition of the whole Bible in quarto was issued in 1569, the one edition of the Bishops' that could be said to have been carefully printed.

In the meanwhile Giles Lawrence, one of the most famous teachers of Greek in his day, favoured the Archbishop with his criticisms, and apparently his services were utilized in a further revision of the New Testament. This Revised New Testament appeared in the 1572 Bible, often called the Leda Bible because of the ornamental initial letter at *Hebrews*—blocks intended for Ovid's *Metamorphoses* had been used, and, of course, critics made great capital out of the accident.

Careless printing dogged the Bishops'. The 1572 edition was set up from the corrupt 1568 and not from the correct 1569. The probable reason was that the 1569 edition, being a small-sized volume, was inconvenient for a record of alterations, not at all as good for the purpose as the large 1568 folio. But every edition of the Bishops' suffered from the printers and in every one of them unauthorized alterations were introduced and Genevan notes imported into the margin. Perhaps in this latter the printers could not help themselves; the Bibles had to be sold and the public demanded commentary.

Many readings introduced by the Bishops' of 1568 and 1572 in the New Testament have stood the test of time. Some excited considerable controversy. One novelty must be noticed here since Shakespeare offers evidence of interest in it.

One of the matters in dispute between Sir Thomas More and Tindale was the latter's refusal to translate the Biblical and ecclesiastical word $\dot{a}\gamma\dot{a}\pi\eta$ by " charity "—he translated it by " love " or " kindness "—although he introduced the adverb " charitably " ($\kappa a\tau\dot{a}$ $\dot{a}\gamma\dot{a}\pi\eta\nu$) into *Romans*. As in the case of all Greek words for which no exact English equivalents exist, there can be no final determination of the argument; it is possible on historical and other grounds to offer objections to either "charity" or "love." The Revisers of 1881 decided in favour of Tindale, but that decision has not commanded the unanimous consent of scholars and some of them have gone so far as to suggest the coining of a new word by transliterating the Greek.

Whittingham was the first to re-introduce "charity" in *Jude*, and the Genevans confirmed it. The Bishops' in 1568 adopted it in *Romans* as well as in *Jude*, and in 1572 extended it to *1st Corinthians*, and the other passages in which the Authorised has made the term familiar. The action of the Bishops' evoked considerable comment by Puritans. Shakespeare plays on this conflict of opinion in *Titus Andronicus*, as well as in *Love's Labour's Lost*.

The last quarto edition of the complete Bishops' Bible was, as far as it has been possible to discover, that of 1584, though handy volumes of the New Testament continued to be printed, even after the publication of the Authorised in 1611. Large costly folios (the 1585 folio was one of the most magnificent Bibles printed in England) were still turned out, the last being in 1602, but what ordinary man was likely to buy an expensive heavy folio Bible? The only sort of man that would do so would be one wanting a copy for an official purpose, as, for instance, for reading in church, or for reading at school prayers, which was the presumable object for which the Headmaster of Heath Grammar School, Halifax, determined to procure a Bible of the largest size, *circa* 1600. The cessation of the quartos means that virtual possession of the field was left to the Genevan and its Tomson Revision. If anybody bought a complete Bible it was one of these two. The Bishops' New Testament had an independent public, but the Bishops' complete Bible had not.

RHEIMS, 1582.

In 1582 appeared the first independent English translation of the New Testament since Tindale. The translators this time were Jesuits, members of the seminary at Rheims, and their translation was from the Latin Vulgate (Stephanus edition of 1546). It should be added that while they translated from the Latin it is abundantly evident, not only from their margin, but also from their skilful management of the Greek definite article that they had the Greek before them. They were, in fact, Greek scholars of no mean order.

Their choice of the Vulgate they justified on the ground that the Greek manuscripts extant were so corrupt that they no longer agreed with Patristic Citation, and that, although the Vulgate was only a translation, yet it represented contact with Greek manuscripts more ancient than any available in the sixteenth century. It is easy to object that, just as the Greek manuscripts were corrupt, so also was the Vulgate, in fact, so much so that it had defied the attempts of Alcuin and Lanfranc to reform it, as it was to defeat the efforts of Sixtus V. and Clement VIII. to improve very much on the text of Stephanus. In our own time, at the behest of Pius X. in 1907, the work has been undertaken by the Benedictines (*Genesis*, *Exodus* and *Leviticus* have appeared, and *Deuteronomy* is nearing completion).

The Rheimists were quite aware of the shortcomings of their copy, but they were able to defend themselves by replying that Beza, the great Protestant authority, had expressed his preference for the Vulgate to any other source for the text.

The Rheims was a more accurate translation of the Latin Vulgate than any of the translations had been of the Greek; it was a most conscientious and scholarly work, but the lines on which it was conceived were altogether too purist and pedantic; at times it was so literal as to become unintelligible to any other than a special student. While its contribution to the Authorised was considerable and valuable, it could not stand as the official version in English of the Latin Church, and it is, therefore, not surprising that, as a perusal of the present Douai Bible will convince, it has been subjected to drastic revision—of all versions it has been the most severely revised.

The version was proscribed; oaths taken upon it were invalid; the extent of its circulation must have been very restricted, and I cannot find any substantial evidence that Shakespeare ever quoted from it. It would almost have been unknown to the revisers of 1611 had it not been for Fulke's *Confutation* of 1589 (reprinted in 1601), which exhibited the Rheims alongside the Bishops'. There was a second edition of the Rheims in 1600.

Those who enjoy whole-hearted abuse in controversy should read the Rheims notes. The castigation of opponents lacks nothing in the way of vigour. In view of the wilful dishonesty attributed to the Genevan and Bishops' texts, it may seem strange that so many readings from those texts were adopted by Rheims. Both the Genevan and Bishops' helped the Rheims very considerably, as the Rheims helped the Authorised, although in neither case was the help ever acknowledged.

BOOK OF COMMON PRAYER, 1559.

With the Douai (the name given to the official Bible of the Latin Church in English of 1609-10 and still attaching to it), and the Authorised of 1611 we are not here concerned. The Authorised marks the close of the second chapter in the evolution of the popular English Bible, and its date practically coincides with the conclusion of Shakespeare's working career. There is no evidence that Shakespeare ever saw either of these versions.

A not unimportant means of acquaintance with portions of Scripture was the Book of Common Prayer. Practically the Elizabethan book was an adoption of the second Book of Edward VI. issued in 1552—the differences between the two Books do not affect us here at all. The Elizabethan Book was slightly revised in 1604, and more extensively in 1662, and its lectionary of the Bible has been rearranged, but, subject to the substitution of the Authorised in the Epistles and Gospels in the Communion Service and in the passages of Scripture quoted in Morning and Evening Prayer, and the addition of a few prayers, for all practical purposes the present Book of Common Prayer is the same as the Elizabethan.

The Book is distinguished among liturgies by its insistence on the systematic reading of the Bible. The Elizabethan lectionary of 1559 (slightly corrected in 1561) provided for the reading at Morning and Evening Prayer in the course of the year of all such parts of the Old Testament (except the *Psalms*), as were considered " edifying "; of portions of the Apocrypha; and for the Second Lesson all of the New Testament (with the exception of *Revelation*) three times in the year—at Matins, the Gospels and *Acts*, and at Evensong, the Pastoral and Catholic Epistles. There were Proper Lessons appointed—namely, for each Sunday and Holy Day a particular portion of the Old Testament or Apocrypha was appointed for each of the two services, but Proper Lessons of the New Testament were only appointed for the Holy Days and a few special Sundays, so that, with the exception of *Revelation*, there was little interference with the reading of the New Testament. But it is important to note the fact that there was considerable interference with the reading of the Old Testament at the Sunday services, which would naturally be the ones the public would attend most. Hence the attention paid to Proper First Lessons in this volume, for, if it is maintained that Shakespeare acquired his knowledge of the Old Testament from what he heard in church, it is important to know what he was likely to have heard there.

The Lessons were supposed to be read according to the Bishops' version, which was the version authorized by the episcopate for the purpose, but there can be no doubt that in some churches the Genevan was read and in a few the Great Bible may still have held its place.

In the course of the month the whole of the *Psalms* were appointed to be sung or said at Morning and Evening Prayer. With a few slight variations these *Psalms* were according to the November 1540 edition of the Great Bible and are as chanted or said in all English-speaking congregations of the Anglican Church throughout the world to-day. The *Psalms* are arranged according to the Hebrew numbering and not according to the Latin; they therefore differ from the numbering in the Vulgate from the 9th to the 148th. Each psalm has as title the opening words of the Latin Vulgate—this is important to remember as there is some evidence that Shakespeare was not unfamiliar with the Latin titles. A list of Latin titles was given in some of the Bishops' Bibles, so that anyone could find the number of the psalm.

In addition to the *Psalms* for the day there were appointed for the daily offices Canticles also taken substantially from the Great Bible—*The Song of the Three Holy Children*, called the *Benedicite*, usually sung in Lent as an alternative to the *Te Deum*, the *Benedictus* (Luke i. 68), *Magnificat* (Luke i. 46) and *Nunc Dimittis* (Luke ii. 29).

Morning and Evening Prayer opened with a passage of Scripture, and the passages provided for the purpose agreed with no known Biblical version but were independent renderings. In all probability these renderings (for which in 1662 texts from the Authorised were substituted) emanated from Hugh Latimer; he resided with Cranmer, undertook no diocesan duties, was known to be engaged in work of the sort, and some of the renderings bear resemblance to those abounding in his sermons. There are clues in Edward's and Elizabeth's Books pointing to him, and they are connected with the way Latimer consistently ignored the English Bible and habitually quoted his texts from the Vulgate, translating them very freely. The first is in the Table of Proper Lessons, where Luke ii. was appointed to be read on Christmas morning down to " And vnto men of good wil." This was a translation of the Vulgate ("hominibus bonæ voluntatis') which, though adopted now by the Revised, was not accepted by any English version then in print nor by any printed Greek Testament of the time. Another clue is in the Commination Service, where the reference was given to Psalm cxviii. (the Latin numbering) instead of to Psalm cxix., the Psalter's numbering and that recognized in the English Bible. Likewise to Psalm x. instead of to Psalm xi. In the Calendar of Lessons, *Susanna* and *Bel* appeared among the Hebrew Canonical Books as Lessons for August 26th under their Vulgate titles, Daniel xiii. and Daniel xiv.

The Lord's Prayer, as in the Prayer Book and as said by nearly all English Protestants (as distinguished from Scottish), whether they are Anglicans or not, does not agree exactly with the Prayer in any printed Bible. Probably Tindale's in Matt. vi. is the nearest.

Isolated passages of Scripture occurring in various of the Services, notably in the Communion Service, were independent renderings. The *Ten Commandments*, as in the Catechism and Communion Service, tally exactly with no Biblical version of Exodus xx.

The Epistles and Gospels (changed in 1662 to the Authorised) appointed to be read in the Communion Service for Sundays and Holy Days, were from the Great Bible, but of no particular edition and with many variations. Whenever a Gospel or an Epistle was otherwise provided it was from the Great Bible.

As many preachers used Genevan texts for their sermons and while the Homilies abounded in independent renderings it can be realized that if Elizabethan churchgoers heard plenty of the Bible, they also heard it in plenty of forms—perhaps the same text in three or four different ways. The variety no doubt caused some confusion, but indisputably it served to stimulate general interest in the quest of the best reading. How great the interest was may be gathered from the fact that Ben Jonson was able in *The Alchemist* to parody Hugh Broughton's *Concent of Scripture* in such a way as to argue that the name, style and matter of this distinguished Hebrew scholar and merciless critic of the Bishops' version were familiar to the audience.

As the Homilies are frequently referred to in this book, it should be explained that they were provided for the clergy who had not " the gift of preaching sufficiently to instruct the people." By Canon 49 of 1604 clergy not licensed to preach were commanded to read the Homilies and not to put forth sermons of their own.

There were 34 of these Homilies (12 of which had first been published in 1547). Each was divided into two or more parts—one or more to be read in the morning and the remainder in the afternoon. When the Book had been read through the minister was to start at the beginning and read it through again. In this way their gist would be very familiar to churchgoers. A Homily was not read when there was a sermon.

There is an amusing reference to the Homilies in *As You Like It*, III. ii. 164-7 by Rosalind: " O most gentle pulpiter, what tedious homily of love have you wearied your parishioners withal, and never cried, ' Have patience, good people ' ?"

CHAPTER II

GENERAL CONSIDERATIONS OF SHAKESPEARE'S BIBLICAL KNOWLEDGE

DIFFERENCES OF OPINION AS TO ITS EXTENT.

Opinion has differed somewhat sharply as to the extent of Shakespeare's Biblical knowledge: some have maintained that he knew much, others that such acquaintance with the Bible as he exhibited was no more than might be expected from an intelligent listener in an age when Biblical subjects were much discussed.

On the one side, Dr. Wordsworth, Bishop of St. Andrew's, claimed that Shakespeare was " in a more than ordinary degree, a diligent and a devout reader of the Word of God " (*Shakespeare's Use and Knowledge of the Bible*). Dr. Thomas Carter, who published a comparison of the plays with the Genevan Bible, asserted that " no writer has assimilated the thoughts and reproduced the words of Holy Scripture more copiously than Shakespeare. . . . Whatever else the poet had or lacked, he must have brought to his work a mind richly stored with the thoughts and words of the English Bible " (*Shakespeare and Holy Scripture*). Dr. Christian Ginsburg, one of the most learned Biblical scholars of the nineteenth century and one of the Revisers of the Old Testament, in the course of a long letter to *The Athenæum* (April 28th, 1883), called Shakespeare a most original interpreter of the Bible and ascribed to him in some particulars a more than ordinary knowledge, having regard to the versions available in his time. Mr. Anders in *Shakespeare's Books* contented himself with naming the Bible as one of the books of which Shakespeare had a special knowledge.

It is fair to point out that all these four men devoted considerable attention to the subject and if, in the cases of Dr. Wordsworth and Dr. Carter, the arguments are vitiated somewhat by the zeal of advocacy, this much must be allowed to all of them, save possibly Mr. Anders, that each of them possessed a very extensive familiarity with the contents of the Bible, far surpassing that of ordinary people. It is important, therefore, that Shakespeare succeeded in impressing them with his knowledge of what might be called their own book.

On the other side, with the exception of Mr. Humbert Wolfe (*The Observer*, January 25th, 1925), it has not been denied that Shakespeare had some Biblical knowledge; what has been doubted is that his knowledge of Scripture was either extensive or profound. Mr. Wolfe was altogether exceptional.[1] Because of the Biblical references in *King Richard II.*, he held there was someone else than Shakespeare, though someone as good as Shakespeare, who had had a hand in the play. He maintained that " Shakespeare was often a metaphysician, never a theologian, nor, for that matter, a Christian." Mr. Wolfe evidently overlooked important theological statements by, among others, Iago (*Othello*, II. iii. 351) and Isabella (*Measure for Measure*, II. ii. 73-5). Mr. Wolfe considered that " the figures of Christian mythology and their significance seem utterly to have passed him by. He never refers to them on his own, hardly ever makes mention of them even in the mouths of characters who might be supposed to feel them most strongly. He is alternately believer in Fate, pagan, or agnostic, never for a moment a believer in Christ. But someone who lent a hand in writing Richard II. was very much a Christian."

Sir Walter Raleigh (*Life of Wm. Shakespeare*) expressed himself with characteristic caution. " He has references to Pilate washing his hands; to the Prodigal Son, to Jacob and Laban, to Lazarus and Dives and the like. But it cannot be inferred from this that he was a deep student of the Bible. The phraseology of his age, like that of later ages, was saturated with Biblical reminiscences. *The Essays of Elia* are a tissue of Biblical phrases; and Shakespeare's knowledge of the Bible, which may be fairly likened to Charles Lamb's, was probably acquired in casual and desultory fashion." It would be hard to controvert this statement of Raleigh's, except that to compare Shakespeare's Biblical knowledge with Lamb's is to place his knowledge on a higher level than one is yet prepared to allow. It would not be easy to subscribe to the implication that Lamb's knowledge of Scripture was " acquired in casual and desultory fashion."

Sir Sidney Lee was less cautious. In his *Life of Shake*

[1]The Author regrets that, by a mistake on his part, the views of another author were wrongly ascribed to Mr. Humbert Wolfe.

speare he wrote, "References to scriptural characters and incidents are not conspicuous in Shakespeare's plays, but, such as they are, they are drawn from all parts of the Bible, and indicate that general acquaintance with the narrative of both Old and New Testaments which a clever boy would be certain to acquire either in the schoolroom or at church on Sundays. Shakespeare quotes or adapts biblical phrases with far greater frequency than he makes allusion to episodes in biblical history. . . . As a rule his use of scriptural phraseology, as of scriptural history, suggests youthful reminiscence and the assimilative tendency of the mind in a stage of early development rather than close and continuous study of the Bible in adult life."

It is evident that Lee assumed that Shakespeare was instructed in the Bible in youth, at school. It is doubtful whether the Bible was taught in Stratford School in Shakespeare's youth. Neither is it possible to accept as an alternative to "youthful reminiscence and the assimilative tendency of the mind in a stage of early development," as though it were the only one, "close and continuous study in adult life." Close and continuous study demands an academic training that Shakespeare affords no evidence of having possessed. His mind was artistic and ever on the lookout for words and phrases as well as other material useful for his purpose. He dipped into Puttenham's *Arte of English Poesie* and Swinburne's *Brief treatise of testaments and last willes*, he may even have fingered the pages of Hooker and have taken from them "admirable dexterity of wit," which he used in *The Merry Wives*, but that is not to say that he read any of these books closely and systematically. Yet of Puttenham and Swinburne he seems to have made great use.

RANGE OF SHAKESPEARE'S QUOTATION AND ALLUSION.

As will be shown in detail in due course, Shakespeare definitely made identifiable quotations from or allusions to at least 42 books of the Bible (18 each from the Old and New Testaments and 6 from the Apocrypha)—*Genesis, Exodus, Numbers, Joshua, Judges, 1 and 2 Samuel, 1 and 2 Kings, Job, Psalms, Proverbs, Ecclesiastes, Song of Solomon, Isaiah, Jeremiah, Ezekiel, Daniel ; Tobit, Judith, Wisdom, Ecclesiasticus, Bel, Susanna ;* the Four Gospels, *Acts, Romans, 1 and 2 Corinthians, Ephesians, Philippians, Colossians, 1 Thessalonians, 1 Timothy,*

Hebrews, James, 1 and 2 Peter, and *Revelation.* The list could easily be expanded, but it is sufficient for the purpose of indicating the remarkably wide range of quotation and allusion, and that too without taking into account what might be found in *Pericles* and the non-dramatic poems, both of which are excluded from our inquiry.

Both Raleigh and Lee give the impression that all Shakespeare's allusions to Biblical incidents are comprehended in a list of proper names actually mentioned. This is far from the fact. Shakespeare often alludes to or makes use of a Biblical incident in some way or other without mentioning any proper name at all; if the audience cares to fill in the name it can do so, but as far as the author is concerned no name which might divert attention from the main issue is indicated.

To take just a few examples. Allusion is made in *King John* to the sun standing still, without mentioning Joshua; there was no need to name him, to do so would have been irrelevant and distracting, but certainly the incident with which his name is associated was being utilized. Likewise in *Twelfth Night* and *Cymbeline* those who cared could identify the allusion to setting the feet on the necks of the five kings, and it should be observed in each case the distinctive words of the Genevan Bible were used. Again without mentioning any names, in *The Tempest* Caliban recalls the incident of Jael driving a nail into the head of Sisera. More humorously, Richard III. in pious horror and out of his charity prays that Heaven may not hear the women railing at the Lord's Anointed, presumably in the way that it had heard Shimei cursing King David. Five times, but most notably by Cleopatra, reference is made to the reply by the Shunamite woman to Elisha's inquiry as to her dead child's health. Richard II. contrasts the reception by Christ of the little children with his attitude to the rich young man who inquired as to the means of salvation. This time, because of the national proverb involved, there is not the least material for dispute as to the reference.

These only comprise a selection, but they are sufficient in quantity to warn anyone that allusions to Biblical incidents are more numerous than might appear at first sight. Shakespeare clearly made use of Scriptural incidents to enrich his language and to provide himself with additional figures. Wisely he abstained from any further emphasis of the incident

3

in view than was strictly necessary for his purpose. The
incident was not important, it was therefore kept in subor-
dination and care was taken lest undue attention might be
bestowed upon it by the audience. If the reader assimilates
this one fact he will understand why so many instances
of Shakespeare's use of Scripture are overlooked. Often
his allusion or quotation takes on the colour of its context
so that it lies undetected even by the eyes of experts. Added
to this is the fact that his Bible was not the one with which
we are familiar. When all this is understood then there is
no wonder that it is a subject on which it is unsafe to express
any opinion unless special study has been devoted to it.

A DRAMATIST'S LIMITATIONS IN ALLUSION.

The dramatist is limited in his use of literary allusion as
compared with ordinary writers. He must not divert
attention from his main purpose; we may forgive ordinary
writers if they take us down an occasional side alley, but if
the dramatist does it he may find his diversion fatal. His
points must be comprehensible to his audience, and if he
aims over their heads so that they fail to grasp his intent he
will miss success as a writer for the stage. That Shakespeare
relied on Biblical allusion for enhanced appreciation of
some of his points argues familiarity with the Bible on the
part of his audience, even if we did not know already that
the Bible was the commonest and most discussed book of
the day.

Still he took care that if the allusion was not seen there
was no mystification; if the audience caught the allusion,
so much the greater their enjoyment, but if they failed,
they yet had something. For instance in *A Midsummer-
Night's Dream*, when Bottom, speaking of his vision, said,
" The eye of man hath not heard, the ear of man hath not
seen, man's hand is not able to taste, his tongue to conceive,
nor his heart to report, what my dream was," because of its
manifest absurdity any member of the audience could be
amused, but those who saw in it a travesty of 1 Cor. ii. 9—
" The eye hath not seene, and the eare hath not heard,
neither haue entred into the heart of man, the things which
God hath prepared for them that loue him "—would enjoy
it all the more.

Or again, in *The Merchant of Venice*, when Portia, speaking
of the Scottish lord, says, " he hath a neighbourly charity

in him, for he borrowed a box of the ear of the Englishman, and swore he would pay him again when he was able: I think the Frenchman became his surety, and seal'd under for another," the skit on the innocuous character, in the eyes of Elizabethans, of the Franco-Scottish alliance against England would be best appreciated by those who associated " neighbourly charity " with " Charitie worketh no ill to his neighbour," of Rom. xiii. 10 (Bishops' version).

Or, in *As You Like It*, when Jaques observed, " There is sure another flood toward, and these couples are coming to the Ark. Here comes a pair of very strange beasts," the humour of the point would be more obvious to those who remembered that the pairs that entered the Ark were unclean, according to Gen. vii. 2; those that were clean entered by sevens.

Or in *Hamlet*, when Rosencrantz protested, " I understand you not, my lord," the wiser sort would relish the Prince's reply, " I am glad of it: a knavish speech sleeps in a foolish ear," more keenly if they connected it with " Whoso telleth a foole of wisedome, is euen as a man which speaketh to one that is a sleepe, when hee hath tolde his tale, hee saith, What is the matter ?" from Ecclus. xxii. 10.

It will be noticed in all these four instances, that the allusion occasions no delay; it is not too marked and, while its recognition enriches the point, if by any chance it is not recognized there is no obscurity and the play does not suffer. If nobody noticed, Shakespeare did not care, everything went on as though no allusion had been made.

Classification of Quotation and Allusion.

It will be inferred from an examination of the foregoing instances that literary allusion involves the reader or spectator in a working partnership with the author, and it may even happen that occasionally he helps the latter to make a better joke than was intended. It may be that Bottom's eloquence had nothing to do with St. Paul; that "neighbourly charity " had no connection with Romans xiii. 10, although Shakespeare elsewhere indisputably quoted the verse; that Shakespeare was unaware that the single pairs of beasts were unclean, in spite of his use of the exact words of the Genevan " couples " and " beasts "; that Hamlet's reply was not inspired by *Ecclesiasticus*, although Shakespeare offers evidence of a close familiarity with that book.

Mistakes in attribution have frequently occurred, sometimes with far-reaching results. Since Shakespeare is not available for examination we may ascribe to him allusions to books he had no intention of making, and also he may have utilized those selfsame books on occasions that have escaped our notice. Our inquiry is in the nature of an Inquest of Documents, where the principal witness is not available for personal interrogation and where all the evidence is contained in existing documents to which it is impossible to add anything. On the one hand there are the plays according to the texts contained in good quartos and the First Folio, and although those texts are not impeccable, abounding as they do in numbers of corruptions and interpolations, yet are they substantially sound and it is possible for any ordinary reader to peruse the first editions without any really serious embarrassment. On the other hand, there are the sources of Scripture available to Shakespeare outlined in the last chapter. The evidence to be gleaned is by comparison of the plays with those Scriptures, and of necessity it is of all kinds ; some of it is very strong, in fact, conclusive, while some is weak and dubious.

For the sake of convenience we might divide the evidence into three classes—certain, probable, possible. There are passages in the plays which can positively be stated to contain Biblical or Liturgical quotations or allusions. These are in the first class. There are other passages containing probable references, which would commend themselves as such to any reasonable man conversant with the Bible and with the plays, having regard to all the circumstances. These would be in the second class. In the third class would be placed those that on a rational showing could possibly be held to be quotations or allusions but about which no one could be dogmatic one way or the other. This third class must be considered if it is desired to estimate the probable extent of Shakespeare's indebtedness to the Bible and Prayer Book.

Examples of Class I.

Very obviously to this class would belong all references that included a Biblical proper name. Thus there would be no doubt that " Nor yet St. Philip's daughters were like thee " (1 *King Henry VI.*, I. ii. 143) contained a Biblical allusion. Similarly in Shylock's " Would any of the stock

of Barrabas," or Antony's " O, that I were Upon the hill of
Basan, to outroar The horned herd !" or the host of others
indicated in our list of Biblical Proper Names.

Of allusions to incidents without mention of a proper
name that would rank in Class I. we might cite Helena's
in *All's Well*:

> So Holy Writ in babes hath judgment shown,
> When judges have been babes: great floods have flown
> From simple sources: and great seas have dried
> When miracles have by the great'st been denied.

Allusion is here made to the raising up of the young child
Daniel in the judgment of Susanna, to the abundance of
water that flowed from the rock smitten by Moses (Numbers
xx. 11) and to the drying of the waters of the Red Sea.

Confessedly these examples were from Holy Writ, but in
the next instance in *Much Ado*, V. i. 185, the allusion is no
less obvious when Claudio, teasing Benedick, says " moreover,
God saw him when he was hid in the garden." No argument would be necessary to show that the comparison was
to Adam hiding from the presence of God in the Garden of
Eden.

Also to the first class belong quotations which are substantially reproductions of the Bible or Prayer Book text.
For instance, in *2 King Henry VI.*, II. i. 34, the Kings's " For
blessed are the peacemakers on earth." Argument would
be superfluous as to this or as to Marcus's in *Titus Andronicus*,
III. i. 244, " To weep with them that weep." The same
applies to Prince Henry's " for wisdom cries out in the streets
and no man regards it " (*1 King Henry IV.* I. ii. 99) from
Prov. i. 21-24, and to Othello's " Peace, and be still " and
Ariel's " Not a hair perish'd." No less certain is Lear's
" ' Ay ' and ' No ' too was no good divinity," in its allusion
to 2 Cor. i. 18, 19. From the Psalter in the Prayer Book we
might cite as belonging to this class, Pistol's

> He wooes both high and low, both rich and poor,
> Both young and old, one with another,

in *The Merry Wives*—an obvious adaptation of Ps. xlix. 2.

A couple of examples from the Prayer Book may be taken
in illustration of this class. The first is where Hamlet
refers to his hands as " these pickers and stealers " in very

clear allusion to the phrase in the Catechism—" to keep my hands from picking and stealing." The other is Cardinal Wolsey's " vain pomp and glory of this world " which is, excepting " this " for " the," a word for word quotation from the Anglican Baptism Service.

If all Shakespeare's references to the Bible and Prayer Book were as easy as these, our task would be extremely simple. But Shakespeare was fond of paraphrase, like a man that loves words and tries his hand at free translation into English from Latin or French, so he often took his Biblical phrase and turned it, expressing the same thought otherwise. Sometimes he would embellish, as for instance in *King Richard II.* when he took from Luke xviii. 25, " For it is easier for a Camel to goe thorow a needeles eye," and transmuted it into

> It is as hard to come as for a camel
> To thread the postern of a small needle's eye.

There was some pleasure in thus dressing the phrase with its skilful play. In this case he left the quotation sufficiently obvious as to admit of no controversy as to its character.

But it is not so obvious in *Macbeth*, IV. iii., where Macduff says,

> the Queen that bore thee,
> Oft'ner upon her knees than on her feet,
> Died every day she liv'd.

That it was inspired by St. Paul's " I die dayly " (1 Cor. xv. 31) is certain.

The well-known passage from Portia's speech—

> The quality of mercy is not strain'd,
> It droppeth as the gentle rain from heaven
> Upon the place beneath—

is a more difficult example. There would be no dissentient from the view that Shakespeare was indebted to Ecclus. xxxv. 19, " O howe faire a thing is mercie in the time of anguishe and trouble ? it is like a cloude of raine that commeth in the time of drought." The position is complicated here by the fact that there is another candidate for the inspiration of the passage. The figure " It droppeth as the gentle rain " may have been suggested by the *Song of Moses* (Deut. xxxii. 2), " My doctrine shall drop as doeth the raine: and my speache shall flowe as doeth the dew, as the showre vpon the hearbes, and as the droppes vpon the grasse." There is no reason why both passages should not have operated, but in any case the texts should unite in convincing anybody that Portia's speech had a Scriptural base and so, therefore, whether it was *Ecclesiasticus* or *Deuteronomy*, or whether it was both, the excerpt in question would rank in the first class.

Antony's " Kingdoms are clay " (*Antony and Cleopatra*, I. i. 35) is Biblical, although it appears to have escaped notice. The similitude of the weakness in kingdoms to clay is from Dan. ii. 42, " And (as) the toes of the feete (were) part of iron and part of clay: (so) shall the kingdome be part strong, and part broken." The Biblical origin would not be immediately apparent, but none the less it is certain.

EXAMPLES OF CLASS II.

In this class are those which probably are Biblical or Liturgical references but which cannot be said to be indisputable. They can reasonably be held to be allusions or quotations, but the man who refuses to accept them as such cannot be proved to be in the wrong.

The examples in this class consist mainly of striking words and phrases which either contain a figure which is Biblical in kind, or bear a marked resemblance to phrases or words which, as far as can be ascertained, were peculiar to versions of the Bible. A very good one occurs in *Hamlet*, III. iii. 80. Hamlet, as he sees his uncle at prayer, is reminded of how suddenly his father's life was taken, in the midst of his sins without any opportunity for repentance, and exclaims " A' took my father grossly, full of bread." Long ago Malone pointed out Ezek. xvi. 49, where the Genevan reads, " Behold, this was the iniquitie of thy sister Sodom, Pride, fulnesse of bread, and abundance of idlenesse," as the source.

Not quite so strong, but perhaps strong enough, is another in *The Winter's Tale*, IV. iii. 491. Florizel says, " Let Nature crush the sides o' th' earth together." The phrase " sides of the earth " is very peculiar; " sides of the world " would hardly call for comment, but Florizel's catches the eye. It is probable that it was suggested to Shakespeare by the Genevan of Jer. vi. 22, " a great nation shall arise from the sides of the earth." It will be noticed that Shakespeare has used the phrase in a quite different sense from the Bible's ; he has imagined the earth as a building or enclosure.

The next example is stronger. Coriolanus in V. iii. 27-8, addressing his wife, uses these words, " Or those doves' eyes, Which can make gods forsworn ?" As a figure to denote beauty " doves' eyes " is not native to the English, but it is to be found in the Bishops' of *The Song of Solomon.* In i. 11 of that book we find " thou hast doues eyes " and the phrase occurs again in iv. 1. I should regard this evidence as very strong, perhaps everybody would accept it, but it is just short of being absolutely conclusive.

Caliban's " cloven tongues " (*Tempest,* II. ii. 12-14 and Acts ii. 3) and Cæsar's " taste of death " (*Julius Cæsar,* II. ii. 33 and Matt. xvi. 28, Mark ix. 1, Luke ix. 27, John viii. 52) are other examples in this class. In fact it is a question whether this latter is not entitled to higher rank and to be classed as a certainty. It was an innovation of Tindale's, due to his literal translation of the Greek; the translation of the Latin is " taste death " and it was because Whittingham had a Latin text before him that the phrase in Heb. ii. 9 in the Genevan (followed by the Authorised and Revised) became " taste death " instead of " taste of death " as in Tindale and Bishops'. This reversion would argue that the phrase had not been thoroughly acclimatized and would increase the probability that Cæsar's phrase was Biblical.

There are numbers of instances when it might be said that in all probability Shakespeare had a Biblical incident in mind. Some of them have been mentioned already, such as Jael's driving a nail into Sisera's head and the setting of the feet on the necks of the five kings. Anyone familiar with his Bible almost inevitably thinks of the incidents in *Judges* and *Joshua* when he reads the remarks of Caliban, Sir Toby and Belarius. It is almost inconceivable that Shakespeare did not have them in mind also, but it is just possible he did not. Thus it comes about that, unless the incident is very pointedly recalled, as in the case of Helena in *All's Well,* it cannot be classed as a certainty, only at most as a decided probability. Perhaps not quite so decided is the probability in *As You Like It* when Corin informs Rosalind and Celia,

> My master is of churlish disposition
> And little recks to find the way to heaven
> By doing deeds of hospitality.

On one count there is a certain Biblical allusion here to the hospitality enjoined by St. Paul, in Rom. xii. 13, but there is a probability that there is also an allusion to Nabal of Carmel, the wealthy sheep-owner who was " churlish, and of shrewde conditions," one " so wicked, that a man can not speake to him," and who refused hospitality to David and his followers. See 1 Sam. xxv. It is probable that Shakespeare had this Nabal in mind when he referred to Corin's master, but it is no more than probable.

To the same class belong phrases whose exact meaning we conjecture by reference to the Bible. Thus " to go to the world " means " to marry or to be married " and Steevens held it to be in allusion to Luke xx. 34, " The children of this worlde marrie wiues, and are married." Also it might be in allusion to the elder daughter of Lot, who, according to the Bishops' rendering of Genesis xix. 31, said to her younger sister, " There is not a man in the earth to come in vnto vs after the maner of all the worlde."

The phrase is used by Beatrice (*Much Ado*, II i. 332), " Thus goes every one to the world but I, and I am sunburnt." Also by the Clown in *All's Well*, I. iii. 20. We have another variation of it in *As You Like It*, V. iii. 4-5, where Audrey says, " I hope it is no dishonest desire, to desire to be a woman of the world ?" The worldliness of a wife in contrast with the holiness of a virgin is dealt with by St. Paul in 1 Cor. vii. 34, " There is difference betweene a virgine and a wife: the vnmarried woman careth for the things that are of the Lord, that she may be holy both in body and in spirit: but she that is married, careth for the things that pertaine to the worlde, howe she may please her husband." Likewise of the man, in verse 33 he said, " But he that hath married, careth for the things that are of the world, howe he may please his wife."

Beatrice's " and I am sunburnt," which she adds to her complaint that all but her go to the world, is another example of a phrase that belongs to this class. The argument in its favour was advanced as long ago as 1844 by Hunter in *New Illustrations of Shakespeare*, but it seems to have been forgotten. In Shakespeare's time and until the revision of the Prayer Book in 1662, at the Thanksgiving of Women after childbirth, commonly called The Churching of Women, Psalm cxxi. was recited. This psalm, following the Vulgate, reads :

> the Lord is thy defence upon thy right hand; So that the sun shall not burn thee by day: neither the moon by night. The Lord shall preserve thee from all evil. (Genevan has " smite " for " burn.")

As used in this service it was interpreted to mean that the matron surrounded by her husband and family was sheltered. In Beatrice's mouth the phrase may mean that she was unprotected, unlike the matron whom the Psalm, as used in the Service, sought to reassure. But whether, as asserted by Hunter, it commonly had this significance is another matter, although the fact that the Psalm was dropped at the revision of 1662 and Psalm cxvi. or cxxvii. substituted instead would lend some support to the surmise that there was a popular joke attaching to " the sun shall not burn thee." It may have been considered indecorous, in view of some such popular joke, to use the Psalm on an occasion of the sort. While some credence may be given to Hunter's theory in this case, it must be remembered that " sunburnt " often referred to ruined complexions (See *Troilus and Cressida*, I. iii., " The Grecian dames are sunburnt ").

EXAMPLES OF CLASS III.

In the third class are included all those passages which contain possible Biblical references—that is to say, references which are capable of being reasonably supported but about which it would be improper to be dogmatic. They might be due to Biblical influence, but also they might not. Shakespeare enriched his language from all sources ; he was not writing an argumentative essay for students, but plays for public entertainment. He had no incentive to quote exactly or to make unambiguous allusions. Hence he paraphrased or otherwise quietly incorporated portions of Scripture that he had read or heard in conversation, so that the Biblical sources in many cases can only be recognized with effort and even then they can only be surmised, they cannot be categorically stated. If this fact is remembered trivial and very doubtful instances will not irritate the reader. It is necessary that possibilities as well as certainties and probabilities should be considered, but it is no less necessary that the spirit in which they are advanced should be clearly understood. It is open to anyone, without any reflection on his intelligence, either to accept or reject any or all of them and no more can be said.

A very good example of this class occurs in *King Lear*, III. vi. 84-6, where Lear says to the ragged Edgar, "You, sir, I entertain for one of my hundred: only I do not like the fashion of your garments: you will say they are Persian; but let them be chang'd." Dr. Carter in *Shakespeare and Holy Scripture* maintained that here was an allusion to the immutable character of the laws of the Medes and Persians (Dan. vi. 8) and consequently he italicized " but let them be chang'd." He ridiculed the idea that Lear was speaking ironically, that Edgar might be supposed to imagine that his rags were gorgeous robes. In default of clear evidence that Persian robes were topical, I incline to Dr. Carter's opinion, blended with a suggestion made by Mr. Blunden (*Shakespeare Significances*), that Shakespeare was indebted to " Persicos odi ... apparatus " of Horace. It is an excellent instance where differences of opinion must exist and where there can be no last word.

Our next example of a possible reference is one that is dangerously near to being no more than a parallel, and a parallel that contains no thought that is uncommon. In *All's Well*, III. ii. 90-1, the Countess, with reference to the wicked Parolles, says, " My son corrupts a well-derived nature With his inducement." Was this inspired by St. Paul's famous quotation from Menander, " Euill wordes corrupt good maners " (1 Cor. xv. 33) ? It is a verse Shakespeare could hardly have helped hearing, for the chapter was read in the Burial Service. A careful reading of the Countess's remark with the " well-derived nature " as a paraphrase of " good maners " might enhance the possibility.

A famous example is to be found in *Measure for Measure*, II. ii. 170-2, where Angelo, referring to Isabella, says:

Having waste ground enough,
Shall we desire to raze the sanctuary,
And pitch our evils there ?

Again in *King Henry VIII.*, II. i. 66-8, Buckingham protests:

> Yet let 'em look they glory not in mischief;
> Nor build their evils on the graves of great men:
> For then, my guiltless blood must cry against 'em.

It is the word " evils " that is in question. Steevens and other eighteenth-century scholars identified " evils " as jakes or privies, and connected the passages with 2 Kings x. 27: " And they brake the image of Baal, & brake the house of Baal, and made a draught house of it, vnto this day." Nebuchadnezzar threatened the wise men and magicians with the same indignity: if they could not solve his dream not only would their bodies be drawn in pieces, but their " houses made a iakes " (Dan. ii. 5). Steevens maintained that this Eastern idea of converting to the abject uses of nature a despised or hated object was in Shakespeare's mind.

Such has been the importance of the conjecture that even the great Oxford Dictionary has had to pay attention to it. The editors of that dictionary concluded that " evils " might just as well have meant " hovels," or, indeed, anything else that the word " evils " might imply. They were evidently not impressed by the doubtful examples advanced by Steevens and Malone.

I have never been able to accept the suggestion made by Steevens. The word "evils," as used by Angelo, appears to have no other meaning than wickedness. He used it as an antithesis to " sanctuary," and therefore as the abode of vice. Why was vice not content with its own indulgence without destroying that which was holy ? When there were so many willing to accommodate vicious inclination, why could it only make its pitch where goodness dwelt ? It follows on what he had previously said, " Can it be, That modesty may more betray our sense Than woman's lightness ?"

Steevens and the others missed the real point of 2 Kings x. 27. It was not merely that Jehu destroyed the house of Baal and used the site for a jakes. It was that the sanctuary of Baal was converted into a jakes, and its materials used for the grossest acts of nature.

In *King Henry VIII.* it is still more difficult to take " evils " to signify " jakes." Buckingham speaks of those who brought about his death, and bids them desist from contriving their wicked conspiracies at the cost of great men's lives. The reference to the " graves of great men " is clearly figurative. If his enemies persisted in their evil course, then, as did Abel's, his blood would call from the ground for retribution.

Owing to the importance assumed by Steevens' conjecture, against my own judgment I have treated it as a possibility. It must be borne in mind that Steevens loved to read a curious meaning into the simplest words, and often chose to do so in the names of his two clerical ghosts, Amner and Collins. In the two passages concerned the simplest interpretations appear to give the best and most consistent sense, and on the stage, where words can only be used in a sense that is easily intelligible, that is a material consideration.

Sometimes the possibility of there being a Biblical inference depends entirely on the reader's or auditor's personal reaction. If a number of readers or spectators, without consultation with each other, independently experience similar reactions, the question naturally arises, Did the author himself have these reactions? Did he intend that the spectators should have them? We may take it that Shakespeare would wish his audience to share his own reactions and, if he intended a Biblical reference, it would be all to the advantage of the play that it should be recognized.

Bishop Wordsworth remarked that when Hamlet (III. iv. 82) said to his mother, " O shame, where is thy blush?", he immediately thought of the famous phrase, " O death, where is thy sting?" (1 Cor. xv. 55), which occurred in the Burial Service in Elizabethan Liturgies as " Death, where is thy sting?" Very many have experienced the same reaction. We are then justified in asking, Did Shakespeare intend that the sound of Hamlet's question should recall that of St. Paul? Or was it even in his mind when he penned it? Who can say? Obviously no answer is possible. The fact that Troilus addresses a somewhat similar question to Cressida—" O beauty, where is thy faith?" (V. ii. 65)—and that that play is of about the same date as *Hamlet* is interesting, but of no assistance in reaching a conclusion. Troilus's question recalls Christ's question (Luke viii. 25), and so has a Biblical interest of its own.

Many will, no doubt, be able to cite other passages where they have experienced Scriptural or Liturgical reactions on evidence that is altogether insufficient to support any allusion or quotation. One well-known student confessed to me that when Hamlet plays with Rosencrantz and Guildenstern as to the disposal of the body of Polonius and says, " The body is with the King, but the King is not with the body," he irresistibly thinks of St. Paul (see 2 Cor. xii. 2-4), or of the Athanasian Creed. But who on this evidence would venture to accuse Shakespeare ?

Occasionally it happens that whether there is a Biblical or Liturgical reminiscence or not depends on the reading of the Shakespearian text accepted. If a passage is suspected of corruption and an emendation involving a Scriptural or Liturgical allusion is proposed, unless the conjecture is *lectio certissima*, the allusion it entails can only be considered as possible.

An example occurs in *Othello*, IV. ii. 152-3. All turns on a single letter, on " or " for " of." Desdemona protests:

> If ere my will did trespass 'gainst his love,
> Either in discourse of thought, or actual deed.

This is the reading of the Folio, the *editio princeps* of the play: the passage is not in the 1622 Quarto. " Discourse of thought " is the difficulty. It is a very bad habit to transform difficult phrases into easy ones; the Shakespearian text has been littered with corruptions because each ingenious editor has sought to make our path smooth, and I have no wish to aggravate the evil.

Here the question is, Should we read " discourse or thought " ? The 1630 Quarto of the play enjoys no authority, although the fact that it amalgamates the 1622 Quarto with the Folio and that there is a superficial suggestion of an editor with independent information has led to its being consulted more frequently than is the case with other reprints. That Quarto reads " discourse or thought," but whether due to a compositor's slip or an editor's deliberate emendation, it is impossible to say.

For " discourse or thought " there is independent support. It may have been that Shakespeare paraphrased the Liturgy. Compare the General Confession in the Communion Service: " We acknowledge and bewail our manifold sins and wickedness, Which we, from time to time, most grievously have committed, By thought, word, and deed, Against thy Divine Majesty." It can be argued that Desdemona is denying having offended against her marriage vow, first in either of two and then in the third of the ways enumerated in the Confession. " Either in discourse or thought, or actual deed " is a paraphrase of " in word or thought or deed," which would be the natural way of expressing " by thought word and deed," when denying a charge and not confessing to its commission. If the emendation is accepted (and I am not recommending it) then Desdemona first denies offence " either in discourse or thought," and then adds " or actual deed." *Cf.* " discourse of reason " (*Troilus and Cressida*, II. ii. 116).

Occurring both in the plays and in contemporary Bibles are phrases rare in their application, but not sufficiently rare to be absolutely distinctive. Shakespeare may have been indebted to the Bible for them, and they ought to be noted, but not in any dogmatic temper. Examples of such are " without redemption," meaning " utterly " (*King Richard II*, III. ii. 129 and Deut. xx. 17 *B*); " spring of day," meaning " morning " or " dawn " (*2 King Henry IV.*, IV. iv. 35 and 1 Sam. ix. 26, and Hosea vi. 3 *B*).

PARALLELS.

A great difficulty is presented by parallels—that is to say, by Shakespearian passages which, while they contain no quotation of Scripture, yet exhibit a more or less close resemblance in thought to some Biblical passages. Should they be included or excluded ? Obviously, in a professedly Christian country and in an age keenly interested in Biblical and theological topics, it would be exceedingly strange if Shakespearian characters did not reproduce many ideas expressed by Biblical writers, whether suggested directly by those writers or by intermediates. As it is not an object here to create a harmony between Shakespeare and the Scriptures, but rather to inquire into Shakespeare's literary knowledge, it will be readily conceded that to include parallels indiscriminately would confuse all the evidence.

On the other hand, ought parallels to be excluded, and should we adhere strictly to passages which by some verbal resemblance can be argued to be Biblical references ? If we do, we may then be guilty of withholding evidence which ought to be submitted where a character deals with a Biblical theme in such a way as to suggest a paraphrase or a development.

It has been thought advisable to steer a middle course, and only to admit parallels with discretion and for some particular reason. One reason for admission might be that where we found numbers of parallels with passages in the same Biblical book, we might be entitled to regard such an aggregation as evidence that Shakespeare derived them from reading the book in question.

A book that answers this qualification is *Ecclesiasticus*. It is now only known to a few, although several generations back it was read with avidity by many who loved shrewd observations of life and manners. It figures very largely in the Homilies. Not only did Shakespeare quote directly from it—"Who so toucheth pitche, shall be defiled withall"—but he constantly expressed thoughts bearing remarkable resemblance to utterances of the son of Sirach. A stray one would be of no account, but we meet them in all sorts of plays, from the earliest right up to *Measure for Measure*, and even later. Only one conclusion is possible. *Ecclesiasticus* was a book read by Shakespeare.

A feature of *Ecclesiasticus* is its deprecation of needless sorrow. It warns against overmuch grief for the dead, while allowing such mourning as is expedient for the sake of reputation and for the worthiness of him that is dead. Did Lady Capulet or Hamlet's uncle or Lafeu have this warning in mind when they reproved prolonged mourning? Or again, when Sir Toby Belch, irritated with Olivia's over-affectation of grief for her dead brother, said, "I am sure care's an enemy to life," had Shakespeare in mind Ecclus. xxx. 24: "Zeale and anger shorten the dayes of the life, carefulnes and sorow bring age before the time"?

Or in the *Induction*, ii. 137-8, of *The Taming of the Shrew*, compare:

> And frame your mind to mirth and merriment,
> Which bars a thousand harms, and lengthens life

with Ecclus. xxx. 22: "The ioy and chearefulnes of the heart is the life of man, and a mans gladnesse is the prolonging of his dayes." This almost ceases to be a parallel and becomes a paraphrase on Shakespeare's part.

Ecclesiasticus comments on the popularity of the rich and the unpopularity of the poor. One famous passage is in chapter xiii. (the same that contains the remark about pitch)—" when the poore falleth, his acquaintance forsake him." In *Troilus and Cressida*, when his sometime friends pass him strangely by, Achilles asks:

> What ? am I poor of late ?
> 'Tis certain, greatness once fall'n out with fortune
> Must fall out with men too.

Is the parallel admissible ? Of if not that, is the Player King's in *Hamlet*:

> The great man down, you mark his favourite flies;
> The poor advanced makes friends of enemies ?

I do not care to be an advocate in doubtful cases, but the spirit of this remark of the Player King's is so exactly that which permeates *Ecclesiasticus* that, having regard to other facts in the plays, I cannot dissociate Ben Sirach from the passage in *Hamlet*. There are many other topics of Ben Sirach's dealt with by Shakespeare.

Another book very well known by Shakespeare was *Job*, and he quotes from it both in the Bishops' and Genevan versions, and he may even, in one instance, have been influenced by a marginal note in the Bishops'. When, therefore, we find a resemblance between Shakespeare and *Job*, we are justified in considering the inclusion of the passage concerned as a parallel.

It is a well-known fact that some minds, when they begin to darken and lose their grip, have a tendency to resort to Scriptural parallels. They are apt to create Biblical parallels to their own circumstances. Shakespeare thought fit to introduce a hint, perhaps more than a hint, of this weakening of intellect in his delineation of Richard II. in misfortune. Richard in prosperity had not quoted Scripture, but at the first blast of misfortune he seems, to the consternation of his friends, to bethink himself of the precedent of Job. The following speech of his delivered almost immediately on his return from Ireland suggests the influence of *Job*:

> Discomfortable cousin ! know'st thou not,
> That when the searching eye of heaven is hid
> Behind the globe, that lights the lower world,
> Then thieves and robbers range abroad unseen
> In murders and in outrage boldly here;
> But when from under this terrestrial ball
> He fires the proud tops of the eastern pines
> And darts his light through every guilty hole,
> Then murders, treasons, and detested sins,

4

The cloak of night being pluck'd from off their backs,
Stand bare and naked, trembling at themselves?

Compare this with Job xxiv. 13-7:

Those are they that flee from the light, they knewe
not his wayes, nor continue in his pathes. The murderer
riseth earely, and killeth the poore and needy, and in
the night is as a thiefe. The eye of the adulterer waiteth
for the darknesse, and sayeth, There shall no eye see
me: and hideth his face. In the darke they dig through
houses, which they marked for themselues in the day
time: they know not the light. The morning is to them
euen as the shadowe of death: if one knowe them
(they are) in the terrours of the shadowe of death.

Considering all the circumstances, the parallel seems good
enough to rank as almost a certainty. If we accept it, is
it not of interest to note the way one poet handles the theme
of another poet?

A more difficult question is presented by Constance in
King John. She, too, is addicted to a quotation of Scripture,
though the spirit in which she uses it is one of ferocity.
Fighting desperately against odds, she scolds in terms of Scripture and sometimes wrests from its pages more than a fair
construction could yield. When Constance denounced law:

when law can do no right,
Let it be lawful that law bar no wrong.
Law cannot give my child his kingdom here
For he that holds his kingdom holds the law:
Therefore, since law itself is perfect wrong,
How can the law forbid my tongue to curse?

was Shakespeare making her develop St. Paul's well-known
disparagement of law? Compare Rom. iii. 19: " Nowe
we know that what things so euer the law sayth, it sayeth
it to them which are vnder the lawe: that euery mouth
may be stopped, and that al the world may be endangered
to God," or *ibid.*, iv. 15: " Because the lawe causeth wrath:
For where no law is, there is no transgression." Perhaps
the suggestion is no more than fanciful, and merely an instance
of personal reaction. Constance denounces the law that would
restrain her, St. Paul disparages law and there, perhaps, the
resemblance ends. But it is legitimate to advance the possibility for consideration, although at that point it must be
left. Like other passages of the kind, it can only be noted.

CHAPTER III

OTHER GENERAL CONSIDERATIONS

How Was Shakespeare's Biblical Knowledge Acquired?

It was possible for Shakespeare to have acquired the Biblical knowledge he exhibited in any or all of five different ways:

1. By reading the Bible.
2. By hearing the Bible read in church or elsewhere.
3. By hearing Homilies, preachers' texts and passages quoted in services.
4. In the course of general secular reading.
5. In the course of general conversation.

All five of these agencies could have operated at any time in his life. There does not appear to have been anything to have prevented his hearing the Bible read in church; whatever his private opinions may have been, and whether his father was a Roman recusant as maintained by the late Dr. Smart, or a Puritan recusant as Dr. Carter has it, it is fairly clear from his familiarity with various portions of Common Prayer and the Homilies that outwardly he was a Conformist.

If it is desired to stress Shakespeare's church attendance as his principal means of imbibing Scriptural knowledge, it is pertinent to inquire how often is it supposed he attended church? Did he attend other than on Sundays? Did he attend at Evensong as well as at Matins and Holy Communion? Evensong was held in the afternoon. He could hardly have attended Evensong when in London during the theatrical season, for the performances took place on Sunday afternoons. Some attempt must be made to answer these questions before propounding the theory. If it is concluded that normally Shakespeare attended on Sunday mornings, then, in our list of Biblical books, the portions of the Old Testament occurring as Sunday Morning Proper Lessons are very important.

Let us grant that he was an attentive listener. Still, even

in the case of the most attentive listener, hearing a Lesson
read once and perhaps not hearing it again is not equal to
hearing constantly the same thing over and over again as in
the case of the Prayers or the Canticles.   The Lessons were
not even like the *Psalms*, the whole of which were said or
chanted twelve times a year and read or sung, not merely
heard.   It is reading that most impresses on the mind, and
next to that constantly hearing.   Even on a mind so receptive
as Shakespeare's it is hardly possible to imagine once hearing
to have much effect.   Now and again a phrase well-read
at the lectern floats in the mind, but it would be the exception.

That is not to deny that odd phrases might stick and
phrases distinctive of the Bishops' version, such as " redeeming time " (*1 King Henry IV.*, I. ii.), and " death is to
him advantage " (*King Henry V.*, IV. i.) might owe their
existence in the text to his having heard them at Evening
Prayer.   More exactly we can seize upon a phrase distinctive
of an Epistle read in the Communion Service, as " I come
in kindness and unfeigned love " (*3 King Henry VI.*, III. iii.).
Shakespeare might have heard the Epistle read in that form
once every year, but he might as well have read it in a 1568
or 1569 edition of the Bishops'.   Some deal very simply
with the Bible he heard and the one he read.   They just
assume that all Bishops' readings were heard in church,
and all Genevan readings were perused at home.   Such
simplicity will not do.   Some of the distinctive Bishops' readings, mentioned in Chapter IV., occur in Biblical chapters
never read in church, while some Genevan readings belong
to Sunday Morning Proper First Lessons.

That Shakespeare imitated other authors in the use of
some Scriptural phrases is practically certain.   For instance,
it is my firm belief that the habit numbers of his characters
evince of referring to life as a " pilgrimage " is one acquired
from *Euphues*, and the same would be true of " weaker
vessel," as applied to a woman or wife, or of " temple " as
a term for the human body.   That is not to say Shakespeare
did not know the terms in Scripture ; it is most improbable
that he did not, but as they occur in his plays they appear
to be Euphuisms rather than Biblical quotations.

We cannot ignore the influence of ordinary conversation.
We do not know the manner of speech of Shakespeare's
acquaintance, for we have no examples.   But it is not

unreasonable to suppose that phrases out of the Bible figured in their talk. We all make literary references which we have never read in their proper context. How many who quote " Music hath charms " have read *The Mourning Bride* ? Of those who speak of " two kings of Brentford " how many have read *The Rehearsal* or even *The Task* ? Multitudes speak of leviathans who are ignorant of the Biblical origin of the creatures. How many are conscious that when they mention the " skin of their teeth " they are quoting Job xix. 20 ? Accordingly, we might not be surprised if phrases such as " men of mould," " they know not what they do," " the leopard's spots," etc., were popular as far as Shakespeare was concerned rather than literary.

But before rashly adopting any such conclusion even about these simple phrases, there is a point to remember about them. A man who knew a Biblical phrase through the medium of ordinary speech would not know that it was Biblical and he would use it indiscriminately. The phrases specified are not used without discrimination or deliberation. Pistol, who says " men of mould," is an oily rascal given to unctuous speech ; Henry VI. in his piety often quotes the Bible, especially the Gospels ; and Norfolk's reference to the leopard's spots is not his solitary Biblical allusion, and he is, moreover, spoken of by the saintly Bishop of Carlisle as a devout man. Shakespeare evidently knew these phrases were Biblical. In addition, we have to bear in mind that we have behind us 400 years of the English Bible, and are the heirs of many Bible-quoting generations. Thus we have inherited Biblical phrases. Shakespeare had no such inheritance; his was only the second generation to whom the Bible in English was easily accessible.

SHAKESPEARE READ THE BIBLE.

That Shakespeare read at least some of the Bible does not admit of any doubt whatever, apart altogether from the fact that the Bible was the commonest book of the time. It is strange that there should exist a disinclination to allow that he might have perused such a very readable book as the Bible. Partly it may be due to a fear lest such an admission might be held to argue that he was a devout man, forgetting that the English Bible is capable of affording worldly pleasure as well as spiritual delight, and that many, who would not in any sense be called religious, have been fond of reading it. But partly it is due to a superstition. Ben Jonson had said of him that he had " small Latin and less Greek "; Milton spoke of him as warbling " his native wood-notes wild "; this developed into a supposition that his debt was to nature and not to art; finally, in time, he came to be represented as one almost untutored, who only reluctantly opened a book to extract from it materials for a play. The truth is that he was no exception to the race of great poets; he was an avid reader of books. By no other means could he have acquired his remarkably extensive vocabulary. He read difficult books (neither Puttenham nor Swinburne was an easy book). There are at least three indications that he may have read Hooker's *Ecclesiastical Polity*, and that is not a book for everybody. It is not difficult to demonstrate that occasionally, at least, he read the Bible.

First let us take the very simplest proof. It is only when we assemble all the references to Adam and Eve that we realize how intimately he knew that narrative; the isolated references do not impress at all, but when they are gathered together, it is borne in on the collector that there is hardly a phase of the story as narrated in the first three chapters of *Genesis* that has been missed.

If we go on further to another very popular incident, the Flood, we are convinced that Shakespeare was aware that the unclean animals, or beasts as they are called in the Genevan, went in by couples, as that version has it. This is a point that would escape him who only knew the story from hearing it read.

His reading of *Genesis* is still more apparent when we read Shylock's " What says that fool of Hagar's offspring ?" with reference to his former servant Launcelot, whom, as Sarah did Ishmael, he suspects of mocking him. From hearing the chapter read, no one would gather the incident in all its significance, to say nothing of the perfect aptness of Shylock's allusion in view of all the circumstances.

But the matter is clinched finally, and all doubts of Shakespeare's having read *Genesis* are dissipated when we come to Shylock's account of the deal between Laban and Jacob. The deal is not free from complications, but Shakespeare gets it accurately. Not only does Shylock add the concluding verse of the chapter as to the blessing that attended Jacob, but Antonio refers to the succeeding chapter. The man who had only heard the story read might have a vague idea of one chapter, but he would not know the next. Dr. Ginsburg even went so far as to assert that Shakespeare read the marginal note in the Bishops'. Anyway, it is abundantly clear that Shakespeare actually read the account.

That he knew the prologue to the Book of *Job*, the references at the end of *The Merry Wives*—the slander of Satan, Job's poverty and the wicked counsel of his wife—prove. The matter extends to two chapters. The allusion to the wickedness of Job's wife might have been due to the Bishops' marginal note.

We may leave out of account the *Psalms*—his knowledge of the Psalms, according to the Prayer Book version, will be proved in due course, with something to spare. He displays such a familiarity with *Job*, *Proverbs* and *Ecclesiasticus*, and in later years with *Isaiah*, as can only have been acquired by reading. *Job* and *Ecclesiasticus* especially seem to have attracted his attention—*Job* had been read by Falstaff (he knew that life was as a weaver's shuttle); by Duke Vincentio (it furnished the burden of his counsel to Claudio); and by Constance (it gave tone to her cursing of the day). As for *Ecclesiasticus*, it served Constance in her welcome of death, Portia in her great Court speech, Hamlet's uncle in his reproof of his nephew's mourning, and is apparent in numbers of other places.

If we agree that Shakespeare had favourite books in the Old Testament—and it is almost impossible to conclude that *Job* and *Ecclesiasticus* were not favourite books—it is an argument that he sometimes read the volume containing them. A man does not have special favourites in books he has not read but only heard. My own impression is that the wisdom of *Ecclesiasticus* appealed to Shakespeare. Probably its keen observation of human society provided him with a parallel to his own, and a man of his temperament would enjoy its reprehension of immoderation, whether it concerned grief, food, wine, or the pursuit of revenge. So I think now and again he refreshed himself with a perusal of its pages. It was in this spirit of recreation that it seems to me he mostly read the Bible.

In the next chapter it will be shown that at first he quoted mainly from the Bishops', but in later plays from the Genevan. This change of version indicates reading the Bible during the course of his career. But we do not need to rely on inference that in manhood Shakespeare read the Bible; we have concrete proof.

In adult life he consulted the Bible, as we know from *King Henry V.*, III. vii. 71-2, where the Dauphin quoted in French *2 Peter* ii. 22, as detailed in the next chapter. It is a substantial reproduction of the verse as it appears in the de Tournes Testament printed at Lyons. Obviously Shakespeare copied it out. He had used the same text in English in *2 King Henry IV.*, so he knew it and the context, and evidently could find his way about the Testament.

Another proof that he had a reading acquaintance with the Bible in adult life is afforded by *Measure for Measure*, IV. ii. 69-70:

> As fast lock'd up in sleep, as guiltless labour,
> When it lies starkly in the traveller's bones.

This is based upon Eccles. v. 11: "The sleepe of him that trauelleth, is sweete." This reading is peculiar to certain roman letter Genevan-Tomson Bibles, and it has not been traced in any Bible printed before 1595; the only other one in which it has been found is that of 1598.

Was Shakespeare taught the Bible at School?

It is sufficiently clear that Shakespeare read the Bible in adult life, and it may be that he did so fairly frequently. It is not so clear that he read it in youth, or rather that his acquaintance with it extended beyond what he could have acquired by attendance at service or by occasional perusal of the volume that was provided in the church for members of the public to read.

Sir Sidney Lee took it for granted that he was instructed in the Bible at school (see page 20). Unfortunately this view seems to have been based on nothing more substantial than a confident assumption; there is nothing to show that he took any special pains to confirm it by means of inquiry. Dr. Carter was less positive. He believed that " the spontaneous flow of Scriptural ideas and phrases which are to be found everywhere in the plays reveals the fact most clearly that the mind of Shakespeare must indeed have been ' saturated ' with the Word of God." This being his opinion, he laid it down that " the power of apt and literal quotation is seldom acquired after the earlier days of manhood have been passed, and no man can quote instinctively and correctly unless he has been well grounded in his childhood."

If, as assumed by Sir Sidney Lee and Dr. Carter, there was at Stratford School instruction in the English Bible in Shakespeare's youth the fact is of very great importance for our purpose. Any such instruction would have been in the hands of the masters and ushers. In this connection it is well to bear in mind that the only account, with any sort of pedigree that would entitle it to our credence, of Shakespeare's early occupation that we possess is to the effect that he was a schoolmaster in the country. Beeston, the authority for the statement, as the son of one of Shakespeare's colleagues, has some claim to be regarded as well informed in such a matter. The occupation of schoolmaster would not only develop Shakespeare's power of assimilation and his ability to make a little knowledge go a long way, but it would also make him more perfect in the subjects figuring in the school curriculum. If the English Bible was one of those subjects, then it would not be unreasonable to expect him to be well grounded in portions of Scripture and his mind to be saturated in Biblical phrase and thought.

Unfortunately there are many doubts to be satisfied. There has been as yet no adequate proof adduced that the English Bible was taught generally in country schools between 1572 and 1580, or if we agree that Shakespeare served as an usher, even as late as 1586.

Perhaps some have been misled by confusing Biblical instruction with religious instruction. There is no doubt whatever that pupils at schools like Stratford Grammar School received religious instruction. Professor Foster Watson (*The English Grammar Schools to 1660*) devoted considerable attention to the place of the Bible in the schools. He remarked, " It may be safely asserted that the Statutes of Schools much more frequently include the teaching of the Catechism, Primer and A B C than they explicitly name the Bible. The most important consideration was that the child should know the articles of the faith."

We have evidence of religious instruction in schools from Shakespeare himself. In *King John*, I. i. 192-6, the Bastard refers to an Absey Book. An Absey Book was an A B C Book to which was attached the " Little Catechism," by which name the Catechism in the Book of Common Prayer was distinguished from other catechisms commonly in vogue.

It would be a mistake to imagine that, because English Reformers emphasized the need of a Bible in the vernacular, it immediately occurred to them on their accession to power that that Bible should be taught to pupils in schools. The movement to give the Bible a place in the curriculum was of gradual growth.

The first indication of the entrance of the English Bible into schools is in 1547 from the Injunctions of Commissioners to Winchester. Foster Watson noted four references prior to 1586 to the introduction of Bible-teaching into schools—at East Retford in 1552, Hartlebury 1565, Rivington 1566 and St. Bees 1583. As time went on the movement gathered force, manifesting itself in different schools with all the variety characteristic of the English, until at last in 1604 the Bible was definitely and officially fixed as a school subject (Canon 79).

There is good reason for believing that the English Bible was not taught at schools like Stratford during Shakespeare's youth and adolescence. There were practical difficulties in the way of any such general instruction. For the purpose, an ample supply of Bibles of handy size and small cost would have been requisite. How many copies would have been required may be gauged from Foster Watson's statement that 10,000 copies, and in one year at least considerably more, of the Latin Grammar were printed annually to supply the schools. Even if we admit that Bibles would not be exposed to the same hard usage as were the Latin Grammars yet how many copies of the Bible would require to be printed annually to meet a general demand by schools in addition to that of the ordinary public ?

Anyway there was no prodigious number of Bibles printed in the earlier years of Elizabeth. Before 1575 no great efforts were made to push the Genevan Bible, whose handy size and small cost would have made it the version most convenient for school use. In fact, it was not until 1587, when the Tomson New Testament began to supersede the ordinary Genevan Testament, that large quantities of Bibles began to appear on the market, and it was not until the nineties that those quantities were such as to prove a considerable school demand.

A portion of Scripture may have been read at school

prayers; there is no evidence for denying such a proposition, but also there is none conclusively supporting it. For such a purpose any version might have been used. But if the Bible was taught at Stratford in Shakespeare's boyhood, then beyond all reasonable doubt the version used would have been the Genevan. If so the influence of that version would be manifest in Shakespeare's earliest plays. This subject must be left to the next chapter, where the evidence submitted will tend to the conclusion that in his earlier plays Shakespeare quoted rather from the Bishops' than from the Genevan.

Those who, like Dr. Carter, ascribe to Shakespeare's boyhood a good grounding in Scripture do so under the impression that Biblical phrases and thoughts flowed spontaneously and unconsciously from his pen. As far as the earlier plays are concerned, with the exception of the *Psalms*, it is not my impression that Shakespeare used Biblical phrases and thoughts other than consciously. I have found that in the earlier plays Scriptural allusions are fairly easy to detect but that as the plays progress the references become more idiomatic and more closely woven into the text and in consequence their discovery is rendered more difficult. In our lists under the plays an examination of quotations, apart from those that might be expected to be excerpts from popular speech, will reveal in the Elizabethan plays, as distinguished from the Jacobean, that a very large proportion of them are uttered by a comparatively small number of characters. It will also be observed that while some plays, like the Historical Plays, *Love's Labour's Lost* and *The Merchant of Venice*, abound in Scriptural quotation and allusion, others, like *The Two Gentlemen of Verona* and *The Taming of the Shrew*, for no obvious reason, have remarkably few of them. We should not have had this contrast had it been Shakespeare's instinct to fall back upon Scripture for assistance in expression as do those writers who have been nursed in Scripture. Ginsburg, in the letter already cited, disclaimed any idea that Shakespeare " derived his thoughts or style from the Bible."

A saving clause in favour of the *Psalms* has been entered. From first to last there is not a play in the Folio entirely free from a suggestion of a use of the *Psalms*. In two plays, 2 *King Henry VI.* and *King Henry VIII.*, the allusions to the *Psalms* run into double figures. Even the Sonnets are not devoid of quotations from the *Psalms*. If Shakespeare made instinctive and spontaneous use of any part of Scripture it was of the Psalter.

His indebtedness to the Psalter struck Mr. Anders very forcibly when reviewing the subject in his *Shakespeare's Books*, and he hazarded the suggestion that perhaps he had sung the Psalms in church as a choir-boy. Certainly his knowledge of the Psalms is greater than the ordinary layman might be expected to acquire by attendance at church, and Mr. Anders' suggestion has its attractions. It would account for his acquaintance with some of the elements of vocal music.

It is more likely, however, that Shakespeare knew certain of the Psalms in the Prayer Book thoroughly from having learnt them by heart at school. The Psalter in the school was no innovation at the Reformation; traditionally pupils had been taught several of the Psalms and even in our own time the custom has not died out. It is not at all improbable that some exercise of the sort was a part of the curriculum at Stratford Grammar School. The difficulty that attended the teaching of the Bible would not be applicable to Psalters. As they were required for the services of the Church, a good supply might be expected to be on hand, or Psalms may have been written out by pupils from dictation and then committed to memory.

SHAKESPEARE'S HOME AND THE BIBLE.

Did Shakespeare's parents give him instruction in the Bible ? We may ignore the fact that John Shakespeare signed certain documents with a mark. Even in our own day such a signature would not be a conclusive proof of illiteracy, although it might rank as a strong presumption in favour of it. But in Elizabethan times it would not even be a presumption; making the sign of the cross for a signature was not an extraordinary method of attesting a document. In any case illiteracy would be inconsistent with John's reputed ability in accounts. We may very safely assume that John suffered no literary disability which would have prevented his instructing his son in the Bible narrative. About the mother we know nothing, but from her connections we should not suppose that she could not read. We may take it for granted that neither parent was disabled by lack of education from giving Biblical instruction if so minded.

What we cannot overlook is the assertion that John Shake-

speare was recusant—that is, that he refused to conform with
the established ecclesiastical order—a Roman recusant as
maintained by Dr. Smart (*Shakespeare : Truth and Tradition*),
a Puritan recusant according to Dr. Carter (*Shakespeare :
Puritan and Recusant*). Neither Dr. Smart nor Dr. Carter can be said to have
established his case with any degree of conclusiveness; if
anything, Dr. Smart's is the more probable. There was a
Roman party at Stratford whose strength we may infer
from the fact that Simon Hunt, who was headmaster of the
Grammar School from 1570-5, became one of the Jesuits
at Douai and was afterwards at the penitentiary in Rome
(Sir E. Chambers' *Shakespeare*, vol. i., p. 10). There was
also a strong Puritan party whose influence finally dominated
Shakespeare's own family.

If John Shakespeare opposed the Elizabethan Church
settlement from Roman motives, then nothing more need
be said as to his son's being instructed in the Bible at home.
The English Bible was prominently associated with the
Elizabethan Church, and accordingly it would be viewed
with suspicion by adherents of " things as they used to be."
It would not be treasured.

On the other hand, if John's religious convictions were of
the Genevan persuasion and were sufficiently robust to induce
recusancy, then it would be incredible that he would fail
to secure Biblical instruction for his son. It would be probable, though not absolutely certain, that he would choose the
Genevan version as the medium of instruction. As in the
question of school instruction, the version quoted in the early
plays would naturally be expected to throw some light on
the matter. As already stated, the early plays do not seem
to me to favour the Genevan, but readers can determine
this for themselves.

More important is the respect with which Shakespeare
treated excerpts from the Bible. A child of a home where
the Bible has been treated with veneration, no matter how
his opinions may afterwards develop, has a tendency to
entertain an instinctive respect for the Scriptural writers
and for their utterances. It will be bred in his bones and
he will not rid himself of it unless he is wilfully at war with
his inheritance, and such a rebellious disposition Shakespeare
does not afford evidence of having possessed. The question
then to be put is, Does he give the impression of handling

his Biblical quotations as though he had an inbred respect for their source ?

Evidently Dr. Bowdler thought not, for he laid a heavy hand on many of the Biblical references in the plays. Dr. Bowdler is hardly a fair criterion. His unbending attitude has been repudiated by many devout people and by none more strongly than by Bishop Wordsworth.

A fairer witness is Dr. Carter. He was anxious to establish the good principles that attended Shakespeare's upbringing, and therefore what he says as to the character of his allusions is worthy of respectful attention. He says, " Not that he always quotes with a religious object in view; on the contrary, he is often unmindful of the meaning or association of the words, and becomes so daring and indiscriminate in his use that he shocks the sensitive mind. He may be said to use Scripture on any and every occasion, to dignify the thought of a king, to point the jest of a wit, or to brighten the dulness of a clown." Dr. Carter might have added that Shakespeare did not hesitate to allow the profligate sons of Tamora to use Scriptural controversy to make a jest of their lust (*Titus Andronicus*, IV. ii. 43). Occasionally he seems to have shocked moderate contemporaries, as in his profane allusion to Matt. xxv. 34 (see *2 King Henry IV.*, II. ii. 26-8).

Sometimes he used Biblical ideas in a way our present Censor would consider blasphemous. Let us take an example from *Othello*. Cassio, made drunk, turns theological, a by no means uncommon phenomenon. He exclaims, " Well, God's above all; and there be souls must be saved, and there be souls must not be saved." (Views of the kind were expounded in the Catechism on Predestination prefixed to Genevan [not Tomson] Testaments from 1579 onwards.) Then Cassio proceeds :

For mine own part—no offence to the General, nor any man of quality,—I hope to be saved.
IAGO. And so do I too, lieutenant.
CASSIO. Ay, but, by your leave, not before me: the lieutenant is to be saved before the ancient. . . . God forgive us our sins !

However amusing the incident may be, and were it not for the impending catastrophe it would be extremely funny, our Censor in this present year might delete the passage in a new play brought to him for licence as being offensive to religion.

He might be more lenient in *Twelfth Night*, but that would only be on account of the offence being less obvious, though none the less it is there. Sir Toby is drunk and is in a mood of indignant virtue. He defies lechery, of which he imagines he has been accused. Of the visitor at the gate he says, " Let him be the devil an he will, I care not: ' Give me faith,' say I." The point of this jest can be better appreciated from an extract from some contemporary verse on the Puritan quoted by Nares in his *Glossary* (vol. ii. 700):

His followers preach all faith, and by their workes
You would not judge them catholickes, but Turkes.

In the play that intervened between *Twelfth Night* and *Othello*—*Troilus and Cressida*—the colloquy between the Servant of Paris and Pandarus might have attracted our Censor's attention (see *Troilus and Cressida*, III. i. 1-16).

It is submitted that, had Shakespeare been instructed by his parents to respect the Bible, the influence of that early teaching might have been expected to act as a deterren- and he might have hesitated before presenting certain chert ished opinions in a ridiculous light. It is not denied that the opinions thus made ludicrous were those entertained by types who had made themselves very objectionable to theatre folk and that they deserved all they got.

It is advisable to exercise caution as to these passages and to refrain from drawing any rash conclusion as to Shakespeare's inward convictions from them. It should not be forgotten that the characters made to utter these pieties are not represented as hypocrites; one of them, Cassio, is a splendid type of manhood and would do honour to any cause to which he belonged.

The impression made on my mind by these sallies of Shakespeare is not that he favoured this or that doctrine, or that he was hostile to some other, but that he regarded the contents of the Bible dispassionately. If he was guilty of profanity, he was unaware that a little innocent mischief did anyone any harm and that he had committed any offence. Such an attitude might be regarded as inconsistent with a mind impregnated in youth with Scriptural teaching. It would be reasonable, therefore, to doubt that Shakespeare was grounded in the Bible in his home.

SHAKESPEARE'S USE OF SCRIPTURE FOR DRAMATIC EFFECT.

If occasionally the sensitive religious mind is wounded by some of Shakespeare's lighter references to things treasured as sacred, there is no doubt there are other occasions on which he more than makes amends. That is very largely why Dr. Bowdler in his elimination of what he considered blasphemies has been unable to command the support of the great body of devout men and women. Shakespeare often paraphrased or otherwise made use of a Biblical text or incident in a way that delights a lover of Scripture, and that was one reason that made the learned Ginsburg call him " a most original interpreter of Scripture."

Specially pleasing to the devout is when Shakespeare utilized Scripture to produce a ring of sincerity. In *The Winter's Tale* Polixenes enhances his protest of innocence by his reference to the betrayal of Christ:

> and my name
> Be yok'd with his, that did betray the Best.

Or again, the tragic intensity of the ending of *Othello* is rendered all the more telling by the Moor's probable double reference to Judas Iscariot and the pearl of great price :

> of one whose hand,
> Like the base Judean, threw a pearl away
> Richer than all his tribe. . . .
> I kiss'd thee, ere I kill'd thee.

It is not only in the later plays that Shakespeare caused characters to appeal to Scripture and to make use of its teaching to enhance emotional effect. It is a feature of his work throughout his career. Thus in one of the earliest, *The Two Gentlemen of Verona*, a comedy, as already remarked, strangely bare in Biblical allusion, the generosity of Valentine's forgiveness of Proteus is made all the more touching by his reference to Divine pardon of penitents :

> Who by repentance is not satisfied
> Is nor of heaven, nor earth; for these are pleas'd:
> By penitence th' Eternal's wrath's appeas'd.

Shakespeare's audience of church-goers would be familiar with the point of Valentine's allusion in a way, perhaps, that a modern audience would not be. (See the note in the play.)

Is it not understandable that a devout Christian should regard the Duchess's petition to Bolingbroke in *King Richard II.* as " full of the spirit of true prayer " ?

> Pleads he in earnest ? Look upon his face;
> His eyes do drop no tears, his prayers are in jest;
> His words come from his mouth, ours from our
>   breast.
> He prays but faintly, and would be denied;
> We pray with heart and soul and all beside:
> His weary joints would gladly rise, I know;
> Our knees shall kneel till to the ground they grow:
> His prayers are full of false hypocrisy;
> Ours of true zeal and deep integrity.
> Our prayers do out-pray his: then let them have
> That mercy, which true prayer ought to have.

There is what some would term " real Catholic feeling " in the opening speech of the weary Bolingbroke in *1 King Henry IV.*

> To chase those Pagans in those holy fields
> Over whose acres walk'd those blessed feet
> Which fourteen hundred years ago were nail'd
> For our advantage on the bitter cross.

To a man who has known what spiritual struggle means, Hamlet's Uncle is one of the wonders of Shakespeare's invention. It has often been said of Shakespeare that he failed to give the world a single religious character. It might have been said in reply that King Henry VI. exhibited all the attributes of a deeply religious character— he was gentle, dispassionate in his own worldly affairs, without rancour to his enemies and with a mind given to spiritual contemplation. If that was not satisfactory then it might be said that the failure to discover a religious character was due to the fact that the critics in question had lifted their eyes to heaven and had not peered among the damned in Shakespeare's hell. If only they had turned in the latter direction they might have discovered a soul that was religious in its understanding, a soul that might have ranked among great divines had it not been for the

5

consuming power of physical love and of the ambition which
so often accompanies that passion.

Bishop Wordsworth has hinted that Hamlet's Uncle
influenced Pearson, the eminent Anglican divine born in
the last year of Shakespeare's working life. The wretched
King in the misery of his toils confesses :

> In the corrupted currents of this world
> Offence's gilded hand may shove by justice,
> And oft 'tis seen the wicked prize itself
> Buys out the law. But 'tis not so above;
> There is no shuffling; there the action lies
> In his true nature and we ourselves compell'd
> Even to the teeth and forehead of our faults
> To give in evidence.

Pearson used the figure in his argument on conscience.
" It followeth," he wrote, "that this conscience is not so
much a judge as a witness, bound over to give testimony for
or against us, at some judgment after this life to pass upon us."
Hamlet's Uncle, if anything, put it more powerfully than the
divine, although his source was possibly Juvenal whereas
Pearson referred his argument to Rom. ii. 14-16.

No less notably another villain, Iago, is an exponent of
divinity, and there is in his case no doubt as to the source of
his inspiration. It is Iago who gives Holy Writ its highest
title in " confirmations strong As proofs of Holy Writ."
There has been no better summary than his of the Anglican
doctrine that Baptism is accompanied by forgiveness of sins
and the gift of the Spirit :

> were't to renounce his Baptism,
> All seals and symbols of redeemed sin.

It might be concluded that Iago had been an angel once.
In the play that followed *Othello* Shakespeare developed the
study and there we are asked to watch the angel in course
of his fall.

Many admirers of Shakespeare are pleased or disappointed
with him because they sometimes forget that his purposes
were purely theatrical. His aim was the entertainment of
an audience in a playhouse, and for the purpose he had to
be amusing or to be thrilling, or in some other way to provide

the actors with the means of commanding attention. It was not his conscious task to be either instructive or improving.

As an auxiliary to command the attention of the audience the Bible served him admirably. It was a book in which many were read, and with whose leading features all in some way were more or less familiar. Accordingly, the effect of an ordinary phrase could be heightened by giving it a Biblical touch, and what otherwise might have been flat and undramatic would become vivid and arresting. This will be best illustrated if we take a play for which Shakespeare derived his material from North's *Plutarch*, and in which we do not normally expect Biblical allusion or quotation. The most popular of the Roman plays in the theatre is, without doubt, *Julius Cæsar*. It occurs in the middle of Shakespeare's career, its date can be taken as 1599, and it will serve our purpose very well.

Two passages from the play will suffice. In the life of Marcus Brutus, Portia says (I am quoting from Skeat's *Shakespeare's Plutarch*), " I confess that a woman's wit commonly is too weak to keep a secret safely." Evidently the phrase, " a woman's wit commonly is too weak," caught Shakespeare's attention. He did not use it in Portia's colloquy with Brutus in Act II. i., but employed an adaptation of it in her final soliloquy in Act II. iv., and to make her feverish apprehension more real he imparted a Biblical touch to it. In the play Portia says:

> Ay me ! How weak a thing
> The heart of woman is !

Compare with this Ezek. xvi. 30:

> How weake is thine heart, sayeth the Lord God, seeing thou doest all these, (euen) the woorkes of a presumptuous whorish woman.

The chapter was read in church at Matins on the 17th Sunday after Trinity.

In the same Life of Brutus we read, "And therefore he greatly reproved Brutus, for that he would shew himself so straight and severe, in such a time as was meeter to bear a little than to take things at the worst." In Act IV. iii. 86-8, Shakespeare transmuted the words of Cassius into:

> Brutus hath riv'd my heart:
> A friend should bear his friend's infirmities,
> But Brutus makes mine greater than they are.

" To bear infirmities of others " was a familiar Biblical allusion which Mrs. Quickly misquoted. It was from the Genevan of Rom. xv. 1: " We which are strong, ought to beare the infirmities of the weake." There is no doubt that Shakespeare's skilful use of the familiar Biblical phrase here made the words of Cassius immediately arresting and well calculated to enlist something of the sympathy of the audience with him in his quarrel with Brutus. It would appeal to them and so it could be understood that it would find a soft spot in Brutus.

As a means of suggesting scholarship the Bible was invaluable to Shakespeare. To portray a scholar convincingly is possibly the hardest task a dramatist or novelist can be set. The writer's possession or lack of scholarship is not the point; even if he is as great a scholar as his hero how is he to make his figure comprehensible to his auditor or reader? The mere assertion that the character is a scholar or that he is learned is futile; the scholarly learning must be suggested some way or other, and that, too, within the comprehension of the unlearned patron who has paid to be entertained.

Shakespeare evidently contemplated the portrait of a scholar with some pleasure, judging from the frequency of his efforts in that direction. Especially he delighted in scholar princes, as his portraits of Henry VI., Hamlet, Orsino, Vincentio and Prospero would suggest, to say nothing of the dabblers in learning we meet in *Love's Labour's Lost*. Of the five scholar princes, Henry VI., Hamlet and Vincentio show considerable familiarity with the Bible, and their quotation from that book contributes to the impression of contemplative scholarship. If, in the case of *Hamlet*, many of the spectators recognized anything from Juvenal, it is certain that very many more would know the Biblical references, possibly everybody present.

This was where the Bible was extremely convenient to Shakespeare. It was a book recognized by all as affording scope to the learned, a book that required commentary and trained exposition, and so it was one which could serve as the study of a scholarly character. Quotation from it could denote thoughtful reflection, both in *Hamlet* and *Measure for Measure*, and yet the audience could be relied upon to follow without confusion.

On the lighter side there is a curious fact connected with the Authorised Version which, in these days of attaching serious significance to coincidences in Elizabethan writings, may amuse a number of people. Lord, then Mr. Gerald, Balfour once mentioned that some industrious student had made an extraordinary discovery in one of the Psalms in the Authorised Version. In that version (which was in course of printing when Shakespeare was forty-six years of age), and in no other version previously, in the 46th Psalm, the 46th word from the beginning combined with the 46th word from the end (not counting the direction Selah which is no part of the text) makes the name Shakespeare.

CHAPTER IV

WHICH VERSION DID SHAKESPEARE USE?

SOME DOUBTFUL CLAIMS.

It is beyond all shadow of doubt that on occasions Shakespeare used the Genevan, just as on others he used the Bishops', and on others, again, a rendering found in the Prayer Book. It is not certain that he used the Rheims; there are specks of evidence in favour of that version in *All's Well* and *The Tempest*, and, on the other hand, there are many instances where the version quoted was any but the Rheims. It has not been possible to identify a use of the Great Bible which might not also have been a use of the Prayer Book or of the unrevised Bishops' of 1568 and 1569, or of the Genevan. Neither has it been possible definitely to distinguish a Tomson reference which might not also have been a Genevan, although the evidence is in favour of Shakespeare's possession of a Genevan Old Testament bound up with a Tomson New Testament, and there is also an indication that he may have been influenced by a Tomson marginal note. On the other hand, there are a couple of instances where the reference might have been either to the Genevan or the Bishops', but certainly not to the Tomson. Broadly the issue is triangular and concerns the Genevan-Tomson (*i.e.*, a Genevan Old Testament and Apocrypha bound up with a Tomson New Testament), the Bishops' and Common Prayer—every one of the identifiable English Biblical quotations or allusions in Shakespeare's plays conforms more or less to passages to be found in one or more of these versions.

As all these three versions, with the exception of a few passages of Scripture found in the Book of Common Prayer, belong to the same family, and are very closely related, the task of identifying the particular version is not always easy, and is at times quite impossible. In this connection it may as well be reiterated that even the Rheims is not entirely unrelated to the Genevan and the Bishops', despite the abuse its editors poured upon them. The great resemblance thus existing has led numbers to false conclusions, and the influence of particular versions on particular occasions has been claimed on inadequate grounds.

For instance, it happens that numbers have cited the Genevan version in several cases as Shakespeare's source, without considering sufficiently the possibilities of other versions that were also accessible to him. This remark applies to the four great examples, the accumulative force of which has been held to point decisively to the use of the Genevan Bible; not one of the four is watertight owing to the fact that the search has not been thorough enough. The great four may be taken to be Shylock's " parti-coloured lambs " (*Merchant of Venice*), Prince Henry's " good amendment of life " (*1 King Henry IV.*), Norfolk's reference to the leopard's spots and the Bishop of Carlisle's " dead men's skulls " (both from *King Richard II.*). A fifth might be added in " Sathan avoid " in *The Comedy of Errors*, though strangely Dr. Carter overlooked this instance and quoted the Authorised for it.

Let us take the passages in order. First there is the speech of Shylock (*Merchant of Venice*, I. iii. 72-89):

When Jacob graz'd his Uncle Laban's sheep . . .
Mark what Jacob did.
When Laban and himself were compromis'd
That all the eanlings which were streak'd and pied
Should fall as Jacob's hire, the ewes, being rank,
In th' end of Autumn turned to the rams,
And, when the work of generation was
Between these woolly breeders in the act,
The skilful shepherd peel'd me certain wands
And, in the doing of the deed of kind,
He stuck them up before the fulsome ewes,
Who then conceiving did in eaning time
Fall parti-colour'd lambs, and those were Jacob's.

This battle of craft is related in Gen. xxx., and here are the accounts according to the Genevan and Bishops':

Geneva, 1587.	Bishops', 1585.
32. I will passe through all thy flockes this day, and separate from them all the sheepe with litle spots & great spots, and all blacke lambes among the sheepe,	I will goe about all thy flockes this day, & separate from them all the cattel that are spotted, and of diuers colours: and all the blacke among the sheepe, and

and the great spotted, and litle spotted among the goates: and it shalbe my wages. . . .

37. Then Iaakob tooke rods of greene popular, and of hazell, and of the chesnut tree, and pilled white strakes in them, and made the white appeare in the rods. . . .

39. And the sheepe were in heate before the rods, and afterward brought foorth yong of partie colour, and with small and great spots.

the partie and spotted among the kiddes, (the same) shalbe my reward. . . .

Iacob tooke rods of greene populer, hasell, and chessenut trees, and pilled white strakes in them, and made the white appeare in the roddes. . . .

And the sheepe conceiued before the rods, and brought foorth lambes ringstraked, spotted, and partie.

The 35th verse may be given as in the Great Bible of 1569, as the expression " partie coloured " also occurs there.

Therefore he toke out the same day the hee goates that were partie and of diuers colourre, and all the shee goates that were spotted and partie coloured. . . .

The term " parti-coloured " was no monopoly of the Genevan as some have appeared to think. In all the versions Joseph's coat, as in Gen. xxxvii. 23, was parti-coloured.

The Bishops' describes the lambs as " partie," which is not a far remove from " partie coloured," having regard to the mention of " diuers colours." Shylock speaks of the eanlings as " streaked " (Bishops' " ringstraked," the Genevan has not the term); of the ewes as " then conceiving " (Bishops' " conceiued," Genevan " were in heate "); of the young dropped as " lambs " (Bishops' " lambes," the Genevan " yong "); and the name of the patriarch is spelt Iacob, and not as Iakob or Iaakob as in the Genevan.

Dr. Ginsburg inferred from Antonio's speech that Shakespeare had been inspired by the Bishops' marginal note. Antonio protested:

This was a venture, sir, that Jacob serv'd for,
A thing not in his power to bring to pass,
But sway'd and fashion'd by the hand of heaven.

The marginal note in the Bishops' of 1568, 1569 and 1572 runs (as also in later editions), " It is not lawful by fraude to seeke recompence of iniurie: therefore Moses sheweth afterwarde that god thus instructed Iacob, Gen. 31.b." From 1568-72 in Bishops' Bibles the chapters were divided into lettered paragraphs as well as into verses, and " Gen. 31.b "

means Genesis xxxi., verses 7-13. Antonio regarded Shylock, like Satan, as making a partial statement of Scripture,
and he therefore reminded him of the next chapter to which
the Bishops' marginal note called attention.

It is interesting that Shylock's speech should afford a proof
to several that Shakespeare used the Genevan, and at the
same time that in Antonio's protest Dr. Ginsburg should
discern the influence of the Bishops'. On points, I think
the Bishops' has the better of it.

The next instance is in *1 King Henry IV.*, I. ii. 114, where
the Prince says to Falstaff, " I see a good amendment of
life in thee." In the New Testament, " amendment of
life " is peculiar to the Genevan of Luke xv. 7 (" which neede
none amendement of life " as also Matt. iii. 8 and Acts
xxvi. 20). But the phrase is also found in the Exhortation
in the Communion Service—" confess yourselves to Almighty
God, with full purpose of amendment of life." It abounds
in the Homily on Repentance. In addition, the rendering
of Matt. iii. 2, prefixed to Morning and Evening Prayer,
cannot be overlooked—" Amende your liues, for the kyng-
dome of God is at hande." The phrase " amend your lives "
also occurs in the Communion Office and " amend our
lives " in the Litany as well as similar phrases in the Genevan of Luke xiii. 3, etc. Altogether the idea of " amendment of life " was far too common to admit of the source
of the Prince's remark being confined to a few verses in the
Genevan.

The third and fourth are from *King Richard II.* In Act
I. i. 174-5, the King says, " Lions make leopards tame," to
which Norfolk replies, " Yea, but not change his spots."
This reply of Norfolk's is according to the Genevan of
the famous verse of Jer. xiii. 23—" Can the blacke More
change his skin? or the leopard his spots?" Instead of
" leopard " the Bishops' gave " the catte of the mountaine."
In *Euphues* occurs, " Can the Aethiope chaunge or alter
his skinne? or the leopard his hiew?" The phrase about
the leopard and his spots, from its occurrence in *Euphues*,
sounds as though it was proverbial and hence gives the
impression that it was from popular speech rather than from
any Biblical version that Norfolk quoted.

In Act IV. i. 144, in the speech of the Bishop of Carlisle
we find, " and this land be call'd The field of Golgotha
and dead men's skulls." In the Genevan of Mark xv. 22

we have " Golgotha, which is by interpretation, the place of dead mens skulles," and so also in Matt. xxvii. 33 and John xix. 17. The Bishops' has " place of a skull " and the Rheims " the place of Caluarie." As there is no evidence pointing exclusively to the Great Bible we can leave it out of account, but there is the Prayer Book Gospel appointed for Good Friday (a very important service). It is of John xix. 17: " & went furth into a place, whiche is called the place of dead mennes sculles: but in Hebrue Golgotha."

No claim has been advanced by Genevan champions on behalf of " Sathan, avoid ! I charge thee, tempt me not " (*Comedy of Errors*, IV. iii. 47), owing apparently to an oversight. It is clearly in reference to Matt. iv. 10, which is in the Genevan, " Auoyde Sathan."† This is also the rendering in the 1568 and 1569 Bishops' but not in the Revised Bishops' of 1572 *et seq.* which runs " Get thee hence behinde me, Satan." " Auoide Sathan " is the reading contained in the Prayer Book Gospel for the 1st Sunday in Lent. The Rheims has " Auant Satan."

From these examples it will be seen that some caution must be exercised in making any claims for any version. Because a passage in Shakespeare can be identified as corresponding with a passage in a particular version, it does not of necessity follow that that has been Shakespeare's immediate source. He may have been indebted to another version or to some intermediate, or to some other part of the Bible not noticed by the student.

One example will be sufficient to enforce the lesson. In *King Richard II.*, II. ii. 76, the Queen says, " Uncle, for God's sake, speak comfortable words." The phrase " comfortable words " is very familiar to devout Anglicans in the Communion Service after the Absolution: " Hear what comfortable words our Saviour Christ saith unto all that truly turn to him." It also occurs in the Genevan of Zech. i. 13: " with good wordes and comfortable wordes." There is no doubt about the resemblance and there is no question of the plenitude of opportunity of either hearing the phrase in church or of reading it in the Liturgy or Genevan Bible. Yet I do not believe either was Shakespeare's immediate source. I think his mind was elsewhere.

When Shakespeare came to write *King Richard II.*, he seems to have turned to the Bible for material wherewith

† See Note, p. 280.

to illustrate the darkening wits of the distracted King. Almost the King's first words in Act III. ii. suggest this search. When Aumerle tried to persuade Richard to adopt some measure of ordinary forethought, the King rounded on him with " Discomfortable cousin !"

" Discomfortable " in the sense of " disheartening "— *i.e.*, causing depression—is extremely rare in our language, in fact it may be said to have been obsolete ever since its birth and only to have been employed by those who loved curiously applied words. Coverdale preserved it in Ecclus. xviii. 14. It was retained both by the Bishops' and Genevan, but rejected by the Authorised in favour of " uncomfortable." The Bishops' renders the verse, " My sonne, when thou doest good, make no grudging at it: and whatsoeuer thou giuest, speake no discomfortable wordes." The Bishops' of Tobit x. 4 has " she wept with discomfortable teares," but that sense "inconsolable" is not so rare and striking. Decidedly " speake no discomfortable wordes " would make an impression on anyone, like Shakespeare, interested in words and phrases ; it is the kind of expression the eye would catch ; it checks the reading as " uncomfortable " does not do and gives an incomparably intimately personal effect to the whole verse. As an orator Coverdale knew what he was doing when he chose the word.

When Shakespeare was endowing the Queen with speech in Act. II. ii., he had already seized upon the " discomfortable " of *Ecclesiasticus* and marked it for his own. Actually I believe the Queen's words were not inspired by the Liturgy or by the Genevan of *Zechariah* but by the antithesis of " comfortable " found in *Ecclesiasticus*, and " speake no discomfortable wordes " became in her mouth, " speak comfortable words," meaning words calculated to raise her spirits.

Whether this conjecture be accepted or not, at least it will be conceded that a plausible case has been made against what must seem to be the obvious source of the Queen's remark. Consequently, it is urged, no instance by itself is secure, it is the aggregation of instances that really is important: one stray example of a resemblance to a version unsupported by others, means nothing, there is no saying what was Shakespeare's immediate influence; it is when there is a number of sound examples that the argument becomes significant, every additional example enforcing the probability.

Readers will be well advised to remember this when they

peruse the succeeding pages. Examples will be presented to them, but they should not be regarded otherwise than as pieces of evidence tending to a certain cumulative effect. Also it should be borne in mind that all pieces of evidence are not of equal value, some are more valuable than others and some are very dubious; it is for the reader to determine for himself the value he attaches to each.

Of one type of evidence the reader will be well advised to be particularly cautious. Differences in spelling Biblical names will be noted, but it is impossible to attach much weight to them. No one can say precisely whose spelling we have in Quartos and Folios, but even if it is Shakespeare's we do not know from where he derived his spelling of Biblical proper names; probably it was derived from no particular Biblical model either consciously or unconsciously. Most likely popular usage was followed.

The Genevan-Tomson Bible, the Bishops' of 1572 *et seq.*, and Common Prayer are taken as our starting point; it is assumed Shakespeare used these three. As the Great Bible figures in the ancestry of all three (a few sentences in Common Prayer excepted) it is not necessary to point out its agreements, especially since no passage in Shakespeare has been found to be exclusively identified with it. Differences of the genuine Genevan New Testament from the Tomson are noted. In every New Testament passage the Rheims is given, where it disagrees, that all may satisfy themselves how far from or how near to that version the Shakespearian passage is. The examples given comprise only a selection; any reader who desires to make a complete list of passages involving one version rather than another can do so from our lists under the Plays and of the Proper Names.

THE CASE FOR THE GENEVAN-TOMSON.

In *Love's Labour's Lost*, Salomon is as in the Genevan and Prayer Book. In the Bishops' it is Solomon.

The Genevan introduced " Iudea " for Jewry, and throughout Elizabeth's reign the term remained peculiar to it and its Tomson revision. " Like the base Judean " in *Othello* can be looked upon accordingly as a Genevan reading.

In *2 King Henry VI.*, Henry says, " O graceless men ! they know not what they do." This occurs in various forms in several of the plays. It is derived from the Genevan and the Rheims of Luke xxiii. 34, " for they know not what they doe." Other versions read " wote not." Possibly, like the leopard's spots, it was a popular phrase.

In the references to the Parable of the Prodigal Son by Falstaff in *1 King Henry IV.*, IV. ii., and by Orlando in *As You Like It*, I. i., the Genevan and the Rheims have been followed. The Genevan reads (Luke xv. 16): " And hee would faine haue filled his bellie with the huskes, that the swine ate," and this is substantially repeated by the Rheims. Instead of " huskes " the Bishops' and its predecessors read " cods."

The Genevan begins definitely to manifest its influence in *2 King Henry IV.*, whose date might be taken to be about 1596-7. In Act I. i. 47, if the figure of a steed devouring or swallowing the ground—" He seem'd in running to devour the way,"—was suggested by the Bible to Shakespeare then the medium was the Genevan of Job xxxix. 27: " He swalloweth the ground for fiercenesse and rage." The reading in the Bishops', " Yet rusheth hee in fiercely, beating the ground," has not nearly the same thrill. The figure is not uncommon and it might occur to anyone owning a highly mettled horse.

The next is also from the Book of *Job*. In Act I. ii. 7, Falstaff says " this foolish compounded clay man." The Genevan of Job xxxiii. 6 is " I am also formed of the clay." The Bishops' has " moulde."

In Act II. ii. 52, the Prince's " let the end try the man," although apparently a proverbial remark, has a base in the Genevan of Job xxxiv. 36, " I desire that Iob may be tried, vnto the ende touching the answeres for wicked men." The Bishops' " let Iob be wel tryed."

In Act II. iv. Mrs. Quickly turns the Genevan of Rom. xv. 1 topsy turvy. She says " you cannot one bear with another's confirmities. . . . One must bear, and that must be you: you are the weaker vessel." The Genevan has, " We which are strong, ought to beare the infirmities of the weake." It is also quoted in *Julius Cæsar* by Cassius in his altercation with Brutus. Instead of " infirmities " the Bishops' reads " frailenesse." The Rheims renders thus, " And vve that are the stronger, must susteine the infirmities of the vveake." The " weaker vessel " is in 1 Pet. iii. 7, but it is also a Euphuism. It is, however, in the Genevan form that Mrs. Quickly applies it. In the Genevan it is the woman who is the weaker vessel while in the Bishops' it is the wife. The Rheims has " the vveaker feminine vessel."

In Act IV. i. the Archbishop applied the Parable of the Tares among the Wheat to the King's delicate position :

> That, plucking to unfix an enemy,
> He doth unfasten so and shake a friend.

The word in the Genevan of Matt. xiii. 29 is " plucke ": " Nay, lest while yee goe about to gather the tares, yee plucke vp also with them the wheate." So also the Prayer Book Gospel for the 5th and 6th Sundays after Epiphany. Bishops' and Rheims, " roote vp."

In *King Henry V.*, IV. vii. 66, the King says, " Enforced from the old Assyrian slings." Obviously anything Assyrian is, or is intended to be, Biblical. The way " Assyrian slings " occurs here would lead one to suppose that, like those of Benjamin, Assyrian slingers were famous and that they were prominently mentioned in the Bible. It is, therefore, surprising that only one reference can be found to Assyrian slings, and that a very obscure one, in the Genevan of Judith ix. 7, " they trust in shield, speare, & bow, and sling." The Bishops' omits any reference to slings or slingers.

Jaques makes a remark in *As You Like It*, V. iv. 35-6, arguing acquaintance with the Genevan, " There is sure another flood toward, and these couples are coming to the Ark. Here comes a pair of very strange beasts." The Genevan of Gen. vii. 2 is " Of euery cleane beast, thou shalt take to thee by seuens, the male and his female: but of vncleane beasts by couples, the male and his female." The Bishops' is " but of vncleane cattel, two, the male and his female." The Genevan note explained that of the seven clean beasts, " sixe were for breed, and the seuenth for sacrifice."

Hamlet affords evidence of the use of the Genevan. First, we might take Laertes', " A double blessing is a double grace." The phrase " double grace " is found in the Genevan of Ecclus. xxvi. 15 and is there applied to " A shamefast & faithfull woman." It should be noted that " grace " is also another term for a blessing before a meal and so Laertes makes the play.

The Genevan of Job x. 21, " Before I goe and shall not returne, euen to the land of darknesse, and shadow of death: Into a land, I say, darke as darknesse it selfe, and into the shadow of death, where is none order, but the light is there as darknes," is the nearer to Hamlet's

> But that the dread of something after death,
> The undiscover'd country from whose bourne
> No traveller returns,

in Act III. i. 78-80.

Strongest of all is in Act III. iii. 80, when Hamlet in his excitement drops into the vernacular and utters, " A' took my father grossly, full of bread." It is in Ezek. xvi. 49 in the Genevan, " Behold, this was the iniquitie of thy sister Sodom, Pride, fulnesse of bread, and abundance of idlenesse was in her, and in her daughters." The other versions read " meate " instead of " bread."

The next example is, in Act V. ii. 232-3, where Hamlet observes, " There is special providence in the fall of a sparrow." The word " fall " occurs in the Genevan of Matt. x. 29, " Are not two sparrowes sold for a farthing, and one of them shall not fall on the ground without your Father ?" The Bishops' has "light on the ground." The Rheims agrees with the Genevan.

It is interesting to note that Sir Toby's invitation to Maria (*Twelfth Night*), " Wilt thou set thy foot o' my neck ?" as a token of his complete subjugation by her accords with the Genevan of Josh. x. 24, which records the incident of the five kings that has given rise to the figure, " Come neere, set your feete vpon the neckes." The Bishops' has " put." Belarius in *Cymbeline*, III. iii. 91, uses the same phrase, " Thus mine enemy fell And thus I set my foot on's neck."

Our next is the comparison of Desdemona in *Othello*, IV. ii. 58-61 to a fountain and a cistern :

> The fountain from the which my current runs
> Or else dries up: to be discarded thence !
> Or keep it as a cistern for foul toads
> To knot and gender in.

Thus the Genevan of Prov. v. 15-18 :

> Drinke the water of thy cisterne, and of the riuers out of the middes of thine owne well. Let thy foun-taines flowe foorth, and the riuers of waters in the streetes. But let them bee thine, euen thine onely, and not the strangers with thee. Let thy fountaine bee blessed, and reioyce with the wife of thy youth.

The Genevan note says, " Thy children which shall come of thee in great abundance, shewing that God blesseth mariage and curseth whoredome." The Bishops' has neither " fountain " nor " cistern " in the passage. In the Homily on Idleness the 15th verse is quoted in its Genevan form, but there the " cistern " is not taken as a wife.

In *Measure for Measure*, I. ii. 131, Claudio's " The words of heaven: on whom it will, it will," agrees with the Genevan of Rom. ix. 15 rather than with the Bishops'. The former reads, " I will haue mercie on him, to whom I will shewe mercie: and will haue compassion on him, on whom I will haue compassion." The Bishops' is less emphatic, " I will shewe mercie, to whom so euer I shew mercie: and will haue compassion, on whom so euer I haue compassion." The Rheims substantially follows the Genevan.

In *Timon of Athens*, IV. iii. 174, Timon answers the assertion of Alcibiades that he never did him any harm by " Yea, thou spok'st well of me." This is according to the Genevan variant of Luke vi. 26, " Wo be to you when all men speake well of you." The Bishops' variant " praise " is found in *Twelfth Night*, V. i. 11-19. The Rheims has " VVo, vvhen al men shal blesse you."

Menenius in *Coriolanus*, Act V. iv. 25, observes, " He wants nothing of a god but eternity and a heaven to throne in." These attributes of the Deity are mentioned in the Genevan of Isa. lvii. 15, " For thus sayth hee, that is hie and excellent, hee that inhabiteth the eternitie, whose Name is the Holy one "; and of Isaiah lxvi. 1, " Thus sayth the Lord, The heauen is my throne." In these passages the Bishops' reads " euerlastingnes " and " seate." The fact that the two words occur in the same book and pretty much in the same part of the book would increase the presumption that Shakespeare was indebted to the Genevan of *Isaiah*.

In the dirge in *Cymbeline*, IV. ii., " Home art gone and ta'en thy wages " is owing to the comparison of our life with a task appointed to a hired labourer to whom reward will be given. The most prominent instance in the Bible is the Parable of the Labourers in Matt. xx. 1-16, where all the versions speak of " hire." But the idea is also taken up by St. Paul in 1 Cor. iii. 8 and the Genevan reads " euery man shall receiue his wages, according to his labour." The other two versions read " rewarde."

The Winter's Tale, IV. iii. 491, offers interesting evidence on behalf of the Genevan. Florizel says, " Let Nature crush the sides o' th' earth together." The Genevan of Jer. vi. 22 reads, " a great nation shall arise from the sides of the earth." Other versions read " endes."

The final instance to be cited in favour of the Genevan is connected with Eccles. v. 11. In 1560 the Genevans made this verse read, " The sleepe of him that trauaileth, is sweete," and so it was reprinted in all black letter editions of the Genevan that I have examined. In the roman letter editions at some time or other this " trauaileth " became " traueileth " and in this form it was printed in editions appearing in 1576, 1587, 1590, 1591, 1592, 1593, 1594. lt may have been so printed in other roman letter editions, I am only speaking of those actually examined. In 1595, in at least one roman letter edition, a Genevan-Tomson Bible, this " traueileth " became " trauelleth " and thus it was printed also in a Genevan-Tomson of 1598. The first year of the appearance of " trauelleth " was 1595, as far as I have been able to find out, and the collections in the possession of the British and Foreign Bible Society, British Museum and Glasgow University have been searched for the purpose. Both the Bibles in which the variant has been found were Genevan-Tomson Bibles.

Shakespeare would seem to have read such a Bible and to have mistaken the import of the verse, for in *Measure for Measure*, IV. iv. 69-70, Claudio, with the verse evidently in mind, says of Barnardine that he is

As fast lock'd up in sleep, as guiltless labour,
When it lies starkly in the traveller's bones.

The Bishops' rendering of the passage is " A labouring man sleepeth sweetely."

THE CASE FOR THE BISHOPS'.

As to the spelling of proper names, in *The Merchant of Venice*, it is Iacob as in the Bishops' and not Iaakob or Iakob of the Genevan. In *2 King Henry IV.*, Falstaff says, " A whoreson Achitophel." So the name is spelt in some of the later Bishops', in the 1584 and 1585 for example. But in the 1572 it is spelt as in the Genevan—" Ahithophel." Nothing could illustrate more the futility of ascribing to Shakespeare's reading certain versions because of agreements in spelling.

6

In *King Henry VIII.*, V. v. 25-6, Cranmer speaks of the Queen of Sheba as Saba and this is often quoted in favour of the Bishops' as in that version her land is called " Saba " whereas in the Genevan text it is " Sheba." But the argument is far from watertight. The Genevan page and chapter headings have " Saba." " Saba " was the ordinary popular name from the Vulgate and in that form it appears in the Psalter, Ps. lxxii. 10.

Perhaps more important is the fact that Shakespeare nowhere has " Judæa " although he has " Judean." Instead, he has Iewry or Iury or Iurie (except in *Antony and Cleopatra*, when he was copying North, he does not use Iewry in the later plays). In some such form the name will be found in the Bishops', Prayer Book and Rheims, never as Iudæa. The name Iuda occurs in the Gospel narrative but not the other.

1 King Henry VI., I. v. 9, offers evidence for the Bishops' when Talbot exclaims " Heavens, can you suffer hell so to prevail ?" It is a reference to Matt. xvi. 18, which in the Bishops' reads " & the gates of hel shal not preuaile against it." The Prayer Book Gospel for St. Peter's Day and the Rheims are in agreement, but the Genevan has " shall not ouercome it."

In *2 King Henry VI.*, III. i. 69-71, the King declares that Gloucester is as innocent of treason " As is the sucking lamb, or harmless dove." The Biblical allusion is obvious; " harmelesse as the Doues," is the Bishops' of Matt. x. 16 and it is peculiar to that version. The Genevan has " innocent " and the Rheims " simple."

It is in *Love's Labour's Lost* that quotations from the Bishops' most abound. First there is the famous one in IV. iii. 363-5, where the resourceful Berowne argues:

> It is religion to be thus forsworn,
> For charity itself fulfils the law
> And who can sever love from charity ?

There can be no doubt as to either the identity or the source of this quotation, for in the form cited by Berowne it is without paraphrase and is to be found in the Bishops' and, as far as known, nowhere else, not even in the Wicliffite or the Rheims. The Bishops' of Rom. xiii. 10 is " Charitie worketh no ill to his neighbour, therefore the fulfilling of the law is charitie." This is quoted here from the 1585

Folio, but it is the same, except for spelling, in which the variety is extreme, in all Bishops' Bibles and Testaments examined. In all other known versions it is "loue." As the previous verse had ended "Thou shalt loue thy neighbour as thy selfe," the change over from "love" to "charity" was extraordinary and possibly aroused some pointed comment. We have a suggestion of this in *Titus Andronicus*, IV. ii. 43, where Chiron remarks jocularly on the expressed lust of Demetrius for a thousand Roman dames, "A charitable wish, and full of love."

There is another variation on the verse in *The Merchant of Venice*, I. ii. 84, when Portia says of the Scottish lord, in sly allusion to the Franco-Scottish entente against England, "That he hath a neighbourly charity in him." Altogether the verse served Shakespeare fairly well and the possibility that he was aware of its controversial feature is of interest.

There is no doubt about another reference in *Love's Labour's Lost*, I. ii. 95, where the lively young Moth says of Delilah that "she had a green wit." The play on the Bishops' of Judg. xvi. 8, "And then the lords of the Philistines brought her seuen withs that were yet greene, and neuer dried, and she bound him therewith," is fairly obvious. Instead of "withs" the Genevan had "cordes," which would deprive Moth's remark of its point. The chapter did not figure as a Lesson for a Sunday or Holy Day. It was not likely, therefore, that Shakespeare heard it read in church.

In the first scene of the play Berowne asks, "What is the end of study?" and proceeds to make game of study, and finally, in the spirit of *Ecclesiastes*:

> Why, all delights are vain, but that most vain,
> Which with pain purchas'd, doth inherit pain,
> As painfully to pore upon a book
> To seek the light of truth.

Compare with this Eccles. xii. verses 9 and 12 as in the Bishops': "All is but vanitie (saith the preacher) all is but plaine vanitie. . . . Therefore beware my sonne of that doctrine that is beside this: for to make many bookes, it is an endlesse worke: and too much study wearieth the body." The Genevan has "and much reading" instead of "study" which is the point of Berowne's argument.

Berowne's "like a rude and savage man of Inde" is based on Jer. xiii. 23 as found in the Bishops', "May a man of

Inde chaunge his skinne." The Bishops' retained substantially the reading of the Great Bible, whilst the Genevan
substituted " blacke More." No doubt the phrase became
popular to denote outlandish people, although the chapter
was not read in church on a Sunday. It also occurs in
The Tempest, II. ii. 61. In that same play we have " cat
o' mountain," but whether it is in allusion to " and the
catte of the mountaine her spots ?" mentioned in the Bishops'
instead of " leopard," is quite impossible to determine.

In Act IV. iii. of *Love's Labour's Lost* there is an interesting
use of *The Song of Solomon*, which seems to be decidedly after
the Bishops' rather than the Genevan.

> BER. O ! 'tis the sun that maketh all things shine.
> KING. By heaven, thy love is black as ebony.
> BER. Is ebony like her ?   O wood divine !
> A wife of such wood were felicity.
> O, who can give an oath ? where is a book ?
> That I may swear beauty doth beauty lack,
> If that she learn not of her eye to look,
> No face is fair that is not full so black.

The Bishops' of The Song of Solomon i. 4-5 reads: " I am
blacke (O ye daughters of Hierusalem) but yet fayre and
well fauoured, like as the tents of the Cedarenes, and as
the hangings of Solomon. Maruaile not at mee that I am
so blacke, for why ? the Sunne hath shined vpon mee."
The Genevan has: " I am blacke, O daughters of Ierusalem,
but comely, as the tents of a Cedar, and as the curtaines
of Salomon. Regard ye me not because I am blacke: for
the sunne hath looked vpon mee." The point made by
Berowne is " No face is fair that is not full so black," and
there the . Bishops' lends him some support, whereas the
Genevan has " comely " and the delightful paradox is lost.
There is also the point as to the sun shining and not looking
upon her.

Also from the Bishops' of the Song of Solomon v. 10,
Armado's " My love is most immaculate white and red "
(I. ii. 96) might have been taken. The Bishops' has " As
for my loue, he is white and red coloured," instead of the
Genevan's " My welbeloued is white and ruddie."

In the last scene in line 292 " and leap for joy " the phrase
is found in the Bishops' of Luke vi. 23, " and leape ye for
ioy." The Genevan has " Reioyce yee in that day, and be

glad," and the Rheims " Be glad in that day and reioyce."
" Leape ye for ioy " in Luke vi. 23 was peculiar to the
Bishops'; it was not in the Great Bible, but was in the Genevan
margin.

The predilection for the Bishops' found in this comedy
is very curious. Were it confined just to one part of the
Bible, it would not be so remarkable. A glance over the
quotations just mentioned will show that the Books concerned
are well spread—*Judges, Ecclesiastes, Song of Solomon, Jeremiah,
Luke* and *Romans*. Not one of the Old Testament chapters
figured as a Lesson read on Sundays. The cumulative
evidence is such that only one conclusion is reasonably
possible—Shakespeare had read portions of the Bible in the
Bishops' version before he wrote the comedy. It would not
even be too much to say that he had read considerable
portions, for he would not use a tithe of what he had perused.

In *King Richard II.*, I. iii. 202, Norfolk protests, " My name
be blotted from the Book of Life." This agrees with the
Bishops' of Rev. iii. 5, " and I wil not blot out his name out
of the booke of life." Both the Genevan and the Rheims
have " put " for " blot." Later in the play Richard says
" Mark'd with a blot, damn'd in the Book of Heaven."

In addition to the name Chus, instead of Cush, *The Merchant
of Venice* affords some evidence of the use of the Bishops'.
The account of Laban and Jacob, although on the whole
it is favourable to the Bishops', can be left on one side as it
is open to debate. Also Portia's use of " neighbourly charity "
need not be repeated. Gobbo's " the boy was the very staff
of my age," in Act II. ii. 71-2, is our first instance. In the
Bishops' of Tobit v. 23 we have with reference to Tobias
" his mother began to weepe, and said, The staffe of our age
hast thou taken away." Also Tobit x. 4, " thou staffe of
our age." In the Genevan of Tobit v. 17 Tobias is said to
be " the staffe of our hand."

Again in Act III. v. 21, Jessica asserts, " I shall be sav'd
by my husband, he hath made me a Christian." This
would agree with the Bishops' of 1 Cor. vii. 14 rather than
with the Tomson. The former reads, " the vnbeleeuing
wife is sanctified by the husbande." The Genevan proper
and the Rheims adopt the same rendering, but the Tomson
has " to " for " by " and such a reading would not accord
with Jessica's remark.

In *1 King Henry IV.*, I. ii. 99-100, the Prince, taking up the line offered him by Falstaff about the old lord of the council who had " talked very wisely, but I regarded him not: and yet he talked wisely, and in the street too," made the reply he was expected to make from Prov. i. 20, 24: " Thou didst well: for wisdom cries out in the streets and no man regards it." In the Bishops' it runs, " Wisedome cryeth without, & putteth forth her voyce in the streetes. . . . Because I haue called, and yee refused, I haue stretched out my hand, and no man regarded." Instead of " and no man regarded " the Genevan reads " and none would regard."

In the same scene there is another instance where a phrase occurs that is common to the Bishops' and Genevan but is not to be found in the Tomson. In the last line of this scene the Prince says, " Redeeming time when men think least I will." " Redeeming the tyme, because the dayes are euill," is a notable phrase from the Bishops' of Ephes. v. 16, and the Genevan proper agrees substantially. Again in Col. iv. 5 the Bishops' has " Walke in wisedome toward them that are without, redeeming the time," and the Genevan has " redeeme the time." In each instance the Rheims agrees with the Bishops' but the Tomson reads " season " for " time."

Passages which look like echoes of Bishops' renderings crop up in *King Henry V*. First, there is one that attracted the curiosity of Canon Todd because of the rendering of the Greek in the Authorised. In Act II. ii. 42 the King says " It was excess of wine that set him on." There may be nothing in it, but " in excesse of wines " occurs in the Bishops' of 1 Pet. iv. 3, where the Genevan has " drunkennesse " and the Rheims has practically the Bishops'.

A little stronger, perhaps, in the same scene is the King's

> The mercy that was quick in us but late,
> By your own counsel is suppress'd and kill'd:
> You must not dare, for shame, to talk of mercy.

It has some affinity with the Bishops' rendering of Ecclus. xxviii. 4, " Hee that sheweth no mercie to a man which is like himselfe, howe dare hee aske forgiuenes of his sinnes ?" The Genevan has " will " for " dare."

We have Pistol's " men of mould," probably a popular phrase. It occurs in the Bishops' of Job xxxiii. 6, " made euen of the same moulde." The Genevan has " clay."

Also in the Bishops' of Tobit viii. 8, " Thou madest Adam of the moulde of the earth " (the Genevan has simply " Thou madest Adam ").

In Act IV. i. 193 there is a decisive instance in favour of the Bishops'. The King says " and dying so, death is to him advantage." This is an application of Phil. i. 21, as in the Bishops', " For Christ (is) to me life, and death is to me aduantage." The Genevan adopted Whittingham's alteration, " For Christ is to me both in life, and in death aduantage." The Rheims is as in modern Bibles, " For vnto me, to liue is Christ: and to die is gaine."

In *Twelfth Night*, V. i. 19, the Clown quotes the Bishops' variant of Luke vi. 26, " Woe vnto you when men shal prayse you," Genevan, " speake well of you " and the Rheims, " blesse."

There is an interesting possible use of the Bishops' in *Timon*, IV. i. 25-8, where Timon curses the Athenian youth:

<blockquote>
Lust and liberty
Creep in the minds and marrows of our youth,
That 'gainst the stream of virtue they may strive,
And drown themselves in riot.
</blockquote>

Compare this with the Bishops' of Ecclus. iv. 28, " And striue thou not against the stream: but for righteousnesse take paines with all thy soule, and for the trueth striue thou vnto death." The Genevan omits altogether " And striue thou not against the stream."

Of the Bishops' account of the Shunamite woman's reply as to her dead child's health, Shakespeare seems to have made use on five occasions, *Romeo and Juliet*, IV. v. 76, *2 King Henry IV.*, V. ii. 3, *Macbeth*, IV. iii. 176-9; *Antony and Cleopatra*, II. v. 31-3 and *Winter's Tale*, V. i. 30. We take the last but one, where in reply to the messenger's assurance that Antony is well, Cleopatra says, " But, sirrah, mark, we use To say the dead are well." See 2 Kings iv. 26, " Is all well with thee, and with thy husband, and with the ladde ? And she answered, All is well." The Genevan variant is " Art thou in health ? is thine husband in health ? & is the childe in health ? And she answered, We are in health."

From a perusal of these two lists of the principal Genevan and Bishops' quotations it will be perfectly clear that Shakespeare used both versions, in the earlier plays the Bishops' rather than the Genevan and in later years more of the Genevan. It is improbable that in many of the instances Shakespeare was indebted to attendance at church for his knowledge of the Bishops', for many of the passages concerned do not occur in chapters read on Sundays. He might have owned one of the Bishops' quartos, the last of which, so far as is known, was issued in 1584. It is not beyond the bounds of possibility that he may even have owned a folio. The argument against such ownership is that the folio was very cumbrous; even to-day its transport is not easy. But whatever may have been the fact, there can be no reasonable doubt that some way or other he had access to a copy of the Bishops' Bible. He also appears to have had access to the Genevan-Tomson, which there would have been no difficulty in carrying about.

THE CASE FOR THE BOOK OF COMMON PRAYER.

A. THE PSALTER.—It has already been mentioned that Shakespeare quoted more from the Psalter than from any other book of the Bible. There is no doubt that a large proportion of such quotations can be identified as according with the version in the Prayer Book rather than with any other.

There are two apparent exceptions, both found in one play, to a statement that all allusions to the *Psalms* agree with the version to be found in the Psalter, and both these relate to a psalm to be found elsewhere in the Bible as well as in the Book of *Psalms*. The Psalm is the 18th in the Psalter and it is also contained substantially in 2 Sam. xxii.

In *2 King Henry VI.*, II. iii. 25, the King, on relieving Humphrey of the seals of his office, makes use of a number of phrases out of *Psalms* and says, " God shall be my hope, My stay, my guide and lantern to my feet." All these phrases, with the exception of God as " my stay," are to be found in the Psalter. Instead of " my stay," the Psalter has " my upholder " in Ps. xviii. 18. We have to turn to the Genevan and Bishops' versions of Ps. xviii. 17 for the phrase, in the Genevan, " but the Lord was my stay " and in the Bishops' " but God was vnto me a sure stay." Or we can find it in the version of the psalm in 2 Sam. xxii. 19, in the Genevan, " but the Lord was my stay " and in the Bishops', " the Lord staied me vp."

The other concerns " pangs of death," a phrase that seems

common enough to us now and of which Shakespeare made frequent use: *2 King Henry VI.*, III. iii. 24; *3 King Henry VI.*, II. iii. 17; *King John*, V. iv. 59; *Merry Wives*, III. v. 112; *Twelfth Night*, I. v. 81 and III. iv. 265. It is to be found in the same psalm in the Bishops' as contained " God was vnto me a sure stay "—namely Ps. xviii. 3, " The panges of death haue compassed me about " (Psalter and Genevan, " sorrows of death ")—and both occur in the same play of *2 King Henry VI.* The phrase is also found in both the Genevan and Bishops' versions of 2 Sam. xxii. 5.

Both phrases, " my stay " and " pangs of death," could have been taken from Ps. xviii. as in the Bishops', or from the same psalm as in 2 Sam. xxii. in either the Genevan or the Bishops'. If we assume that the Bishops' version of the *Psalms* was the source, we have an immediate difficulty. That version of the *Psalms* was only printed three times, in the large folios of 1568, 1572 (alongside the Psalter version) and 1585. The alternative that Shakespeare was indebted to 2 Sam. xxii. seems to be more reasonable.

As for the rest of the passages in the plays which seem to have been suggested by the *Psalms*, as far as it has been possible to judge, they could all have had the Psalter as their source, and in the case of a large proportion of them they are nearer to that version than to the Genevan.

Our first instance, from *The Comedy of Errors*, IV. iv. 19, is decisive. Dromio of Syracuse protests, " Nay, 'tis for me to be patient: I am in adversity." It is obvious that the source of this is in Ps. xciv. 13, " That thou mayest give him patience in time of adversity." With this the Bishops' agrees though it gives the Genevan in the margin. The Genevan reads, " That thou mayest giue him rest from the dayes of euill."

Of the wits of the Court of Navarre, Rosaline says, " Well-liking wits they have: gross, gross: fat, fat " (*Love's Labour's Lost*, V. ii. 269). The conjunction of " well-liking " and " fat " is found in Ps. xcii. 13, " They also shall bring forth more fruit in their age: and shall be fat and well-liking." The Genevan and Bishops', " they shalbe fat and flourishing."

In *Romeo and Juliet*, V. iii. 229-30, the Friar says:

> I will be brief, for my short date of breath
> Is not so long as is a tedious tale.

This comparison of a life to a tale was a favourite of Shake-speare's. In *King John*, III. iv. 108, Lewis says, "Life is as tedious as a twice-told tale," and Macbeth in V. v. 26-7 says that life "is a tale Told by an idiot." The source of the figure is to be found in Ps. xc. 9, "we bring our years to an end, as it were a tale that is told." The Genevan is far removed from this and has "wee haue spent our yeeres as a thought," and the figure in the Bishops' is "word."

In *King Richard II.*, I. ii. 43, Gaunt refers his sister-in-law to "God, the widow's champion and defence." God is thus spoken of in Ps. lxviii. 5, "He is a Father of the father-less, and defendeth the cause of the widows," and in Ps. cxlvi. 9, "he defendeth the fatherless and widow." The Genevan speaks of God in the former psalm as "a Iudge of the widowes," and in the latter as "he relieueth the father-lesse and widow." The Bishops' copied the Genevan.

In the same play, III. i. 34, we have the phrase "pains of hell" and it is to be found also in *King John*, IV. iii. 138; *All's Well*, II. iii. 244, and in the mouth of Iago in *Othello* I. i. 155, as "hell pains." Ps. cxvi. 3 has "and the pains of hell gat hold upon me," with which the Bishops' agrees, but the Genevan has "the griefes of the graue caught me."

"The fire seven times tried this" in the scroll of the silver casket in *The Merchant of Venice* may be indebted to Ps. xii. 7, "even as the silver, which from the earth is tried, and purified seven times in the fire." The Genevan, followed by the Bishops', has "as the siluer, tried in a fornace of earth, fined seuen folde."

There is no doubt about the version adapted by Pistol in *The Merry Wives*, II. i. 115-6, "He wooes both high and low, both rich and poor, both young and old, one with another." Obviously Ps. xlix. 2, "High and low, rich and poor: one with another." The Genevan runs, "As wel low as hie, both rich and poore," without any mention of "one with another." The Bishops' is an amalgam of the two.

Pedro's "Runs not this speech like iron through your blood?" in *Much Ado*, V. i. 257, seems to be derived from Ps. cv. 18, "the iron entered into his soul." The Bishops' repeated the error of the Psalter. The Genevan, "and he was layd in yrons."

In *Julius Caesar*, IV. i. 50-1, Octavius adapts Ps. xxviii. 3, "And some that smile have in their hearts, I fear, Millions of mischiefs." The Psalter has "which speak friendly to their neighbours, but imagine mischief in their hearts." The Genevan has "when malice is in their hearts," and the Bishops' has " mischiefe."

Shakespeare was very fond of likening a lifetime to a span, a figure he took from Ps. xxxix. 6, " Behold, thou hast made my days as it were a span long " (Genevan, " as an hand bredth," as also Bishops'). The figure occurs in the paper read by Celia in *As You Like It*, III. ii. 138-41:

> Some, how brief the life of man
> Runs his erring pilgrimage,
> That the stretching of a span
> Buckles in his sum of age.

Again " Man's life's but a span," in Iago's song in *Othello*, II. iii. 75. Also in *King Henry VIII.*, I. i. 223-4, where Buckingham even elaborates the figure and suggests the 7th verse, " For man walketh in a vain shadow ":

> My life is spann'd already;
> I am the shadow of poor Buckingham.

In *Antony and Cleopatra*, V. i. 15-7, the meaning of

> The round world
> Should have shook lions into civil streets,
> And citizens to their dens

is made clearer by reference to Ps. xciii. 2, " He hath made the round world so sure: that it cannot be moved." (Both the Genevan and Bishops' omit " round.") It means that, though the round world was so fixed that it could not be moved, yet Antony's death was such a calamity that one side of the world should have changed with the other.

In *Timon*, V. i. 170, First Senator says, " Who, like a boar too savage, doth root up." This is reminiscent of Ps. lxxx. 13, " The wild boar out of the wood doth root it up " (Genevan "hath destroyed it," but Bishops' as Psalter).

Leontes (*Winter's Tale*, I. ii. 111-2) affords one of the best examples of the use of the Psalter, " my heart dances, But not for joy: not joy." There is nowhere in the whole of the plays a surer indication of a text, for it checks as though to disappoint those who thought they knew what he was going to say after " my heart dances." The reference is to Ps. xxviii. 8, " therefore my heart danceth for joy." The Bishops' substituted " skippeth " for " danceth " and the Genevan had " therefore mine heart shall reioyce."

There is another good example of the phraseology of the Psalter in *King Henry VIII.*, II. i. 128-30, where Buckingham, complaining of the instability of friends, says that

> when they once perceive
> The least rub in your fortunes, fall away
> Like water.

In this variation on the theme of Ben Sirach, Shakespeare resorted to Ps. lviii. 6, " let them fall away like water " (Genevan, " melt," Bishops' " dissolued ").

Different from the foregoing is an instance in *The Tempest*, noticed by Mr. Anders. Most people are aware of the passage in Act II. i., where Gonzalo, after Florio's Montaigne, dilates on his ideal commonwealth. He rendered Florio's " no use of wine, corne, or mettle," as " No use of metal, corn, or wine, or oil." Mr. Anders commented on the transformation of the phrase into its Biblical form with " corn, wine, oil " in this order. The instance that will spring to most men's minds will be in Ps. iv. 8, " since the time that their corn, and wine, and oil, increased." Neither the Genevan nor Bishops' has the phrase here. In the same order the phrase occurs both in the Genevan and Bishops' in other parts of the Bible, notably in Deut. vii. 13, but the chances are that it was the phrase of the Psalter that was in Shakespeare's head and that it was his instinct to render Florio's phrase accordingly.

From all these instances in favour of the Psalter it will be plain that it was a version of which Shakespeare had considerable knowledge. It may be interesting, therefore, to mention an instance where that knowledge led him astray.

Holinshed relates that after the Battle of Agincourt the King " gaue thanks to almightie God for so happie a victorie: causing his prelats and chapleins to sing this psalme: ' In exitu Israel de Ægypto'; and commanded euerie man to kneele down on the ground at this verse: ' *Non nobis*, Domine,

non nobis, sed nomini tuo da gloriam.' Which doone, he
caused *Te Deum*, with certeine anthems to be soong ''; etc.
(Boswell-Stone's *Shakespeare's Holinshed*).

There was very good reason for the choice of *In exitu
Israel*, for it is a very important psalm in the Latin Church,
being said at Vespers in each week-day, except in Lent,
and was therefore very likely to be well known to the troops.
What confused Shakespeare was the reference to *Non
nobis, Domine*. He evidently knew the Latin titles in his
Psalter (they were listed in alphabetical order in some of the
Bishops' folios) and he looked up *In exitu Israel*, which is there
Ps. cxiv., and he could not see anything in it to justify the
inclusion of " Non nobis, Domine, non nobis " etc.   But he
saw the title of the next psalm, Ps. cxv., *Non nobis, Domine*.
He appears to have concluded that his authority had made
a mistake, that it could not have been *In exitu Israel* and that
what was meant was that the prelates and the chaplains
sang *Non nobis, Domine*.   Accordingly in Act IV. viii. 128 he
makes the King say, " Let there be sung *Non Nobis* and *Te
Deum*."

Had the King given any such order the probability is that
there would have been some confusion, as there was neither
in the Vulgate nor in the Service Books any separate psalm
so entitled.   In the Vulgate and Service Books *In exitu
Israel* (Vulgate, Ps. cxiii.) includes *Non nobis, Domine* (in
the Anglican Psalter, Ps. cxv.).   Shakespeare evidently
assumed that they were separate psalms in the Latin Service
Books, as they were in the Psalter of the English Church, and
so he corrected Holinshed.

Shakespeare's error ought to do something towards dis-
posing of the idea that he was careless.   His error here was
due to too much care.   Had he known less and been less
painstaking, he would not have corrected his authority.

B. GOSPELS, EPISTLES, SENTENCES.—In the 1559 edition
of Common Prayer, Barrabas, Jacob, Salomon and Sathan
are spelt as in the plays.   But the spelling of that book is
no criterion as to how other editions chose to write the names.
The Prayer Book was issued in a variety of forms, some of
them unauthorized and some very much garbled.   It is,
therefore, quite impossible to set any store by the spelling
affected by the First Book of Elizabeth.

It would be legitimate to claim that Cleomenes's remarks,
The Winter's Tale, V. i. 1-5, were inspired by the rendering

of Ezekiel xviii. 21-2, prefixed to the daily offices, when he said:

> Sir, you have done enough, and have perform'd
> A saint-like sorrow: no fault could you make
> Which you have not redeem'd; indeed, paid down
> More penitence than done trespass. At the last
> Do, as the heavens have done, forget your evil.

It is difficult not to associate this last with " I wil put al his wickednes out of my remembraunce sayeth the Lord."

Mention has already been made of " Auoide Sathan " in the Gospel for the First Sunday in Lent and of " the place of dead mennes sculles: but in Hebrue Golgotha " in the Gospel for Good Friday. It will be sufficient to mention one of the Epistles, although even in this the Liturgy was not unique as its rendering is also agreeable with the First Bishops'. In *3 King Henry VI.*, III. iii. 51, Warwick says, " I come in kindness and unfeigned love." The rendering of 2 Cor. vi. 6 for the First Sunday in Lent was " in kyndnesse, in the holy Ghost, in loue vnfained." The Genevan read like the Revised Bishops', " by kindnesse, by the holy Ghost, by loue vnfeigned," and the Rheims, " in svveetenes, in the holy Ghost, in charitie not feined."

C. THE VARIOUS OFFICES.—It is not usually recognized that while within limits prescribed by public opinion any use might be made of the Bible—*i.e.*, before 1605—by the Act of Uniformity of 1559 disrespectful liberties with the Prayer Book were prohibited in Interludes, Plays, Songs and Rhymes. However profane a playwright might be, his profanity had to stop short of bringing the Prayer Book into disrepute.

It is not surprising under these circumstances that we can observe a certain restraint on the part of Shakespeare in any references made to the services of the Church. It is natural that the Lord's Prayer should be utilized by him, but in the form found in the Prayer Book it is always with respect. It is pertinent to remark that in *Othello*, II. iii. 117, when Cassio in drink falls on his knees and he begins to pray " God forgive us our sins," or the tipsy Trinculo, frightened by Ariel's invisible tabor, also falls on his knees and utters " O forgive me my sins," in neither case is the Prayer Book form, " And forgive us our trespasses," used.

Instead the clause as found in Luke xi. 4 was used, although the other form would have been the more natural.

Iago in *Othello*, III. iii. 203-4, may have alluded to a well-known passage in the daily offices when he said of women " their best conscience Is not to leave't undone, but kept unknown." The possibility of a reference to " We have left undone those things which we ought to have done " of the General Confession needs no stressing.

The Litany provided Shakespeare with some material. There is the well-known one in *The Shrew*, " From all such devils, Good Lord, deliver us." Or in *Love's Labour's Lost* Longaville's " to hear meekly " in allusion to the petition, " That it may please thee to give to all thy people increase of grace to hear meekly thy word," etc. The best reference is in *The Merry Wives*, where Sir Hugh failed to recognize a phrase from the Litany and termed it as " affectations." Pistol's " He hears with ears," drew from the parson the angry comment, " The Tevil and his Tam ! What phrase is this, ' He hears with ear ' ? Why, it is affectations." Parson Evans forgot the very familiar phrase from the Litany, which also occurs in Ps. xliv. 1: " O God, we have heard with our ears."

Two references to the Commination Service may be noted. In *King John* III. i. 181-2, when Constance calls upon the Cardinal " cry thou ' Amen ' To my keen curses," the allusion is to the leading feature of the service, where the congregation say " Amen " to the curse pronounced. The other is in *King Richard III.*, I. iv. 141-2, where 2nd Murderer complains of conscience, in evident allusion to the seventh curse, " he cannot lie with his neighbour's wife, but it detects him."

Allusions to distinctive features, words and phrases of Holy Matrimony are extremely numerous. Even Hamlet is acquainted with one of its phrases. Allusions to the service occur in *The Shrew*, *3 King Henry VI.*, *Love's Labour's Lost*, *Romeo and Juliet*, *Much Ado*, *As You Like it*, *Hamlet* and *Twelfth Night*.

Shakespeare also made considerable use of the Baptism Service. The more Protestant section of the Church were insistent on this sacrament being performed in the presence of the congregation, and in the liturgy issued with the 1578 Genevan the service for private Baptism was omitted. Usually Baptism was carried out in the course of Sunday Matins, so that details of the service would be very familiar with the public.

Notably Shakespeare fell back upon this service to embellish the vows of the King and his companions in the opening of *Love's Labour's Lost*. It figures in *King Richard II.* in the reference to Norfolk made by the Bishop of Carlisle, and even Cardinal Wolsey culls from it one of its most famous phrases.

Shakespeare often uses phrases reminiscent of the Burial Service, but there is nothing concerning that service calling for comment here, except the interment of Ophelia. The interest of her burial lies principally in the suggestion that Shakespeare took pains to be acquainted with mediæval usage, for the rite in mind seems to be Roman and not Anglican.

The preliminary circumstances are peculiar and revision is a possibility. First the Queen's direct evidence, laid before the audience, was that Ophelia's death was accidental. The gravediggers were suspicious, but even the 2nd Gravedigger was positive that, as the result of the coroner's inquest, Ophelia was to have the benefit of the Church. It is from Hamlet the audience has its first intelligence of the denial of full benefit: " And with such maimed rites ? This doth betoken The corse they follow did with desp'rate hand Fordo its own life."

The priest (described in the principal edition as " Doctor ") declared that Ophelia's " death was doubtful " and that had it not been for " great command " the body would have been lodged " in ground unsanctified." As it was he refused " To sing a requiem, and such rest to her As to peace-parted souls."

Although the Elizabethan liturgy, like its Edwardian predecessors, made no provision for refusal of Church benefit to suicides (the present rubric was added in 1662), custom prescribed the refusal. The Canon of 1604 would suggest this, although it made no provision for doubtful cases. Canon 68 provided that no minister was to refuse to bury any corpse brought to the churchyard unless " the party deceased were denounced excommunicated majori excommunicatione, for some grievous and notorious crime, and no man able to testify of his repentance." Any minister refusing burial otherwise was to be suspended by the Bishop for three months. It will be noticed that the crime had to be denounced—that is, proclaimed; a mere doubt was insufficient ground for refusal. Although this Canon was later than the first production of *Hamlet* probably it only formulated what had been the prevalent practice in the Church of England in the closing years of Elizabeth.

" Maimed rites " (not provided for in the Prayer Book and contrary to the Act of Uniformity) in a case where death is doubtful (as Ophelia's was said to be) are provided for by the Roman rite, as reference to Canon 1240, par. 2, in the *Codex Juris Canonici* would show. " Occurrente prædictis in casibus aliquo dubio, consultatur, si tempus sinat, Ordinarius; permanente dubio, cadaver sepulturæ ecclesiasticæ tradatur, ita tamen ut removeatur scandalum." This latter is exactly the procedure followed in Ophelia's case and the suggestion is very strong that Shakespeare, as he did elsewhere, took extraordinary pains to be accurately informed.   If we hold this view we shall not be inclined to consider that the Doctor is using the word " requiem " in other than its strict sense.   The Prayer Book makes no provision for a requiem mass, and taken in conjunction with the other features—" maimed rites " and " death was doubtful "—the refusal of a requiem would point clearly to Roman usage.

Dr. Michell, of St. Stephen's House, Oxford, in the course of a personal letter, suggests that " there is a possible analogy in modern R.C. practice in cases where a dispensation is given to marry a non-R.C. partner.   In such cases a service is held, but no nuptial mass is allowed and there may be some minor restrictions.   The principle seems to be the same in either case—*i.e.*, the marriage or burial is not wholly satisfactory, but yet not wholly unsatisfactory, the most sacred item in the ideally complete rite is withheld, but what is *necessary* for Christian marriage or burial is allowed. If the marriage or burial is wholly unsatisfactory, no rites at all are allowed."

The term " Doctor " is a costume direction to distinguish his rank.   (Neither the Second Quarto nor the Folio gives any direction as to the entrance of a priest and the 1603 Quarto indicates only one priest.)   Presumably he would not be in full canonicals.   Dr. Michell asks if " the hypothesis of Shakespeare's curiously accurate (almost recondite) knowledge of mediæval custom is correct may not the description ' Doctor ' mean or hint at canonist—doctor legis canonici ? and if hostile be aimed at pettifogging distinctions ?"   A Doctor of Divinity would appear to have

7

been intended, although Dr. Michell's suggestion is very interesting.

D. THE CATECHISM.—Shakespeare could not have avoided contact with the Little Catechism, as the Catechism contained in the Confirmation Service was called. It was bound up with the A B C Book, referred to by the Bastard as the Absey Book.

The Ten Commandments, as contained in the Catechism and as recited in the Communion Service, differ in the wording of the Second and Sixth from that of Exod. xx. in any printed Bible of Shakespeare's time. In the Catechism the Second runs, " and visit the sins of the fathers," and the Sixth, "Thou shalt do no murder." In the Second the Bishops' has "visite the sinne of the fathers" and the Genevan "visiting the iniquitie of the fathers," and in the Sixth both read "Thou shalt not kill." Whenever Shakespeare has occasion to make a character allude to either of these commandments, it is to the distinctive form in the Catechism and not to that in the Bibles. For the Second Commandment see *King John*, II. i. 179-82 and *Merchant of Venice*, III. v. 1, and for the Sixth, *King Richard III.*, I. iv. 206.

There used to be a prelude to Confirmation (which contained the Catechism) and when Falstaff pleaded "Thou seest I have more flesh than another man and therefore more frailty," he may have been referring to a phrase in that prelude: "partly by the frailtie of their own flesh." But there is no doubt at all that in the first scene of *Love's Labour's Lost* Berowne was quoting from the Catechism when he said, "Not by might master'd, but by special grace."

But the best use of the Catechism must be allowed to Hamlet, when he protests (holding out his hands) that he still loves Guildenstern "by these pickers and stealers" in reference to the reply by the catechumen that it was his duty "To keep my hands from picking and stealing."

FRENCH VERSION.

In *King Henry V.*, III. vii. 71-3, according to the Folio, the Dauphin says, *Le chien est retourne a son propre vemissement est la leuye lauee au bourbier.* This is meant as a quotation from 2 Pet. ii. 22 and it contains at least three mistakes apart from lack of accents. Obviously "vemissement" should be "vomissement" and "est la leuye" should be "et la truye." There may be others: a colon may have been omitted after " vomissement " and the second " est retournee " may have been left out by the printer without the authority of his copy.   If we assume that these two omissions were the blunders of somebody other than Shakespeare, then we know the exact source of the Dauphin's remark.   It is from the Lyons Olivetan version, the one that preceded the French Genevan.   The reading in the Lyons Bible printed by Jean de Tournes in 1551 and now in the British Museum is, " Le chien est retourné a son propre vomissement: & la truie lauee est retournee au bourbier."   In the Lyons New Testament of 1603 printed by Antoine de Harsy, and in the same collection, the verse is printed the same except " truye " for " truie."   I am indebted to Mr. K. G. Rendall of the British Museum for calling my attention to the existence of these two volumes.   Mr. Anders discovered this reading of de Harsy's Testament in the Lyons Bible printed in 1550 by Balthazar Arnoullet.   Unfortunately, he did not state where the volume was to be consulted.

The normal French Genevan reading follows the 1560 de Tournes New Testament (British and Foreign Bible Society's Collection): " Le chien est retourné à son propre vomissement: & la truye lauée est retournée à se veautrer au bourbier."   In the same collection is the Louvain Bible of 1550 with the reading: " Le chien est retourné à son vomissement, & la truye lauée est retournée à se touiller en la fange."   The Le Fèvre edition of 1521 differs still more.

It should be noted that 2 Pet. ii. 22 was quoted by the Archbishop in *2 King Henry IV.*, just a little while before *Henry V.*

LATIN VULGATE.

Shakespeare makes one quotation from the Vulgate in *2 King Henry VI.*, II. i. 53, when Beaufort flings at Gloucester, " Medice, teipsum " in evident allusion to " Medice, cura teipsum " of the Latin Vulgate of Luke iv. 23.   It is certain that the phrase was proverbial.   Unlike Bacon, who quoted the Vulgate frequently, sometimes inaccurately, Shakespeare did not use the Vulgate and in *King Henry V.* he showed that he was ignorant of one of its most elementary features.

THE RHEIMS VERSION.

As mentioned in Chapter I., Shakespeare had not good facilities for consulting the Rheims New Testament.   The version became more accessible in Fulke's *Confutation*, but that was a book for specialists and scholars and it would be very surprising had Shakespeare been one of its readers.

The Rheims in a good many places adopted readings to be found in its English precursors, with the result that in numbers of instances it might be taken with the others to rank as a source for Shakespeare. In a couple of cases it could be held to be nearer to Shakespeare than any other. In *The Tempest*, I. ii. 217, Ariel says of the passengers and crew of the shipwrecked vessel, "Not a hair perish'd." The phrase is familiar to everybody in all the versions by reason of Luke xxi. 18, "And there shall in no case one haire of your head perish." However, many associate the passage in *The Tempest* with St. Paul's hortatory address to his comrades in the ship. If that incident was in Shakespeare's mind, then the nearest to Ariel's remark would be the Rheims of Acts xxvii. 34, "for there shal not an heare of the head perish of any of you." Both the Genevan and Bishops' read "fall" for "perish." It ought to be noted that it could be argued quite reasonably that the incident in Shakespeare's mind was that of Shadrach, Meshach and Abednego.

Another instance in favour of the Rheims is in *All's Well*, IV. v. 54-9, where the Clown speaks of "the narrow gate" and "the broad gate." This is nearer to the Rheims than to any other version of Matt. vii. 13, where the Rheims reads "Enter ye by the narrovv gate: because brode is the gate." In the other versions one gate is "strait" and the other is "wide." In the Rheims one way is "strait" and the other "large," while in the others the "ways" are "narrow" and "broad."

But it is not by its agreements that we estimate the Rheims as a source for Shakespeare, but by the marked disparity between its renderings and Scriptural figures and phrases quoted by Shakespeare. Thus when Warwick in *3 King Henry VI.* says that he comes "in kindness and unfeigned love" we should never have recognized its origin if we had had only the Rheims of 2 Cor. vi. 6, "in svveetenes, in the holy Ghost, in charitie not feined." Both the allusions of Mrs. Quickly and Cassius to bearing infirmities would lose something of their point if we were to rely solely on "susteine" of the Rheims in Rom. xv. 1 instead of the Genevan's "beare." The Rheims of Phil. i. 21, "to die is gaine," has not the resemblance to King Henry V.'s "death is to him advantage," borne by the Bishops' " death is to me aduantage."

But most marked of all is when Pandarus in *Troilus and Cressida*, III. i. asks, " is love a generation of vipers ?" the Rheims is very much wide.   In all the passages, Matt. iii. 7, xii. 34, xxiii. 33, Luke iii. 7, the Rheims reads either " brood " or " broodes " for " generation " or " generations."   Even in *King Richard II.*, where the King in his fury quotes Matt. xxiii. 33, " O villains, vipers, damn'd without redemption !" the Rheims does not fit so well with its " You serpents, vipers broodes, hovv vvil you flee from the iudgement of hel ?" as " Ye serpents, ye generation of vipers, how will yee escape the damnation of hell ?" of the Bishops'.

Or again, in *King Richard II.*, for " The field of Golgotha and dead men's skulls," the Rheims would fail us, for in none of the texts, Matt. xxvii. 33, Mark xv. 22, John xix. 17, has it " the place of dead mens skulls " or any reading resembling it, but instead " the place of Caluarie."

For " Auoyde Sathan " it reads " Auant Satan," which would not agree with " Sathan avoid " of *The Comedy of Errors*.   Instead of " the weaker vessel " it has " the vveaker feminine vessel."   There is no need to elaborate further. Where distinctive readings come into question, it is clear that it was not the Rheims that was followed.

CHAPTER V

WAS SHAKESPEARE'S BIBLICAL KNOWLEDGE EXCEPTIONAL?

By this question is meant, Was Shakespeare's knowledge of the Bible anything in excess of what might have been expected in an intelligent well-read layman at the close of the sixteenth century, one who was not altogether out of touch with the Church and was given to occasional perusal of Scripture? Dr. Carter and Dr. Ginsburg had no hesitation in giving what might be construed as answers in the affirmative. Unequivocally Ginsburg testified to Shakespeare's Biblical knowledge and credited him with an ability to rise superior to the shortcomings of the English Bibles that were in his day available. Dr. Carter attributed to Shakespeare not only a remarkably close intimacy with the Genevan text of the Bible, but also a knowledge of certain Biblical points which would place him above the ordinary level of those who were not specially Biblical students.

I propose, therefore, to answer the question at the head of this chapter, not by any general survey or argument, but by an examination of one instance put forward by Dr. Carter and two by Dr. Ginsburg. Dr. Carter's is Othello's " the base Iudean " and those of Dr. Ginsburg, Clarence's " To keep that oath were more impiety Than Jephthah's " and Richard II.'s " It is as hard to come as for a camel To thread the postern of a small needle's eye."

THE BASE JUDEAN.

In the Folio, Othello, in Act V. ii. 345-7 and 357, is thus reported:

> Of one, whose hand
> (Like the base Iudean) threw a Pearle away
> Richer then all his Tribe: . . . .
> (l. 357) I kist thee, ere I kill'd thee.

The Quarto, which was printed the year before the publication of the Folio but from which the Folio was not printed, for " the base Iudean " reads " the base Indian." Most editors have adopted the Quarto's reading.

The issue of Judean versus Indian is one of great interest to textual students as it illustrates some elementary rules in textual criticism. In the first place Iudean is the reading in what is generally accepted as the *editio princeps* of the play and the nearer to the author's manuscript. That is always an important consideration: every remove from the original is an additional opportunity for error. If the copy for the Quarto was, as it would appear to have been, an adaptation of the original, then its " Indian " would be badly handicapped at the very start. Secondly it illustrates the famous textual rule enunciated by Bengel in the eighteenth century, " Proclivi scriptioni præstat ardua." " Indian " was a much more familiar word than " Iudean " and therefore a much easier one; a printer or copyist might change " Iudean " into " Indian " but it is improbable that he would change " Indian " into " Iudean." Printers and copyists, like numbers of editors, when puzzled are apt to think of a familiar word and " Indian " is decidedly more familiar as well as more plausible than " Iudean," which is, in whatever light it is regarded, a very difficult reading. At the time Shakespeare wrote the play, Judæa was a rare word, " Jewry " being the usual term, and even by the time the Folio was printed it was only to be found in the Genevan and Authorised as far as Bibles were concerned.

The third point applies to dramatic manuscripts. Where other considerations are equal, the playwright should be given the benefit of the reading which makes for better theatrical effect. If we accept " the base Indian," the objection from a strictly dramatic point of view is that at a most tragic and intensely emotional moment we reduce Othello to an Orsino who could in the very hurricane of his frenzy pause to follow an idle fancy and recall the " savage jealousy" of the Egyptian thief. Othello is not represented as one given to poetical fantasy and here in this final catastrophe he is shown to us as being in deadly earnest. Unfortunately many in constructing Shakespeare's text are not sufficiently alive to the fact that they are dealing with theatrical documents. The great object in a play, and no one was more keenly aware of the fact than Shakespeare, is, as the phrase goes, " to put it across."

So much for " Iudean " as against " Indian " on these

counts. In modern times the case for " Iudean " was revived by Halliwell-Phillipps: he held it referred to Judas Iscariot, who had, like Othello, betrayed the innocent blood (Matt. xxvii. 4) and whose baseness was universally execrated. Furness, after reviewing all other theories, approved of the suggestion and commented on the identity of the first syllable in each of the two—*Jud*as and *Jud*ean.

Dr. Carter developed the case for Judas Iscariot as being the Iudean of the Folio. Not only did he maintain that " I kist thee, ere I kill'd thee " recalled Judas's token of betrayal, but he relied on an old theory as to Iscariot that now commands very wide acceptance and credited Shakespeare with that knowledge. It is held that the surname of Judas, " Iskariotes " or " Ish-Kariyoth," denotes a man of Kerioth (" Kerioth-hezron " in the Revised) which is mentioned in Josh. xv. 25 as one of the villages allotted to the tribe of Judah.

There is evidence (not produced by Dr. Carter) that Shakespeare may have held that Judas was a non-Galilean, of the same Tribe as his Master. The Tomson at Matt. x. 4 has the following Bezan note to Iscariot, " A man of Kerioth. Nowe Kerioth was in the tribe of Iudah, Iosh. 15. 25." The implication of this note is plain enough and it would not be lost on a receptive mind like Shakespeare's. It is not in the ordinary Genevan nor is there any note of the kind in the Bishops' or Rheims. It is when we understand that Shakespeare had access to such a note that we begin to appreciate " Iudean " and " Tribe " and Dr. Carter would have been more convincing had he referred to it.

While it may be agreed that Shakespeare was possessed of this knowledge, which would be exceptional among ordinary laymen to-day, it cannot be regarded as being exceptional in his day, since in the most popular Bible of the day it was there for all to read.

NOTE ON " THREW A PEARLE AWAY."—Reference to the Pearl of Great Price of Matt. xiii. 46 might further strengthen the case for " Iudean." The pearl was one of the commonest figures in Shakespeare's time. It appeared in the motto on the title page of every separately issued Bishops' New Testament. " The pearle which Christ commaunded to be bought: Is here to be found, not els to be sought." The word is used figuratively by Othello, for just as Judas threw away his Saviour, the most precious possession of his Tribe, so he (Othello) destroyed what had been his most precious blessing. Christ was the richest heritage of Jewry; Desdemona was dearer to Othello than all the world.

Othello made the extreme abasement of himself by ranking himself with the worst, and in the same breath he extolled Desdemona in the very highest by association with the Best. None but a very great poet could have so simply and yet so completely achieved the double objective in the one phrase. The tragedy becomes too intense, especially with the final " I kist thee, ere I kill'd thee," as the Moor flings himself on the prostrate body of Desdemona.

To keep that Oath were more Impiety Than Jephthah's.

Dr. Ginsburg held that Shakespeare's " remarkable conception of the import of a passage has often enabled him to get at its true sense when all the English versions of the Bible had positively mistranslated it." Here Ginsburg was referring to the fact that both the Genevan and the Bishops' obscured Jephthah's vow to make a human sacrifice by translating Judg. xi. 31, " Then that thing that commeth out of the doores of my house against me," where the Authorised reads " whatsoever cometh forth " and the Revised has " whosoever " in the margin.

Ginsburg continues: " But though ignorant of Hebrew, and in spite of having wrong versions before him, this almost infallible decipherer of human language clearly saw that Jephthah could never have imagined, and that the evident scope of the passage could never have been designed to convey the idea, that an animal would come forth of the doors of his house to meet him on his victorious return from the battlefield. . . . In the play, therefore, of *King Henry VI.*, third part, Shakespeare rightly assumes that Jephthah's vow was with regard to human sacrifices, and that he duly offered up his daughter. Hence he makes Clarence say to Warwick:

To keep that oath were more impiety
Than Jephthah's when he sacrificed his daughter (V. i.)."

Presumably Ginsburg interpreted Clarence to imply that the impiety of Jephthah's sacrifice of his daughter was due to the vow itself being impious and not merely rash as the Genevan and Bishops' margins called it. Assuming that Ginsburg's interpretation is correct and that all his implications hold, there would have been nothing extraordinary in Shakespeare's believing that Jephthah intended a human victim, no matter how defective the English Bibles might have been.   The idea was a commonplace among church-goers familiar with the Homily against Swearing and Perjury.

In Part II. of the Homily, the writer, in evident reliance on the Vulgate ("quicumque primus fuerit egressus de foribus domus meæ"), informed the congregation, "And Jephthah, when God had given to him victory of the children of Ammon, promised, of a foolish devotion unto God, to offer for a sacrifice unto him that person which of his own house should first meet with him after his return home."   There is no ambiguity here; clearly the writer intimated that Jeph-thah had vowed a sacrifice of a human being.   The Homily proceeds, "Thus the promise which he made most foolishly to God, against God's everlasting will and the law of nature, most cruelly he performed; so committing against God a double offence."

This Homily Shakespeare must have heard many times, for he seems to have taken particular notice of it, judging from the frequency with which he dwelt on its subject in the first half of his career.   Salisbury's speech, *2 King Henry VI.*, V. i. 189-90, "It is great sin to swear unto a sin But greater sin to keep a sinful oath," is a paraphrase of some of its advice.   People were admonished against the performance of "an unlawful and ungodly oath."   It was ignorance of this Homily, which in the light of Article xxxv. must be taken to represent the official view of the Church of England, that led Mr. Bowden (*Religion of Shakespeare*) to base on Salisbury's speech certain claims as to Shake-speare's religion.   The theme of the Homily reappears in *Two Gentlemen of Verona*, II. vi. 11, in Proteus's attempt to justify bad faith.   More amusing are the casuistical develop-ments advanced by Richard, *3 King Henry VI.*, I. ii. 22-7, and by Touchstone, *As You Like It*, I. ii. 68-86.

Everything considered, it is quite plain that Shakespeare was familiar with the Homily and, that being the case, his rising above the bad texts of the Genevan and Bishops' can be very easily explained.

IT IS AS HARD TO COME AS FOR A CAMEL
TO THREAD THE POSTERN OF A SMALL NEEDLE'S EYE.

Ginsburg's other point relates to *King Richard II.*, V. v. 16-7, where the unfortunate King in his distracted way contrasts the invitation "Come, little ones" with "It is as hard to come as for a camel To thread the postern of a small needle's eye." The incidents of the children and the camel are recorded in Matt. xix., Mark x., and Luke xviii. and it is from the last that Richard was probably quoting. Ginsburg takes the narrative as in Matt. xix and also quotes the Folio and not the Quarto, the true text.

He wrote that the passage " where Christ compares the difficulty of a rich man entering heaven to the impossibility of a camel passing through the eye of a needle, has sorely exercised the ingenuity of those commentators who have no taste for poetry nor any appreciation of Eastern hyperbole. Hence we have been told that the original κάμηλος does not mean here camel, but *cable* or thick rope used by mariners in casting anchor, and the figure has thus been reduced to drawing a rope through the eye of a needle. Others, again, will have it that because the narrow gate for foot passengers is called by modern Arabs ' the needle's eye ' in some Syrian cities, in contradistinction to the larger gate close by through which camels and other beasts of burden pass into the town, therefore Christ here means to say that it is as difficult for a rich man to enter heaven as it is for the larger camel to pass through the narrow gate called ' the needle's eye.' An acquaintance with the language of Palestine during the Second Temple would have removed the difficulties and shown these expositors that Christ here quotes a national proverb. To describe an impossibility or to expose a subtlety the common expression was to attempt ' to show a palm-tree of gold or to make an elephant go through the eye of a needle. . . .'

" Without being acquainted with the language of the Talmud, Shakespeare clearly saw that the passage in Matt. xix. 24 was a proverbial saying in which the largest animal and the smallest aperture were selected to express an impossibility. Hence, with the true genius of a great poet, he not only correctly, but most beautifully and poetically, renders it:

> It is as hard to come as for a camel
> To thread the postern of a needle's eye."

Ginsburg would have been on stronger ground had he confined himself to the attempt to reduce the strength of the proverb by producing the word κάμιλος (a cable) to take the place of κάμηλος. There is no trace, that I can find, of any attempt in Shakespeare's time to explain the needle's eye by a narrow gate; the alternative for " camel " in the Genevan margin was " Or cable rope," a sure sign that when Shakespeare was writing the lines he had not recently been perusing the narrative in the ordinary Genevan. The Bishops' had no note, but the Tomson at Matt. xix. 24 (but no note in *Mark* or *Luke*) appended Beza's comment: " Theophylact noteth that by this worde is meant a cable rope, but Caninius alleageth out of the Thalmudists, that it is a prouerbe, and the word, Camel, signifieth the beast it selfe."

I am not convinced that Shakespeare displayed any particular insight in taking the phrase in the Gospel literally to mean a camel and the eye of an ordinary needle. Any intelligent person not misled by commentary would so take it and especially would this be true of a poet. The poet by instinct would refrain from a diminution of a picturesque exaggeration and it is to the poet and not to the student of the Bible that any credit is owing.

WHEREIN SHAKESPEARE WAS EXCEPTIONAL.

Had it been my office to argue in favour of Shakespeare's exceptional Biblical knowledge, I should have concentrated on *The Merchant of Venice*. This was a play in which Shakespeare very evidently taxed his Scriptural knowledge and it is interesting therefore to see what he made of it. In addition to Shylock's very apt references to Scripture there are three points in his character and way of speech that have always convinced me that his creator had assimilated to a remarkable degree Hebrew character and outlook as revealed in the Bible.

First, there is Shylock's conception of righteousness as " justice " and his belief that he was righteous because he had not offended against the law. As one who kept the law, he was entitled to all the privileges of the law: " What judgment shall I dread, doing no wrong ?"; " I stand for judgment: answer: shall I have it ?" This aspect of Shylock's behaviour argues that Shakespeare had noted carefully a feature of Judaism that is in sharp contrast with Christianity. The reward, the indisputable title of the righteous man, the man who does that which is lawful and right, is emphasized as much in the Pentateuch as in the *Psalms* and in *Ezekiel*. Portia in her speech denied any such title.

Second, Shylock refers to his race as " he hates our sacred

nation," " scorned my nation," " the curse never fell upon
our nation." Compare Luke vii. 5, " hee loueth our nation ";
Gal. i. 14, " companions in mine owne nation." It is a
minute point, but sufficient that Shakespeare noticed and
used it deliberately to colour Shylock's character.

The third is possibly highly speculative. It relates to the
fact that of all insults, Shylock resented in very special degree
being called " dog." Marlowe had given a hint in *The Jew
of Malta*, but his Jew passed the insult off; when called
" dog " he said he merely heaved his shoulders. It did not
rankle with him as it did with Shylock. Often elsewhere
in Shakespeare's plays " dog " occurs as a term of abuse, but
on none had it anything like the effect it had on Shylock.
Again and again he harps on the insult. " You call me
misbeliever, cut-throat dog." Twice again in the same
scene he reverts to it. " Hath a dog money ? is it possible
a cur can lend three thousand ducats ?" and " another time
you call'd me dog." Later when he had Antonio in his
custody he snarled, " Thou call'dst me dog before thou
hadst a cause. But, since I am a dog, beware my fangs."
More than anything else having been called " dog " seemed
to spur his enmity and the memory of the epithet made of
him an infuriated devil.

Was Shakespeare influenced by Biblical example in his
choice of a word that would be specially odious to a Jew like
Shylock ? In the Bible " dog " is frequent as a term of
absolute contempt; the Gentiles were " dogs " as were those
who hired themselves out for purposes of unnatural vice.
If, as I believe, Shakespeare used Biblical knowledge, he
utilized a point that a clever schoolboy would not have had
the wit to note and later in adult life to remember. It
would indicate very observant reading.

Professor Stoll in his essay on Shylock remarked on the
use of Scripture in the play. As to Jessica, he asked, Did
not Rachel run away with her father's images ? If Jessica
robbed her father, so did Rachel hers. No question of it,
in this play the advocate of Shakespeare's exceptional
Biblical knowledge will find more material than in any other.

Generally, it may be said, Biblical scholars conversant
with the plays are impressed by their author's Scriptural
knowledge. Ginsburg, it is patent, was dazzled and was
almost ready to credit him with a miraculous gift of tongues
to enable him to decipher Hebrew or Greek. Canon Todd,

generally admitted to be one of the most learned Biblical scholars in the Irish Church to-day, in commenting on an article by Dr. Caroline Spurgeon, wrote to me, " Bacon often misinterpreted and misapplied Scripture, Shakespeare rarely." It was in this interpretation and application of Scripture that Shakespeare was exceptional. His use was apt, often it springs a surprise and the happiness of the application is afterwards a delight, as a perusal of the Proper Names may do something to bring home.

Anyway it is in this ability to apply aptly rather than in extensiveness of knowledge that Shakespeare's excellence in Biblical allusion must be sought. We have no adequate means of gauging the extent of his Biblical knowledge; it could not have been less than he exhibited in the persons of his characters; it must have been much more, since he could only pick and choose amongst all the items with which he was familiar, but how much more, whether it included what might be called recondite knowledge, we cannot say. All we can check is the accuracy or propriety of his quotation or application, and if we are content with this we shall have the satisfaction of choosing ground where he will excel most men, even sometimes men more learned than himself, and where he will compare favourably with any in similar circumstances.

CHAPTER VI

DEFECTS IN SHAKESPEARE'S BIBLICAL KNOWLEDGE

PERHAPS no greater tribute can be paid to Shakespeare's use of the Bible than the comparative paucity of the mistakes it has been possible to trace in the plays. No effort has been spared in the quest; in fact, it must be confessed that the search has been keen with a desire to establish errors; yet the total bag is small, and about one item there would not be general consent.

Sometimes Shakespeare has suffered from the embarrassment of enthusiasts who have wished to ascribe to him quotation from the Bible when it is not at all plain that he was alluding to the Bible. For instance, Dr. Carter, in a desire to strengthen his case, associated with Scripture allusions to the Sword and Word in *2 King Henry IV.*, IV. ii. 10, ("Turning the word to sword") and *The Merry Wives*, III. i. 44-5 ("What? The Sword and the Word? Do you study them both, Master Parson?"). In both these passages Sword and Word are treated as an antithesis, whereas in Eph. vi. 17 they form an identity—" the sword of the spirite, which is the word of God." It is not clear that Shakespeare was quoting directly from *Ephesians*; if he did, then he was misinterpreting and misapplying the text. Ultimately, no doubt *Ephesians* was responsible for the jingle of the two words, but it is much more likely that Shakespeare's immediate source was current controversy, in which the words frequently occur.

His ignorance of the Vulgate I dealt with in Chapter IV., page 80-1, when I was referring to *Non nobis* in *King Henry V.* His error here is elementary. Although warned, in the Prayer Book itself, that its numbering of the Psalms followed the Hebrew and varied from that of the common Latin translation from the 9th to the 148th, he assumed that his Psalter was a better authority than Holinshed for the order given to the troops. We are hardly concerned with such an error here as it is with the English Bible we are dealing, not with the Latin.

99

LUCIFER AS A TITLE OF SATAN.

It is, perhaps, not quite fair to lay at Shakespeare's door the mistake of bestowing on Satan the title of Lucifer. In doing this he was conforming with popular usage and he had good precedents for the attribution. When Malcolm in *Macbeth*, IV. iii. 22, says, "Angels are bright still, though the brightest fell," or Cardinal Wolsey in *King Henry VIII.*, III. ii. 372-3, "And when he falls, he falls like Lucifer, Never to hope again," either may be taken as alluding to Isa. xiv. 12: "Howe art thou fallen from heauen, O Lucifer, thou fayre morning childe?" under the impression that Lucifer refers to Satan instead of to Babylon. Small blame can attach to Shakespeare for the association, since at Luke x. 18—"I saw Satan as it had benne lyghtenyng fallyng downe from heauen"—the 1572 Bishops' (but not the 1585), following St. Jerome, gave the reference to Isa. xiv. 12. There was also the Homily on Rebellion, which identified Lucifer with Rev. ix. 1: "The first author of which rebellion . . . was Lucifer; first God's most excellent creature, and most bounden subject; who, by rebelling against the Majesty of God, of the brightest and most glorious Angel, is become the blackest and most foul fiend and devil; and from the height of heaven is fallen into the pit and bottom of hell." It will be obvious from where Malcolm was quoting.

But still Shakespeare had the means at hand of rectifying any such error. In view of the assertion that he had a more than average knowledge of the Genevan Bible, it is not inequitable to judge him by that Bible's standards. In the Genevan at Luke x. 18 there was no reference to *Isaiah*, but there was the comment (copied by the Bishops'): "The power of Satan is beaten downe by the preaching of the Gospel." At Isa. xiv. 12, this note was attached to Lucifer: "Thou that thoughtest thy selfe most glorious, and as it were placed in the heauen: for the morning starre, that goeth before the sunne is called Lucifer, to whom Nebuchadnezzar is compared." It is evident that Shakespeare had not assimilated the contents of that note when he penned Malcolm's and Wolsey's lines.

THE CONFUSION OF SABAOTH WITH SABBATH.

It would appear that Shakespeare at one time thought that the Sabaoth of the *Te Deum*—"Lord God of Sabaoth"—was identical with Sabbath. In the first edition of *The*

Merchant of Venice, in his opening lines in the Court scene, Shylock says: " by our holy Sabaoth have I sworn " in plain ignorance of the fact that " Sabaoth " means no more than armies or hosts. Shakespeare obviously thought that, in putting the word into Shylock's mouth, he was making him use an emphatic variant of " Sabbath." Although those who were responsible for the second edition and for the Folio, in independence of each other, altered the word to " Sabbath" and therefore it might be argued that " Sabaoth " was never written in the first instance, the answer is that, on the only other occasion in the plays when the word was employed, exactly the same mistake was made.

In the first edition of *King Richard III.*, III. ii. 110, Hastings promised the Priest, " Come the next sabaoth and I will content you." In later editions " sabaoth " became " Sabboth."

No useful purpose is to be served by denying that Sabaoth was the term in each case originally written by Shakespeare. He was not unique in making the blunder. The Puritan Stubbes made the mistake over and over again; Spenser and Bacon both fell into the trap. The most amusing of all was in some of the editions of the metrical psalms bound up with the Genevan Bibles (in those of 1576 and 1598 for example), where, in the metrical version of the Ten Commandments, the Fourth is thus given:

> Remember that thou holie keep,
> the sacred Sabaoth day.

In the 1587 edition, " Sabbaoth." In numbers of editions of the metrical version of the *Te Deum*, " Lord God of Sabaoth " runs " of Sabboth Lord the God." " Sabboth " was quite an ordinary way of spelling " Sabbath "—it was so spelt in the Catechism and in the Bishops' (though not in the Genevan) of Exod. xx.

It was no marvel that Shakespeare and other Elizabethans were confused about the terms; the Bibles then available were largely responsible. Witness these renderings of Rom. ix. 29 and Jas. v. 4.

	Romans ix. 29.	*James v. 4.*
Tindale, 1534 . .	. . Lorde of sabaoth.	lorde Sabaoth.
Great Bible, 1539	. . Lorde of Saboth.	Lord Sabbaoth.
Whittingham, 1557	. . Lord of Sabaoth.	Lord of Armies.
Geneva, 1560 . .	. . Lord of hostes.	Lord of hostes.
Bishops', 1572 . .	. . Lorde of Sabboth.	Lorde of Sabaoth.
Rheims, 1582 . .	. . Lord of Saboath.	Lord of Sabboth.
Authorised, 1611	. . Lord of Sabboth.	Lord of Sabaoth.

8

Can anyone be surprised that numbers went astray when there was such a babel in the texts available? Whether Shakespeare later became wiser in the matter or not, certain it is that after *The Merchant of Venice* he left " Sabbath " and " Sabaoth " severely alone.

THE CANON AND SUICIDE.

In Act I. ii., Hamlet, in his mood of depression, says:

> Or that the Everlasting had not fix'd
> His Canon 'gainst self-slaughter.

Imogen echoes this in *Cymbeline*, III., iv. 78-80:

> Against self-slaughter
> There is a prohibition so divine
> That cravens my weak hand.

A difference of opinion among those competent to judge exists as to whether Shakespeare made a mistake or not in these two passages. In the Bible suicide is comparatively rare and its incidence among Jewish communities in our own day is lower than among Christians. Samson may be reckoned as having taken his life. According to one account, Saul and his armour-bearer committed suicide rather than fall into the hands of the Philistines. Ahitophel hanged himself, as did Judas Iscariot. Zimri perished in the royal palace which he had set on fire. Ptolemeus Macron poisoned himself and Razis preferred to kill himself than suffer the ignominy of falling into the hands of Nicanor's soldiers, and his act apparently met with approval. In none of the cases is there any expressed disapproval of the action.

Those who maintain that Shakespeare made no mistake hold that the commandment, " Thou shalt not kill " or, as in the Prayer Book, " Thou shalt do no murder," sufficiently forbids " self-killing " or " self-murder " to justify Shakespeare. They can rely on the support of the Bishops'. At 2 Macc. xiv. 41, the 1572 Bishops' (as well as later editions) attached this very definite note: " This fact is not to be approoued, for that it is contrary to gods commaundement, Thou shalt not kil. Exo. 20. Deute. 5." There was, therefore, authoritative contemporary opinion that the commandment included suicide.

Those on the other side do not deny that the commandment by implication forbids suicide. Their point is that, if the words of Hamlet and Imogen mean anything, they imply a specific prohibition of suicide, and such a specific prohibition, they argue, does not exist. Bishop Wordsworth, who took this view, hazarded the suggestion that by " canon " was meant a canon of natural religion and he supported this by reference to some of Shakespeare's Pagan characters.

It is possible to suggest another view. I agree with those who hold that Hamlet and Imogen contemplated a specific prohibition but I am unable to conclude that a canon of natural religion was in mind, even though Imogen was a Pagan. In neither case is the Bible named as containing the canon or " prohibition so divine." " Canon " is not the exclusive prerogative of Scripture; it is canon that decides what is Holy Writ and what is not. It was the Church's function to interpret Holy Writ and thus it would be regarded as the living channel whereby God manifested his Will. There was no ambiguity about the Church's attitude to suicide, and Hamlet was well aware that by its canon ecclesiastical benefit was withheld from the remains of those who had wilfully fordone their lives.

We may accept it that in neither passage was Scripture in mind and that in Hamlet's eyes the Church's canon was the Canon of the Everlasting (Dr. Lowther Clarke has suggested to me privately that in the sixteenth century " canon " would imply " canon law "). Its prohibition would be divine and the withdrawal of its benefit would craven the weak hand of Imogen. Under the circumstances, I do not believe that a mistake was made in these two instances.

JUDAS ISCARIOT AND " ALL HAIL !"

Every time Shakespeare alludes to Judas's greeting of betrayal he quotes him as saying " All Hail !" (See 3 King Henry VI., V. vii. 33-4, King Richard II., IV. i. 169.) In the instance in 3 King Henry VI. considerable point of the " All " is made by Richard: " To say the truth, so Judas kiss'd his Master, And cried ' All Hail,' when as he meant ' All Harm.' "

In none of the versions does Judas greet his Master with
"All Hail !" In Matt. xxvi. 49, all the versions from
Tindale to Rheims, with the exception of Whittingham,
Genevan and Tomson, have "Haile master." The three
exceptions have "God saue thee." In Mark xiv. 45, the
Tomson, alone of the versions, has "Haile Master." The
point is that nowhere did any version represent Judas as
saying "All Hail."

In the Gospels "All Hail !" only occurs in Matt. xxviii. 9
as a translation of the verb of greeting in the plural, when
Jesus met Mary Magdalene and the other Mary after the
Resurrection: "All haile " in the Bishops' as also the Rheims,
but "God saue you " in the Genevan and Tomson.

Shakespeare evidently overlooked the actual form of
Judas's greeting and had it firmly fixed in his head that it
was "All Hail." He thus made the Princess (*Love's Labour's
Lost*, V. ii. 340) attach a sinister significance to a phrase
that was Christ's and not Iscariot's.

Chus and Tubal as Countrymen of Shylock.

When Jessica in *The Merchant of Venice*, III. ii. 286, mentioned Chus as a countryman of Shylock's, it is a fair inference from the association with Tubal, that Shakespeare
was indebted to the Bishops' of Gen. x. and that he thought
it suitable to adopt the names of Noah's grandsons as com-
patriots of Shylock.

The son of Ham is called Chus in all the versions except
the Great Bible and Genevan; in the latter his name is
spelt as Cush. The choice of the name for a fellow-country-
man of Shylock cannot be regarded as fortunate. In a
later play, *2 King Henry IV.*, Shakespeare gave evidence that
he was aware that Europeans were supposed to be descended
from Japhet and it seems almost incredible that he was
unaware of the colour of Chus. "Cham and his blacke
sonne Chus " are referred to in George Best's narrative
in Hakluyt. In the Genevan Concordance, Cush is said
to mean "blacknesse, or heate." We may leave out of
account the mention of Chus the Benjamite of Ps. vii.,
associated by the Genevan with Shimei.

The conclusion that must be drawn is that Shakespeare
was unaware of the African significance of the name. Neither
can the name Tubal, a son of Japhet, be regarded as a good

choice for a Hebrew, a member of the same tribe as Shylock. At Ezek. xxxii. 26, both in the Genevan and Bishops', Tubal is identified as symbolizing either an Italian or a Spaniard.

With the exception of Lucifer, it will be noticed that Shakespeare's Scriptural mistakes are confined to the earlier plays.

CHAPTER VII

LIST OF BIBLICAL AND LITURGICAL REFERENCES

EXCEPT in special instances, allusions to the Fall of Man, the Cursing of the Earth, the Tenth Commandment, the Redemption of Man and the Lord's Prayer have been omitted. Numbers of other allusions have been reduced to a minimum.

The list includes several passages whose resemblance to Biblical passages is only slight and for which it is improbable that Shakespeare was directly indebted to the Bible. They have been included chiefly for the sake of completeness.

Any passage or line that might be held to illustrate the use of one version rather than another is marked with an asterisk. The versions involved are the Genevan with its Tomson revision, the Bishops', Rheims and the Book of Common Prayer.

References to Canon Todd in these lists are to personal letters, and those to Dr. Dover Wilson to the New Cambridge Edition of Shakespeare's Plays in progress.

THE COMEDY OF ERRORS

1588-9. First published 1623. This Latin comedy is the shortest of all Shakespeare's plays. Dromio of Syracuse is the principal exponent of Scripture.

Act I. ii. 97-102.

ANT. SYR. (*speaking of Ephesus*). They say this town
is full of cozenage:
As nimble jugglers that deceive the eye:
Dark-working sorcerers that change the mind:
Soul-killing witches that deform the body:
Disguised cheaters, prating mountebanks,
And many such like liberties of sin.

In *Menæchmi*, Shakespeare's main inspiration for this farce, the servant of the second Menæchmus, wishing his master to leave Epidamnum, compiled a list of undesirable creatures who, he said, haunted the town. No doubt Shakespeare acted on the hint. Ephesus, the scene of Shakespeare's play, was notorious for its cheats, as Menander bears witness. As for its magicians, it is interesting to recall that in Acts xix. 19 it is related that as a result of St. Paul's preaching many of the Ephesians addicted to the practice of curious arts publicly burnt their books, to the value, as afterwards found, of fifty thousand pieces of silver. Perhaps Shakespeare had this incident in mind. The possibility is increased by the exorcist Pinch's: " I charge thee, Sathan, hous'd within this man, . . . I conjure thee by all the saints in heaven " (IV., iv. 56, 59), and the resemblance it bears to the adjuration of the exorcists in the 13th verse of the same chapter, " We adiure you by Iesus whome Paul preacheth." Shakespeare possibly used the chapter for local colour.

Act II. i. 20-3.

> Luc. Man more divine, the master of all these,
> Lord of the wide world, and wild wat'ry seas,
> Indued with intellectual sense and souls,
> *Of more pre-eminence than fish and fowls.

Ps. viii. 6-8: " Thou makest him to have dominion of the works of thy hands: and thou hast put all things in subjection under his feet; All sheep and oxen: yea, and the beasts of the field; The fowls of the air, and the fishes of the sea: and whatsoever walketh through the paths of the seas." See also Gen. i. 26. *Cf.* Eccles. iii. 19 *B*, " a man hath no preeminence aboue a beast."

Act II. ii. 178.

> Adr. I a vine.

This comparison of the wife to a vine is Biblical. See Ps. cxxviii. 3: " Thy wife shall be as the fruitful vine: upon the walls of thine house."

Act III. ii. 109-10. See Noah.

Act IV. iii. 13-16, 18. See Adam and Prodigal.

Ibid. 18, 19.

> Dro. Syr. . . . he that came behind you, sir, like an evil angel, and bid you forsake your liberty.

Unlike the good angel in Acts xii. 8.

Ibid. 39-40.

> DRO. SYR. Here are the angels that you sent for to deliver you.

A favourite play on the coins. *Cf.* Acts xii. 11: "that the Lorde hath sent his Angel, and hath deliuered me."

Ibid. 47. See Sathan.

Ibid. 50-7.

> DRO. SYR. Nay, she is worse, she is the devil's dam: and here she comes in the habit of a light wench, and, thereof comes that the wenches say, "God damn me!" That's as much to say, "God make me a light wench." It is written, they appear to men like angels of light: light is an effect of fire, and fire will burn. Ergo, light wenches will burn, come not near her.

2 Cor. xi. 14: "for Satan himselfe is transformed into an angell of light." Notice the "It is written" in the manner of the Gospels. (*Cf.* Matt. iv. 4, 6, 7; Luke iv. 4, 8, 10.)

Ibid. 75-7.

> DRO. SYR. But she, more covetous, would have a chain:
> Master, be wise, and if you give it her,
> The devil will shake her chain, and fright us with it.

Rev. xx. 1, 2: "And I sawe an Angel come downe from heauen, hauing the key of the bottomlesse pit, and a great chaine in his hande. And he tooke the dragon, that olde serpent, which is the deuill and Satanas, and he bound him a thousand yeeres."

Act IV. iv. 19.

> DRO. EPH. *Nay, 'tis for me to be patient: I am in adversity.

Ps. xciv. 13: "That thou mayest give him patience in time of adversity" (*G*, "That thou mayest giue him rest from the dayes of euill"). See page 77.

Any passage like the present which might be held to illustrate the use of one Elizabethan version rather than another is marked by an asterisk.

Act V. i. 98-9.

> ADR. I will attend my husband, be his nurse,
> Diet his sickness, for it is my office.

In allusion to the vow made in *L, Matrimony* by either party: " to have and to hold from this day forward for better for worse, for richer for poorer, in sickness and in health."

See also ii. i. 29 (*L, Matrimony*), II. ii. 67 (Eccles. iii. 1 *G*), III. ii. 102-3 (2 Pet. iii. 12) and Adriana in II. ii. 123-33, 146 in allusion to *L, Matrimony* and Eph. v.

1 KING HENRY VI.

1589-90. First printed in 1623. The allusions to Biblical Proper Names are more numerous than in the other two parts.

Act I. i. 28.

For " King of kings " see God.

Ibid. 29-30.

> WIN. Unto the French, the dreadful Judgment Day
> So dreadful will not be, as was his sight.

For a description of the horrors see Rev. vi. 12-17.

Ibid. 31.

> WIN. The battles of the Lord of hosts he fought.

Thus David was praised. See 1 Sam. xxv. 28: " because my lord fighteth the battels of the Lord."

Act I. ii. 26.

> REIGN. He fighteth as one weary of his life.

Eccles. ii. 17: " Thus began I to be weary of my life "; Gen. xxvii. 46: " And Rebecca saide to Isahac, I am wearie of my life for the daughters of Heth."

Ibid. 27-8.

> REIGN. The other lords, like lions wanting food,
> Do rush upon us as their hungry prey.

Ps. xvii. 12: " Like as a lion that is greedy of his prey."

Ibid. 33, 34, 105, 143.

See Goliath, Samson, Deborah and Philip the Evangelist.

Act I. iii. 39-40.

See Abel, Cain, Damascus.

Ibid. 55.

> GLOUC. Thee I'll chase hence, thou wolf in sheep's
> array.

Matt. vii. 15.   See *2 King Henry VI.*, III. i. 77-8.

Act I. iv. 70-1.

> SALIS. O Lord, have mercy on us, wretched sinners.
> GARG. O Lord, have mercy on me, woeful man.

The opening petition of the *Litany* is: " O God the Father,
of heaven: have mercy upon us, miserable sinners."
The ordinary " Lord have mercy upon us " occurs several
times in the Liturgy, but of course it was otherwise well
known in profane speech.

Act. I. v. 9.

> TALBOT. *Heavens, can you suffer hell so to prevail?

Matt. xvi. 18: " & the gates of hel shal not preuaile against
it " (*G,* " shall not ouercome it "). See page 70.

Ibid. 13.

> JOAN. Talbot, farewell, thy hour is not yet come.

See John vii. 30: " because his houre was not yet come."
The phrase, though it became embedded in popular speech,
has the Gospel as its original source.

Act II. i. 26-7.

> TALBOT. *God is our fortress, in whose conquering
> Name
> Let us resolve to scale their flinty bulwarks.

2 Sam. xxii. 2 *G:* " And he said, The Lorde is my rocke
and my fortresse, and he that deliuereth me " (*B* reads
" castle "); Prov. xviii. 10 *G,* " The Name of the Lorde is
a strong towre " (*B,* " castle ").

Act II. v. 102-3.

> MORTIM. Strong-fixed is the House of Lancaster,
> And like a mountain, not to be remov'd.

Ps. cxxv. 1: " even as the mount Sion: which may not be removed."

Ibid. 116.

> YORK. In prison hast thou spent a pilgrimage.

See Gen. xlvii. 9: " Iacob said vnto Pharao, The daies of my pilgrimage are an hundred & thirty yeres " (*G*, " the whole time of my pilgrimage "). Also Ps. cxix. 54.

Shakespeare was very fond of using the word " pilgrimage " in the Biblical sense of " life." It is thus used in *King Richard II., Midsummer-Night's Dream, As You Like It, Othello* and *Measure for Measure.* Shakespeare probably imitated *Euphues,* and it is therefore in all likelihood a Euphuism and not a Biblical quotation.

Act III. i. 25-6.

> GLOUC. The King, thy sovereign, is not quite exempt
> From envious malice of thy swelling heart.

Cf. L, Catechism: " to bear no malice nor hatred in my heart."

Ibid. 129-30.

> K. HEN. And will not you maintain the thing you
>   teach,
> But prove a chief offender in the same ?

Cf. Rom. ii. 21-3: " Thou therefore which teachest another, teachest thou not thy selfe ? Thou preachest a man shoulde not steale, yet stealest thou ?" etc.

Ibid. 196.

> EXETER. Was in the mouth of every sucking babe.

Ps. viii. 2: " Out of the mouths of very babes and sucklings." See also Matt. xxi. 16.

Act III. ii. 110-11.

> BED. Now, quiet soul, depart when heaven please,
> For I have seen our enemies' overthrow.

There seems to be here a reminiscence of the opening of the *Nunc Dimittis.* See *L, Evening Prayer*: " Lord, now

lettest thou thy servant depart in peace: according to thy
word.   For mine eyes have seen: thy salvation."

Ibid. 112.

BED. What is the trust or strength of foolish man ?

Cf. Jer. xvii. 5: ",Cursed be the man that putteth his trust
in man, and that taketh flesh for his arme."

Act III. iii. 42.

JOAN. *Stay, let thy humble handmaid speak to thee.

Compare the language of Abigail, 1 Sam. xxv. 24 *G*,
" I pray thee, let thine handmaide speake to thee " (*B*,
" in thine audience ").

Act IV. i. 191-2.

EXETER. But that it doth presage some ill event.
'Tis much when sceptres are in children's hands.

Eccles. x. 15: " Woe be vnto thee, O thou land, whose
King is but a childe."

Act V. iii. 10-12.

JOAN. Now, ye familiar spirits, that are cull'd
Out of the powerful regions under earth,
Help me this once, that France may get the field.

A familiar spirit was a link with the powers of hell possessed
by witches.   *Cf.* the incident of Saul's consulting the Witch
of Endor.
I Sam. xxviii. 8: " I pray thee coniecture vnto mee by
thy familiar spirite, and bring mee him vp whom I shal
name vnto thee."

Act V. iv. 37-53.

JOAN. Not me, begotten of a shepherd swain,
But issued from the progeny of kings:
Virtuous and holy, chosen from above,
By inspiration of celestial grace,
To work exceeding miracles on earth.
I never had to do with wicked spirits:
But you, that are polluted with your lusts,
Stain'd with the guiltless blood of innocents,
Corrupt and tainted with a thousand vices,

Because you want the grace that others have,
You judge it straight a thing impossible
To compass wonders but by help of devils.
No misconceived, Joan of Arc hath been
A virgin from her tender infancy,
Chaste and immaculate in very thought,
Whose maiden blood thus rigorously effus'd,
Will cry for Vengeance at the Gates of Heaven.

It will be obvious to anyone that Joan is here drawing
on Gospel narrative, first in the call to the Virgin (Luke i.)
and next in the reference to the way the corrupted Jewish
leaders attributed Christ's miracles to Beelzebub (Matt.
xii. 27). The last two lines are reminiscent of Abel the
first martyr, whose blood called to Heaven for vengeance.

Ibid. 63.

JOAN. . . . the fruit within my womb.

This is a frequent Biblical figure for offspring. See
Gen. xxx. 2: " Am I in Gods steade, which keepeth from
thee the fruite of thy wombe ?" Also Ps. cxxvii. 4.

KING JOHN

1589-90. A play called *The Troublesome Raigne of King John*,
in two parts, was published in 1591, reprinted in 1611, and
again in 1622. I have accepted Mr. Peter Alexander's
suggestion that this was founded on Shakespeare's play, and
not Shakespeare's play on it. It is a theory which meets all
the facts. Accordingly, I give a very early date to the play—
1589-90. The only authoritative text is that of 1623. The
play acts better in the theatre than might be supposed from
perusal. Constance makes considerable use of Scriptural
parallels.

Act I. i. 23.

K. JOHN. . . . and so depart in peace.

Cf. L, *Evening Prayer, Nunc Dimittis:* " Lord, now lettest
thou thy servant depart in peace " (Luke ii. 29).

Ibid. 256.

LADY F. *Heaven lay not my transgression to my
charge.

Cf. Acts vii. 60, where Stephen knelt down " and cryed with a loude voyce, Lorde, lay not this sinne to their charge " (*R*, " lay not this sinne vnto them ").

Act II. i. 179-82.

> CONST. *Thy sins are visited in this poor child,
> The canon of the law is laid on him,
> Being but the second generation
> Removed from thy sin-conceiving womb.

L, Catechism and *Communion*: " and visit the sins of the fathers upon the children unto the third and fourth generation of them that hate me." (This is the Second Commandment: the *G* reads " iniquitie " for " sins " and the *B* " sinne.") See page 86, Ps. li. 5: " and in sin hath my mother conceived me."

Act III. i. 70-4.

> CONST. To me and to the state of my great grief
> Let kings assemble: for my grief's so great
> That no supporter but the huge firm earth
> Can hold it up: here I and sorrows sit;
> Here is my throne, bid kings come bow to it.

Is it unreasonable to suppose that Shakespeare was influenced by Lam. i. 12: " Haue ye no regard al ye that go foreby, behold & see if there be any sorow like vnto mine ?"

Ibid. 77-8.

> K. PHIL. To solemnize this day the glorious sun
> Stays in his course.

In reference to Josh. x. 12-14: " Sunne, stand thou still vpon Gibeon, & thou Moone in the valley of Aialon. And the Sunne abode, . . . So the Sunne abode in the middes of heauen, and hasted not to go downe by the space of a whole day. And there was no day like that before it, or after it."

Ibid. 83-6.

> CONST. A wicked day, and not a holy day !
> What hath this day deserv'd ? what hath it done,
> That it in golden letters should be set
> Among the high tides in the Kalendar ?

" High tides " mean the high festivals. Constance alludes to the Golden Number of the year which was expressed in

Roman numeration and which is a factor in determining the exact date of Easter. Tables for the purpose were contained in Common Prayer.

Ibid. 87.

> CONST. Nay, rather turn this day out of the week.

Cf. Job. iii. 6: " and let it not be ioyned vnto the dayes of the yeere, nor counted in the number of the moneths."

Ibid. 89-90.

> CONST.   let wives with child
> Pray that their burdens may not fall this day.

Shakespeare has evidently paraphrased Matt. xxiv. 19: " Woe shalbe in those daies to them that are with child, & to them that giue sucke."

Ibid. 107-8.

> CONST. Arm, arm, you heavens, against these per-
>   jur'd kings !
> A widow cries, be husband to me, heavens !

See Isa. liv. 4, 5: " yea, thou shalt forget the shame of thy youth, and shalt not remember the dishonour of thy widowhead. For he that made thee, shalbe thy Lorde and husband "; Jud. ix. 3: " helpe me widowe, O Lord my God, I beseech thee " (*G*, " O God, O my God, heare me also a widow "). See also Ps. lxviii. 5 and Ps. cxlvi. 9 for God as the widow's defender.

The passage from *Isaiah* seems to have been the one from which the idea was taken. It is also to be observed that the fancy which represents the heavens as participating in human warfare is Biblical. *Cf.* The Song of Deborah and Barak, Judg. v. 20: " They fought from heauen, euen the starres in their courses fought against Sisera."

Ibid. 181-2.

> CONST. Good Father Cardinal, cry thou " Amen "
> To my keen curses.

A reference to the *Commination Service*, appointed to be said on Ash Wednesday and in Shakespeare's day insisted on being said at least four times a year, in which the principal feature is a recitation of ten curses, of which seven are taken from Deut. xxvii. After each curse it is directed that " the people shall answer and say, Amen."

Ibid. 185-90.

> CONST.   when law can do no right,
> Let it be lawful that law bar no wrong.
> Law cannot give my child his kingdom here
> For he that holds his kingdom holds the law:
> Therefore, since law itself is perfect wrong,
> How can the law forbid my tongue to curse ?

Does this rhetorical frenzy of Constance owe anything to such passages as Rom. iii. 19; iv. 15; vii. 6 ? Shakespeare affords evidence elsewhere of acquaintance with *Romans.* See Chapter II., page 38.

Ibid. 344-5.

> K. PHIL. Thy rage shall burn thee up, and thou shalt turn
> To ashes.

Cf. Wisd. ii. 3: " our bodie shalbe turned into ashes." See also the *Burial Service.*

Act III. iii. 61.

> K. JOHN. He is a very serpent in my way.

Gen. xlix. 17: " Dan shalbe a serpent in the way."

Act III. iv. 25, 28.

> CONST. Death, death . . .
> Thou hate and terror to prosperity.

For this thought see Ecclus. xli. 1: " O Death, howe bitter is the remembrance of thee to a man that seeketh rest and comfort in his substance and riches . . . & that hath prosperitie in all things."
Cf. Ecclus. xli. 2 with the rest of Constance's utterance: " O death, howe acceptable and good is thy iudgement vnto the needefull, & vnto him . . . that in all things is full of care & fearefulnes, vnto him also that is in despaire, and hath no hope nor patience ?"

Ibid. 79. See Cain.

Ibid. 108.

LEWIS. *Life is as tedious as a twice-told tale.

Wisd. ii. 1: " Our life is short & tedious." Ps. xc. 9:
" we bring our years to an end, as it were a tale that is told "
(*G*, " wee haue spent!our yeeres as a thought "). See also
Romeo and Juliet, V. iii. 229-30, *Macbeth*, V. v. 26, 27 and
page 78.

Ibid. 147-8.

PAND. For he that steeps his safety in true blood
Shall find but bloody safety and untrue.

An application of Gen. ix. 5, 6, but see also Hab. ii. 12:
" Woe vnto him that buildeth a towne with blood."
It is interesting to observe how King John repeats the
gist of Pandulph's words in *Act IV. ii.* 104-5.

Act IV. iii. 122. See Lucifer.

Ibid. 138.

HUB. *Let hell want pains enough to torture me.

Ps. cxvi. 3: " and the pains of hell gat hold upon me "
(*G*, " the griefes of the graue caught me "). Ps. xviii. 4 *L.*
See also *King Richard II.*, III. i. 34 and page 78.

Ibid. 140-1.

BAST.   and lose my way
Among the thorns and dangers of this world.

The figure " the thorns . . . of this world " would appear
to be due to the Parable of the Sower, Matt. xiii. 22: " He
also that receyued seede into the thornes, is he that heareth
the word, and the care of this world, and the deceitfulnesse
of riches choke vp the word." See also Luke viii.

Act V. ii. 154-8.

BAST. For your own ladies and pale-visag'd maids
Like Amazons come tripping after drums,
Their thimbles into armed gauntlets change,
Their needl's to lances, and their gentle hearts
To fierce and bloody inclination.

There is a suggestion here that Shakespeare was influenced
by Joel iii. 10: " Breake your plough shares into swordes, and
your sithes into speares, let the weake say, I am strong."

9

Act V. vi. 37-8.

> BAST. Withhold thine indignation, mighty heaven,
> And tempt us not to bear above our power.

Cf. 1 Cor. x. 13: " but God is faithfull, which shall not suffer you to bee tempted aboue that you are able: but shall with the temptation make a way to escape, that ye may be able to beare it."

See also III. i. 208-9 (2 Cor. xi. 14); *ibid.* 265, 266 (Deut. xxiii. 21, 23); IV. i. 92 (Matt. vii. 3).

THE TAMING OF THE SHREW

1590-1. In 1594 a corrupt and degraded version was published (see Peter Alexander, *Times Literary Supplement*, September 16, 1926). First authentic edition 1623. There is a modern tendency to identify this play as the *Love's Labour's Won* mentioned by Meres in 1598. The comedy is frequently acted and is very popular. The Biblical references are, having regard to the character of the play, remarkably few. Only nine allusions to Bible and Prayer Book have been gathered, and of these four can be traced to the *Marriage Service, Catechism,* and *Litany.*

Induction ii. 137-8.

> SERVANT. And frame your mind to mirth and merriment,
> Which bars a thousand harms, and lengthens life.

Cf. Ecclus. xxx. 22: " The ioy and chearefulnes of the heart is the life of man, and a mans gladnesse is the prolonging of his dayes."

Act I. i. 66.

> HORT. From all such devils, Good Lord, deliver us.

L, Litany. A relevant example would be: " From all evil and mischief, from sin, from the crafts and assaults of the devil, from Thy wrath and from everlasting damnation, Good Lord, deliver us."

Act III. ii. 233-5.

> PET. She is my goods, my chattels, she is my house,
> My household stuff, my field, my barn,
> My horse, my ox, my ass, my any thing.

See the *Tenth Commandment* in *L, Catechism* and *Communion*: " Thou shalt not covet thy neighbour's house, thou shalt not covet thy neighbour's wife, nor his servant, nor his maid, nor his ox, nor his ass, nor any thing that is his."

Act IV. i. 6-8.

> GRUMIO. my very lips might freeze to my teeth, my
> tongue to the roof of my mouth.

This looks like a variation of Ps. cxxxvii. 6: " let my tongue cleave to the roof of my mouth."

Ibid. 50-1.

> GRUMIO. . . . and every officer his wedding garment
> on ?

Cf. Matt. xxii. 11, 12: " When the king came in to see the ghestes, he spyed there a man, which had not on a wedding garment, And hee saith vnto him, Friend, how camest thou in hither, not hauing a wedding garment ?"

Act IV. iii. 113.

> PET. Or I shall so be-mete thee with thy yard.

Cf. Matt. vii. 2: " and with what measure yee mete."

Act. V. ii. 147-8.

> KATH. Thy husband is thy lord, thy life, thy keeper,
> Thy head, thy sovereign.

Eph. v. 23: " For the husband is the head of the wife." See also *L, Matrimony.*

Ibid. 156-7.

> KATH. *Such duty as the subject owes the prince,
> Even such a woman oweth to her husband.

This seems a paraphrase of Eph. v. 24 *B*: " as the Church is subiect vnto Christ, likewise the wiues to their owne husbands in all things " (*G* reads " in subiection," which for the purpose here alters the significance somewhat). See also line 165.
Note.—By very hard pressure it might be possible to extract a little more out of the play. Since it concerns

Ecclesiasticus and that therefore Shakespeare was sure to have read it, a good case could be made for Gremio's in

Act II. i. 394-7.

> your father were a fool
> To give thee all, and in his waning age
> Set foot under thy table.   Tut ! a toy !
> An old Italian fox is not so kind, my boy.

Cf. Ecclus. xxxiii. 18-20: " Giue not thy sonne and wife, thy brother & friende, power ouer thee while thou liuest: and giue not away thy substance and good to an other, lest it repent thee, & thou be fayne to aske of them againe. As long as thou liuest and hast breath, let no man change thee.   For better it is thy children to pray thee, then that thou shouldest be fayne to looke in their handes."

2 KING HENRY VI.

1590-1.   With *3 King Henry VI.*, it was first printed in two parts in 1594 and 1595 in incomplete and corrupt form under the titles of " The First Part of the Contention betwixt the Houses of Yorke and Lancaster, with the death of the good Duke Humphrey, etc.," and " The True Tragedie of Richard Duke of Yorke, and the death of Good King Henrie the Sixth, etc."   These are commonly referred to as " The Contention " and " The True Tragedie," and they were reprinted in 1600 and 1619.   First authentic text 1623.   King Henry quotes Scripture on every convenient opportunity and his references to the Psalter are specially numerous.

Act I. ii. 70-3.

> HUME. Jesus preserve your royal Majesty !
> DUCH. What say'st thou ? Majesty ? I am but Grace.
> HUME. But, by the grace of God, and Hume's advice, Your Grace's title shall be multiplied.

In play on 1 Pet. i. 2: " Grace and peace be multiplied vnto you."

Act I. iii. 61.

> Q. MARG. His weapons, holy saws of sacred Writ.

Cf. Eph. vi. 17: " And take the helmet of saluation, and the sword of the spirite, which is the word of God."

Ibid. 145.

> DUCH. I could set my Ten Commandments in your
> face.

Ten Commandments commonly meant the two hands
with whose fingers and thumbs an offender was scratched.
Usually with reference to women, as for instance " my wife's
ten commandments." In allusion, it is thought, to the
tradition that God scratched the Ten Commandments on
the Tables with his nails.

Act I. iv. 28-9.

> WITCH. By the Eternal God, whose Name and Power
> Thou tremblest at.

For the idea that fiends trembled at the Name of God
cf. Jas. ii. 19, " the deuils also beleeue, and tremble."
Emphasized in Homily on Salvation.

Ibid. 43.

> BOLING. *False fiend, avoid !

Cf. " Sathan, avoid," *Comedy of Errors.* See Sathan.

Act II. i. 17, 18.

> GLOUC. Were it not good your Grace could fly to
> heaven ?
> K. HEN. The treasury of everlasting joy.

Luke xii. 33, Matt. vi. 20 *L* (one of the Sentences read
out at the Offertory in the *Communion*): " treasures in heaven;
where neither rust nor moth doth corrupt, and where
thieves do not break through and steal."

Ibid. 35-6.

> CARD. Let me be blessed for the peace I make
> Against this proud Protector with my sword.

Cf. Matt. x. 34: " I came not to send peace, but a sword."

Ibid. 53-4.

> CARD. *Medice, teipsum;
> Protector, see to't well, protect yourself.

Luke iv. 23, Vulgate: " Medice, cura teipsum."
The phrase was probably proverbial and well known. This
is the only quotation from the Latin Vulgate made by Shake-

speare. See *King Henry V.*, IV. viii. 128, for evidence of Shakespeare's ignorance of the Vulgate.

Ibid. 66-7.

> K. HEN. Now, God be prais'd, that to believing souls
> Gives Light in Darkness, Comfort in Despair.

L, Evening Prayer, 3rd Collect: "Lighten our darkness, we beseech thee, O Lord"; *L, Morning Prayer, Benedictus* (Luke i. 79): "To give light to them that sit in darkness"; 2 Sam. xxii. 29: "For thou art my light, O Lorde: and the Lord shall lighten my darkenesse"; Ps. xviii. 28: "Thou also shalt light my candle: the Lord my God shall make my darkness to be light."

Of particular interest is Isa. xlii. 16: "I wil bring the blinde into a streete that they know not, and leade them into a footepath that they are ignorant in: I shal make darknes light before them." *Cf.* also John ix. 5; 2 Cor. vii. 6, *G,* "God, that comforteth the abiect" (*B* and *R,* "humble").

Ibid. 71.

> K. HEN. Although by his sight his sin be multiplied.

Cf. John ix. 41: "If ye were blind, ye should haue no sinne, but now ye say, We see: therefore your sinne remaineth."

Ibid. 74-5.

> K. HEN. Good fellow, tell us here the circumstance,
> That we for thee may glorify the Lord.

Matt. v. 16—*L, Communion, Offertory:* "and glorify your Father which is in heaven."

This is probably the sentence most frequently read at the *Communion Offertory* and therefore the best known.

Ibid. 160.

> SUFF. . . . made the lame to leap.

Cf. Isa. xxxv. 6: "Then shall the lame men leape as an Hart."

Ibid. 184-5.

> K. HEN. O God! what mischiefs work the wicked ones,
> Heaping confusion on their own heads thereby?

Ps. vii. 15-17: " Behold, he travaileth with mischief:
. . . For his travail shall come upon his own head: and his
wickedness shall fall on his own pate." See also Ps. xiv. 8:
" they are all such workers of mischief" (*G*, " workers of
iniquitie "); Ps. cxl. 9: " Let the mischief of their own lips
fall upon the head of them."

Ibid. 193-4.

> GLOUC. . . . and convers'd with such
> As, like to pitch, defile nobility.

This quotation from Ecclus. xiii. 1—" Who so toucheth
pitche, shall be defiled withall "—is a favourite of Shakespeare's.

Act II. ii. 73-4.

> YORK. Till they have snar'd the shepherd of the
>   flock,
> That virtuous prince, the good Duke Humphrey.

Cf. Matt. xxvi. 31: " I wil smite the sheepeheard, and the
sheepe of the flocke shalbe scattered abroad " (*R*, " I vvil
strike the Pastor "). Also Zech. xiii. 7.

Act II. iii. 2-4.

> K. HEN. In sight of God and us, your guilt is great;
> Receive the sentence of the law for sins
> Such as by God's Book are adjudg'd to death.

Exod. xxii. 17 and Deut. xviii. 10-12 provide penalties
for witchcraft and sorcery. For " God's Book " see " Bible."

Ibid. 18-9.

> GLOUC. Ah Humphrey ! this dishonour in thine age
> Will bring thy head with sorrow to the ground.

See also *Two Gentlemen of Verona*, III. i. 19-21.

Gen. xlii. 38: " ye shall bring my gray head with sorowe
vnto the graue."

None of the old versions has the " hairs " of the Authorised;
all read " head." The late Mr. J. M. Robertson considered
these two lines to be reminiscent of Greene's style, to whom
he attributed part authorship of the play.

Ibid. 24-5.

> K. HEN.   God shall be my hope,
> *My stay, my guide and lantern to my feet.

Ps. xxxix. 8: " truly my hope is even in thee." Ps. lxxi. 4:
" thou art my hope, even from my youth." Ps. xviii. 18 *B*:
" but God was vnto me a sure stay " (*G*, " but the Lord was
my stay "; *L*, " upholder "). Note this Psalm is also in 2 Sam.
xxii. Ps. xlviii. 13: " he shall be our guide unto death."
Ps. cxix. 105: " Thy word is a lantern unto my feet " (*B*,
" candel ").

In " lantern to my feet," Mr. Robertson also detected the
hand of Greene.

Act III. i. 69-71.

> K. HEN. Our kinsman Gloucester is as innocent
> From meaning treason to our royal person
> *As is the sucking lamb, or harmless dove.

For the innocence of lambs see Isa. xi. 6 and Luke x. 3,
and for the " harmless dove " see Matt. x. 16: " harmelesse
as the Doues " (*G*, " innocent," *R*, " simple ").

Ibid. 77-8.

> Q. MARG. Is he a lamb ? his skin is surely lent him
> For he's inclin'd as is the ravenous wolf.

Matt. vii. 15: " Beware of the false prophets which come
to you in sheepes clothing, but inwardly they are rauening
wolues."

Ibid. 191-2.

> GLOUC. Thus is the shepherd beaten from thy side
> And wolves are gnarling who shall gnaw thee first.

Cf. Matt xxvi. 31 (see *Act II. ii.* 73-4).

Act III. ii. 76.

> Q. MARG. What ? Art thou, like the adder, waxen
>   deaf?

Shakespeare's belief that the adder is deaf has often been
remarked. His belief was based on the Bible.

See Ps. lviii. 4, 5: " even like the deaf adder that stoppeth
her ears; Which refuseth to hear the voice of the charmer:
charm he never so wisely."

Ibid. 232-5.

> K. HEN. What stronger breastplate than a heart
> untainted?
> Thrice is he arm'd that hath his quarrel just;
> And he but naked, though lock'd up in steel,
> Whose conscience with injustice is corrupted.

Eph. vi. 14: "Stand therefore, hauing your loynes girt about with the trueth, & hauing on the breast plate of righteousnesse" (*R*, "clothed with the breast-plate of iustice"). Wisd. xvii. 11, 12: "For malice is a dreadfull thing that is condemned by his owne witnes: and being pressed with conscience, it euer suspecteth cruell things. For feare is nothing else but a betraying of the succours which reason offereth." Prov. xxviii. 1: "The vngodly fleeth when no man pursueth him: but the righteous are bold as a Lion."

Act III. iii. 24.

> WAR. *See how the pangs of death do make him grin.

Cf. 2 Sam. xxii. 5: "For the pangs of death closed me about"; Ps. xviii. 3 *B*, "The panges of death" (*L*, "sorrows of death," and so also *G*).

It is just possible that Shakespeare took the phrase from the Bible and it is also just possible that he took it from the Bishops' *Psalms*. See Chapter IV., pages 76-7.

Act IV. ii. 18-19.

> HOLL. . . . and yet it is said, "labour in thy voca-
> tion."

A variety of possible sources might be given for this maxim including the *Catechism* and the Homily against Idleness. Latimer in one of his sermons adapted "Let every man labour in his calling" from 2 Thess. iii. As used here and as distinct from Falstaff's in *1 King Henry IV*. there does not appear to be any particular Biblical character about the sense.

Ibid. 146. See Adam.

Act IV. iv. 38.

> K. HEN. *O graceless men! they know not what they
> do.

Luke xxiii. 34 *G*, "for they know not what they doe" (also *R*. *B* reads "wote not," as also *C*).

Act IV. vii. 113-4.

> CADE.   . . . he has a familiar under his tongue: he
> speaks not o' God's name.

See 1 Sam. xxviii. 7 and *1 King Henry VI.*, V. iii. 10-12.

Act IV. ix. 13.

> K. HEN. Then, heaven, set ope thy everlasting gates.

Ps. xxiv. 7: " Lift up your heads, O ye gates, and be ye
lift up, ye everlasting doors."

Act V. i. 160.

> CLIF. Take heed, lest by your heat you burn your-
> selves.

In probable allusion to Dan. iii. 22, Nebuchadnezzar's
furnace, which was so hot that it slew his servants.

Ibid. 213-4.

> RICH. *Fie ! charity ! for shame ! speak not in spite,
> For you shall sup with Jesu Christ to-night.

1 Cor. xiii. 1 *B2*: " Though I speake with the tongues of
men, and of angels, and haue not charitie " (so also *R*.   *G*
reads " loue," as do also *C* and *B1*).
Luke xxiii. 43: " And Iesus sayd vnto him, Verily I say
vnto thee, to day shalt thou bee with me in paradise."
Rev. xix. 9: " Happie are they which are called vnto the
supper of the Lambes marriage."
It is an instance of the consistency with which Shakespeare
has drawn Richard's character throughout the plays, that
thus early after his first introduction he should utter " old
odd ends stol'n out of Holy Writ."

Act V. ii. 33-4.

> Y. CLIF.   O war ! thou son of hell
> Whom angry heavens do make their minister.

For war as one of the judgments of heaven see Ezek. xiv. 21
and Ezek. v. 13.

Ibid. 36.

> Y. CLIF. *Hot coals of vengeance.

Ps. cxl. 10: " hot burning coals " (*G* omits " hot ").

Ibid. 50-1.

> Y. CLIF. My heart is turn'd to stone: and while 'tis mine,
> It shall be stony.

1 Sam. xxv. 37: " and his heart dyed within him, and he became as a stone." Ezek. xi 19: " that stonie heart," but the sense is different, meaning " hard," " barren."

Ibid. 73.

> K. HEN. Can we outrun the heavens ?

Amos ix. 2, 3: (2) " Though they digge into hell, thence shal my hande take them, though they clime vp to heauen, thence will I bring them downe." (3) " And though they hide themselues in the toppe of Carmel, I wil searche and take them out thence: and though they be hid from my sight in the bottome of the sea, thence will I commaunde the serpent, and he shall bite them."
See also Ps. cxxxix. 6-7: " Whither shall I go then from thy Spirit: or whither shall I go then from thy presence ? If I climb up into heaven, thou art there: if I go down to hell, thou art there also."

See also II. i. 34 (Matt. v. 9); III. i. 79 (2 Cor. xi. 14); III. iii. 31 (Matt. vii. 1 and Rom. iii. 22, 23); V. ii. 40-3 (1 Cor. xv. 52); V. ii. 71 (Luke vi. 27-8).

3 KING HENRY VI.

1591-2. First authentic text 1623. For previous imprints see *2 King Henry VI.* Scriptural quotation in this play, in which Richard becomes prominent, though copious, is noticeably less than in *2 King Henry VI.*

Act I. i. 42.

> WAR. *Hath made us by-words to our enemies.

Ps. xliv. 15: " Thou makest us to be a by-word among the heathen " (*G*, " a prouerbe ").

Ibid. 161-2.

> Y. CLIF. May that ground gape, and swallow me alive,
> Where I shall kneel to him that slew my father.

In probable allusion to the destruction of Korah, Dathan and Abiram (Num. xvi. 30-3). 32. " And the earth opened her mouth, and swalowed them vp." See also Ps. cvi. 17 and *King Richard III.*, I. ii. 65. The incident is referred to in the Homily on Obedience.

Act I. iv. 112.

>   YORK. Whose tongue more poisons than the adder's tooth.

Ps. cxl. 3: " They have sharpened their tongues like a serpent: adder's poison is under their lips."

Act II. ii. 163-5.

>   GEORGE. But when we saw our sunshine made thy spring,
>   And that thy summer bred us no increase,
>   We set the axe to thy usurping root.

Cf. Luke iii. 9: " Nowe also is the axe layde vnto the roote of the trees: Euery tree therefore which bringeth not foorth good fruite, is hewen downe, and cast into the fire."

Act II. iii. 15, 23.

>   RICH. Thy brother's blood the thirsty earth hath drunk, . . .
>   WAR.* Then let the earth be drunken with our blood.

Cf. Judith vi, 4, *G*: " and the mountains shall be drunken with their blood."

Ibid. 37.

>   EDW. Thou setter up and plucker down of kings.

Cf. Dan. ii. 21: " he taketh away kings, hee setteth vp kinges."

Act II. vi. 1.

>   CLIF. Here burns my candle out.

Cf. Job xviii. 6, Ps. xviii. 28.

Ibid. 55.

>   WAR. Measure for measure must be answered.

Cf. Mark iv. 24: " With what measure ye mete, with the same shall it be measured to you againe."

Act III. i. 24-5.

> K. HEN. Let me embrace thee, sour adversity,
> For wise men say it is the wisest course.

This may be taken as an allusion to the wise Son of Sirach. *Cf.* Ecclus. ii. 4, 5: "Whatsoeuer happeneth vnto thee, receiue it: suffer in heauines, and be patient in thy trouble. For like as gold and siluer are tryed in the fire, euen so are acceptable men in the furnace of aduersitie." The writers of *Proverbs* and *Ecclesiasticus* are constantly referred to in the Homilies as the wise men.

Act III. iii. 51.

> WAR. *I come in kindness and unfeigned love.

2 Cor. vi. 6—*L, Communion, Epistle (First Sunday in Lent):* "in kyndnesse, in the holy Ghost, in loue vnfained" (as also *C* and *B1*. *B2* reads: "by kindnesse, by the holy Ghost, by loue vnfeigned," as also *G*. *R* reads: "in svveetenes, in the holy Ghost, in charitie not feined"). See Chapter IV., page 82.

Act IV. viii. 49.

> K. HEN. And when the lion fawns upon the lamb.

Although in the famous verse, Isa. xi. 6, it is the wolf that is associated with the lamb, and the lion with the calf, yet, without doubt, Henry is alluding to the general idea contained there.

Act V. i. 90-1. See Jephah.

Act V. ii. 11-15.

> WAR. Thus yields the cedar to the axe's edge,
> Whose arms gave shelter to the princely eagle,
> Under whose shade the ramping lion slept,
> Whose top branch overpeer'd Jove's spreading tree,
> And kept low shrubs from winter's pow'rful wind.

Cf. Ezek. xxxi. 3: "Beholde, Assur is a Cedar in Libanon, with faire branches, & with thicke shadowing boughes of a high stature, and his toppe was among the thicke boughs."

Act V. iv. 74-5.

Q. MARG. My tears gainsay; for every word I speak,
Ye see I drink the water of my eye.

Cf. Ps. lxxx. 5: " and givest them plenteousness of tears to drink."

Act V. v. 8.   See Jerusalem.

Act V. vi. 11.

RICH. *Suspicion always haunts the guilty mind.

Cf. Wisd. xvii. 11: " For malice is a dreadfull thing that is condemned by his owne witnes: and being pressed with conscience, it euer suspecteth cruell things " (*G* reads " doeth euer forecast " for " euer suspecteth " of *B*).

Ibid. 52.

K. HEN. Not like the fruit of such a goodly tree.

Henry here makes use of a Biblical figure to deride Richard. See Matt. vii. 18: " A good tree cannot bring foorth bad fruit."

Act V. vii. 13-4.

K. EDW. Thus have we swept suspicion from our seat,
And made our footstool of security.

For the idea of making of enemies a footstool as a symbol of security, see Ps. cx. 1: " The Lord said unto my Lord: Sit thou on my right hand, until I make thine enemies thy footstool." This is one of the Old Testament passages most quoted in the New Testament. See Matt. xxii. 44, Mark xii. 36, Luke xx. 43, Heb. i. 13.

Ibid. 33-4.   See Judas Iscariot.

See also II. iii. 17* (2 Sam. xxii. 5, Ps. xviii. 3 *B*); II. v. 69, (Luke xxiii. 34); IV. i. 21-3 (*L, Matrimony*).

KING RICHARD III.

1591-2. Printed 1597. Reprinted 1598, 1602, 1605, 1612, 1622. The 1623 Folio printed from the edition of 1622, subject to one important omission and to corrections and additions from other sources. The exact relationship of the Folio text to that of the first edition is accordingly difficult to fix. See Peter Alexander's *Henry VI. and Richard III.*

Of all the Histories, this play has had the most successful theatrical record. If our chronology is followed, then Richard is Shakespeare's earliest successful stage character of great importance. In this play he continues as the devil quoting Scripture.

Act I. ii. 47-8.

> ANNE. Thou hadst but power over his mortal body,
> His soul thou canst not have.

Matt. x. 28: " And feare (ye) not them which kill the body, but are not able to kill the soule."

Ibid. 63.

> ANNE. O earth, which this blood drink'st, revenge his
> death !

See Gen. iv. 11: " And now art thou cursed from the earth, which hath opened her mouth to receiue thy brothers blood from thy hand."

Ibid. 65.

> ANNE. Or earth gape open wide, and eat him quick.

In all probability an allusion to the destruction of Korah, Dathan and Abiram. See Num. xvi. 30-3. See also Ps. cvi. 17: " So the earth opened, and swallowed up Dathan," and *3 King Henry VI.*, I. i. 161-2.

Ibid. 106-10.

> RICH. The fitter for the King of Heaven that hath
> him.
> ANNE. He is in heaven, where thou shalt never come.
> RICH. Let him thank me, that holp to send him
> thither:
> For he was fitter for that place than earth.
> ANNE. And thou unfit for any place but hell.

Cf. Luke ix. 62: " apt to the kingdome of God " (and so all other versions, including *R*. Note the Authorised reading: " fit for the kingdom of God." Note also the popularity of the play in print and on the stage).

Act I. iii. 179.

> RICH. His curses, then from bitterness of soul.

The phrase " bitterness of soul " is frequent in the Bible. See Job xxi. 25: " Another dieth in the bitternes of his soule "; also Prov. xiv. 10, etc.

Ibid. 264.

> RICH. Our aery buildeth in the cedar's top.

Cf. Ezek. xvii. 3: " There came a great Eagle with great wings, yea with a mighty long body, and full of feathers of diuers colours, vpon the mount of Libanus, and tooke the highest branch of a Cedar tree."

Ibid. 272.

> Q. MARG. As it was won with blood, lost be it so.

Gen. ix. 6: "Who so sheddeth mans blood, by man shall his blood be shed, for in the image of God made he man." See also Matt. xxvi. 52: " For all they that take the sworde, shall perish with the sworde."

Ibid. 334-8.

> RICH. But then I sigh, and, with a piece of Scripture,
> Tell them that God bids us do good for evil;
> And thus I clothe my naked villainy
> With old odd ends stol'n out of Holy Writ,
> And seem a saint when most I play the devil.

Richard transforms himself into an angel of light (2 Cor. xi. 14), and like Satan tempting Christ, as in Matt. iv. and Luke iv., quotes sufficient Scripture to suit his purpose and conceal his real intent. Richard makes this self-exposing revelation in no spirit of tragedy, as did Macbeth (a villain by force of temptation and in spite of precept), but in a vein of comedy, in a tone of confidence that expected from his auditors amused appreciation of his wit. Richard should be presented as a comic character. As to rendering good for evil see Matt. v. 43, 1 Thess. v. 15, etc.

Act I. iv. 58.   See Legion.

Ibid. 74.

CLAR. *My soul is heavy and I fain would sleep.

Matt. xxvi. 38: " My soule is exceeding heauy "; *R*, " sor-rovvful "; 43: " he findeth them a sleepe againe: for their eies were heauie."

Ibid. 76-7.

BRAK. Sorrow breaks seasons and reposing hours,
Makes the night morning, and the noon-tide night.

It is possible that Job's affliction provided a hint here. See Job xvii. 11, 12: " My dayes are past, and my coun-sailes and thoughtes of my heart are vanished away, Chang-ing the night into day, and the light approching into darkenesse."

Ibid. 141-2.

2ND MURD. he cannot lie with his neighbour's wife,
but it detects him.

L, Commination: " Minister. Cursed is he that lieth with his neighbour's wife. Answer. Amen."

Ibid. 204-6.

CLAR.   the great King of kings
Hath in the tables of his law commanded
*That thou shalt do no murder.

L, Catechism and *Communion:* " Thou shalt do no murder." (All Tudor versions of the Bible rendered the Commandment in Exod. xx. 13: " Thou shalt not kill "; in Matt. xix. 18 the *R* reads " Thou shalt not murder," and in that verse the Authorised adopted the Prayer Book version.) See page 86.

Ibid. 208-9.

CLAR. Take heed: for he holds Vengeance in his
hands
To hurl upon their heads that break his law.

Deut. xxxii. 35: " Vengeance is mine " (*G*, " Vengeance and recompense are mine "). See also Rom. xii. 19. *Cf.* *L,*Catechism* and *Communion:* " For I the Lord thy God am a jealous God, and visit the sins of the fathers upon the children, unto the third and fourth generation of them that hate me, and shew mercy unto thousands in them that love me, and keep my commandments." In the *Communion Service* the people answer after the reading of each commandment: " Lord, have mercy upon us, and incline our hearts to keep this law." After the last : " and write all these thy laws in our hearts, we beseech thee."

Ibid. 210-19.

> 2ND MURD. And that same vengeance doth he throw
>   on thee
> For false forswearing and for murder too:
> Thou didst receive the holy sacrament
> To fight in quarrel of the house of Lancaster.
> 1ST MURD. And, like a traitor to the name of God,
> Didst break that vow, and with thy treacherous blade
> Unripp'dst the bowels of thy sovereign's son.
> 2ND MURD. Whom thou wast sworn to cherish and
>   defend.
> 1ST MURD. How canst thou urge God's dreadful law
>   to us
> When thou hast broke it in so dear degree ?

The argument of the assassins, with the Scriptural foundation, seems too shrewd to be in character. Injunction against the breaking of vows taken before the Lord—and it is to be noted that Clarence's oath was so taken—are numerous in Lev. xxvii., Num. vi. 2, Deut. xxiii. 21, and are frequently enforced in other books, notably in Eccles. v. 4. The final retort of the 1st Murderer is in the spirit of Rom. ii. 21-3, and might be regarded as a paraphrase of verse 23: " Thou that makest thy boast of the lawe, through breaking the lawe, dishonourest thou God?" Shakespeare makes no distinction between " vow " and " oath." The introduction of a humorous element into a murder scene must excite remark.

Ibid. 224-8.

> CLAR. If God will be revenged for this deed,
> O, know you yet, he doth it publicly.
> Take not the quarrel from his powerful arm:
> He needs no indirect nor lawless course
> To cut off those that have offended him.

See 2 Sam. xii. 12; Deut. xxxii. 35, 43; Rom. xii. 19; Luke xviii. 7, 8.

Ibid. 250-2.

> CLAR. O, do not slander him, for he is kind.
> 1ST MURD. Right:
> As snow in harvest.

The 1st Murderer is applying ironically Prov. xxv. 12: " As the colde of snowe in the time of haruest: so is a faithfull messenger to them that sende him, for he refresheth his masters minde."

Ibid. 282.   See Pilate.

Act II. ii. 107-11.

> DUCH. *God bless thee ! and put meekness in thy mind,
> Love, charity, obedience and true duty.
> RICH. Amen: and make me die a good old man.
> That's the butt end of a mother's blessing:
> I marvel why her Grace did leave it out.

Cf. 1 Tim. vi. 11: " followe after righteousnesse, godlinesse, faith, loue, patience, meekenesse " (*R*, " pursue iustice, pietie, faith, charitie, patience, mildenes "). As for Richard's pious reply, see Num. xxiii. 10: " I pray God that my soule may die the death of the righteous, and that my last end may be like his " (*i.e.*, like Jacob's).

Act II. iii. 11.

> 3RD CIT. Woe to that land that's govern'd by a child !

Eccles. x. 15: " Woe be vnto thee, O thou land, whose King is but a childe."   See also *1 King Henry VI.*, IV. i. 192.

Act III. i. 9-11.

> RICH. Nor more can you distinguish of a man
> Than of his outward show, which, God he knows,
> Seldom or never jumpeth with the heart.

1 Sam. xvi. 7: " For man looketh on the outwarde appearance, but the Lorde beholdeth the heart."   Luke xvi. 15: " Ye are they which iustifie your selues before men, but God knoweth your heartes."

Ibid. 126-7.

> Edw. V. My Lord of York will still be cross in talk.
> Uncle, your Grace knows how to bear with him.

In play on Luke xiv. 27: " And whosoeuer doth not beare his crosse."

Act III. ii. 110.

> Hast. Come the next sabaoth and I will content you.

In the first quarto " sabaoth ": in the third and subsequent editions " Sabboth." See Chapter VI.

Act III. iv. 75-6.

> Rich. Off with his head ! now, by St. Paul, I swear,
> I will not dine until I see the same.

This is from Holinshed and may be taken as in allusion to Acts xxiii. 12, which records the determination of certain Jews neither to eat nor to drink until they had killed Paul. According to Shakespeare, St. Paul (or " holy Paul " or " the Apostle Paul ") was Richard's favourite asseveration; Holinshed is authority for no other instance than the one quoted here.

Ibid. 95-100.

> Hast. O momentary grace of worldly men,
> Which we more hunt for than the grace of God !
> Who builds his hope in air of your good looks
> Lives like a drunken sailor on a mast,
> Ready with every nod to tumble down
> Into the fatal bowels of the deep.

Cf. Jer. xvii. 5: " Cursed be the man that putteth his trust in man, and that taketh flesh for his arme "; Ps. cxlvi. 2: " O put not your trust in princes, nor in any child of man: for there is no help in them." See also *L, Commination.* For lines 97-100, see Prov. xxiii. 31-4: " Looke not thou vpon the wine, howe red it is, and what a colour it giueth in the glasse. It goeth downe sweetely, but at the last it biteth like a Serpent, and stingeth like an Adder. Thine eyes shall beholde strange women, and thine heart shall vtter lewde things: Yea, thou shalt be as though thou laiest in the middest of the sea, or sleepest vpon the toppe of the mast of a ship."

Act III. vii. 72-6.

BUCK. But on his knees at meditation:
Not dallying with a brace of courtesans,
But meditating with two deep divines:
Not sleeping to engross his idle body,
But praying to enrich his watchful soul.

Note " sleeping," " praying " and " watchful." See
Matt. xxvi. 40, 41: " And he cometh vnto the disciples,
and findeth them a sleepe, and saieth vnto Peter, What,
could ye not watch with me one houre ? Watch and pray."

Ibid. 166.

RICH. The royal tree hath left us royal fruit.

Cf. Matt. xii. 33: " For the tree is knowen by his fruite."
The whole of Richard's speech reeks of Scripture but
without particular reference except this.

Act IV. iii. 38. See Abraham.

Act IV. iv. 150-1.

RICH. Let not the heavens hear these tell-tale women
Rail on the Lord's Anointed.

Cf. Shimei's cursing of David, 2 Sam. xvi. 5-14, and
Abishai's remark, 2 Sam. xix. 21: " Shall not Semei die for
this, because he cursed the Lordes anoynted ?" Richard's
tone here is that of horrified piety.

Ibid. 346-7.

RICH. Say that the King, which may command,
   entreats.
ELIZ. That, at her hands, which the King's King
   forbids.

L, Table of Kindred and Affinity " wherein whosoever are
related are forbidden in Scripture and our Laws to marry
together. A Man may not marry his . . . 25. Brother's
Daughter," also Lev. xviii. 16, 17.

Act V. iii. 12.

RICH. *Besides, the king's name is a tower of strength.

This application to himself of the Biblical figure is amusing.
See Prov. xviii. 10 *G*, " The Name of the Lorde is a strong
towre " (*B*, " castle ").

Act V. iv. 37-9.

> RICHMOND. The brother blindly shed the brother's
>   blood;
> The father rashly slaughter'd his own son;
> The son compell'd been butcher to the sire.

Doubtless suggested by Matt. x. 21, but compare Mic.
vii. 6: " For the sonne dishonoureth his father, the daughter
riseth against her mother, the daughter in lawe against her
mother in lawe: and a mans foes are euen they of his owne
houshold."

For reference to the " King of Heaven," " King of kings "
and " High All Seer," see " God," and see " Bible " for
those to " Scripture " and " Holy Writ."

See also I. ii. 68-9 (Luke vi. 27, 28; Matt. v. 44, etc.),
as also I. iii. 316-7; I. iv. 259 (Rom v. 1 *B*); II. i. 49-52,*
(1 Pet. iv. 8 *B2*; Matt v. 9); II. iii. 38-40 (Luke xxi. 26).

TITUS ANDRONICUS

1592-3. Printed 1594 and reprinted in 1600, and 1611.
The 1623 Folio reprinted from the 1611 edition, with the
addition of Act III. ii. This Senecan tragedy, so offensive to
many modern stomachs, was in the closing years of Elizabeth
a very popular play on the stage. Its authenticity is attested
not only by Heminge and Condell, but also by Meres, who
seems to have been one of Shakespeare's personal acquaintance.
Aaron is the atheist of Shakespeare's plays; he believes in no
supernatural power. Like Richard III., he is wilfully wicked,
but he has not that villain's sense of humour.

Act I. i. 55.

> BASS. Commit my cause in balance to be weigh'd.

Cf. Job xxxi. 6: " Let me be weighed in an euen balance ";
Job vi. 2: " O that my complaint were truely weighed, and
my punishment laide in the ballances together." *Cf.* also
Dan. v. 27.

Ibid. 331-2.

> TAM. She will a handmaid be to his desires,
> A loving nurse, a mother to his youth.

Cf. Abigail's reply to David's invitation to become his
wife. 1 Sam. xxv. 40: " Beholde, let thine handmaide be
a seruant to wash the feete of the seruants of my lord."

Cf. also *L, Matrimony*: " Minister. O Lord, save thy servant and thy handmaid."

Act III. i. 16, 22.

> TITUS. O earth ! . . .
> So thou refuse to drink my dear son's blood.

The figure of the earth drinking is Biblical. See Heb. vi. 7: " For the earth which hath drunken in the raine " ; Gen. iv. 11: " the earth, which hath opened her mouth to receiue thy brothers blood."

Ibid. 225.

> TITUS. I am the sea.

Todd draws attention to this curious figure and suggests comparison with Job vii. 12: " Am I a sea ? "

Ibid. 244.

> MARCUS. To weep with them that weep.

Rom. xii. 15: " and weepe with them that weepe."

Ibid. 263-5.

> MARCUS. Now is a time to storm. Why art thou still ?
> TITUS. Ha, ha, ha !
> MARCUS. Why dost thou laugh ? it fits not with this
>   hour.

Cf. Eccles. iii. 4: " A time to weepe, and a time to laugh." That Shakespeare's mind was on the famous passage in *Ecclesiastes* is enforced by Marcus's sharp comment on Titus's hollow laughter. It amounts to " It is not a time to laugh."

Act III. ii. 23.

> TITUS. Has sorrow made thee dote already ?

Cf. Ecclus. xxx. 24: " carefulnes and sorow bring age before the time."

Ibid. 37-8.

> TITUS. She says she drinks no other drink but tears
> Brew'd with her sorrow.

The figure of drinking tears is Biblical. See Ps. lxxx. 5: " and givest them plenteousness of tears to drink." See also *3 King Henry VI.*, V. iv. 75.

Note.—This scene is only to be found in the Folio, it is in none of the previous editions.

Act IV. i. 96-7.

> TITUS. But if you hunt these bear-whelps, then beware !
> The dam will wake and if she wind you once.

The ferocity of the she-bear bereft of her whelps is a frequent figure in the Old Testament. See Hos. xiii. 8, 2 Sam. xvii. 8, Prov. xvii. 12.

Act IV. ii. 32-3.

> AARON. And now, young lords, was't not a happy star
> Led us to Rome ?

Is this an allusion to the star that guided the Magi ? See Matt. ii. 9.

Ibid. 41-3.

> DEM. I would we had a thousand Roman dames
> At such a bay by turn to serve our lust.
> CHIR. *A charitable wish, and full of love.

This seems a play on Rom. xiii. 9-10. *B*, which, in that version, deals with " loue " and " charitie." *Cf. Love's Labour's Lost*, IV. iii. 364. It was one of Shakespeare's favourite passages in his earlier plays.

Act V. i. 147-50.

> AARON. If there be devils, would I were a devil
> To live and burn in everlasting fire
> So I might have your company in hell
> But to torment you with my bitter tongue.

This looks like an allusion to Rev. xx. 10 *T*: " And the deuill that deceiued them, was cast into a lake of fire and brimstone, where that beast and that false prophet are, and shall be tormented euen day and night for euermore " (*B*, " where the beast and the false prophet shall be tormented." *G* and *R* as *B*).

THE TWO GENTLEMEN OF VERONA

1592-3. First published 1623. Very rarely acted. Biblical references are remarkably few, but, what there are of them, they are unmistakable.

Act II. ii. 7.

JULIA. And seal the bargain with a holy kiss.

Cf. 1 Thess. v. 26: " Greete all the brethren in an holy kisse."

Act II. iii. 3, 4. See Prodigal.

Act II. v. 40-1.

LAUNCE. *Thou shalt never get such a secret from me, but by a parable.

Matt. xiii. 34-5: " and without a parable spake he not vnto them: That it might be fulfilled which was spoken by the Prophet, saying, I wil open my mouth in parables, I will speake foorth things which haue bene kept secret from the foundation of the world " (*R*, " I vvil vtter things hidden ").

Ibid. 56-9.

LAUNCE. If thou wilt go with me to the ale-house: if not, thou art an Hebrew, a Jew, and not worth the name of a Christian.

Acts x. 28: " Yee knowe how that it is an unlawfull thing for a man that is a Iewe, to company or come vnto one of another nation."

Act III. i. 19-21.

PROTEUS. . . . heap on your head
A pack of sorrows, which would press you down,
Being unprevented, to your timeless grave.

See also *2 King Henry VI.*, II. iii. 19. Gen. xlii. 38: " ye shall bring my gray head with sorowe vnto the graue."

Ibid. 344-6. See Eve.

Act III. ii. 80-1. See Leviathan.

Act IV. ii. 65-6.

JULIA. it makes me have a slow heart.

Her ear makes her heart sceptical of faith. In this sense
" a slow heart " is Biblical. *Cf.* Luke xxiv. 25: " O fooles,
and slowe of heart, to beleeue all that the Prophets haue
spoken."

Act V. iv. 79-81.

VALEN. *Who by Repentance is not satisfied
Is nor of heaven, nor earth; for these are pleas'd:
By penitence th'Eternal's wrath's appeas'd:

The Bible has much to say about Repentance, but the nearest to Valentine's remark seems to be the rendering of Ezek.
xviii. 21-22, *L, Morning Prayer:* " At what tyme soeuer a
synner doth repent him of his sine, from the botome of his
harte, I wil put al his wickednes out of my remembraunce
sayeth the Lord."

LOVE'S LABOUR'S LOST

1593-4. Printed 1598 and stated to have been " newly
corrected and augmented." Reprinted 1623. Biblical and
Liturgical allusions are in a gay Renaissance spirit. They
are noteworthy not only for their number, but also for the
remarkable proportion identifiable as taken from the Bishops'
version.

Act I. i. 4-10.

KING. When spite of cormorant devouring Time,
Th'endeavour of this present breath may buy
That honour which shall bate his scythe's keen edge
And make us heirs of all eternity.
Therefore, brave conquerors, for so you are
That war against your own affections
And the huge army of the world's desires.

The King and his companions are about to take certain
vows. *Cf. L, Baptism:* " and be made heirs of everlasting
salvation." " . . . Grant that all carnal affections may die
in them, . . . Grant that they may have power and strength
to have victory, and to triumph against the devil, the
world, and the flesh."

See Chapter IV., page 84. Dumaine (lines 28-31) continues the allusion to *Baptism* as well as to Rom. viii. 13 and Col. iii. 5.

Ibid. 70-5.

> KING. *These be the stops that hinder study quite
> And train our intellects to vain delight.
> BER. Why, all delights are vain, but that most vain,
> Which with pain purchas'd, doth inherit pain,
> As painfully to pore upon a book
> To seek the light of truth.

Cf. Eccles. xii. 9, 12: (9) " All is but vanitie (saith the preacher) all is but plaine vanitie." (12) " Therefore beware my sonne of that doctrine that is beside this: for to make many bookes, it is an endlesse worke: and too much study wearieth the body" (*G*, " and much reading is a wearinesse of the flesh "). In *B* a page heading is " All things are vaine." See also Berowne's (*ibid.* 55). " What is the end of study ?"

Ibid. 151.

> BER. Not by might master'd, but by special grace.

See *L, Catechism :* " My good Child, know this, that thou art not able to do these things of thyself, nor to walk in the Commandments of God, and to serve him, without his special grace."

Ibid. 197.

> LONG. To hear meekly.

L, Litany: " That it may please thee to give to all thy people increase of grace to hear meekly thy Word, and to receive it with pure affection."

Ibid. 263-4. See Eve.

Act I. ii. 75, *et seq.* See Samson.

Ibid. 96.

> ARM. *My love is most immaculate white and red.

Cf. Song of Sol. v. 10: " As for my loue, he is white and red coloured " (*G*, " My welbeloued is white and ruddie ").

Ibid. 183. See Salomon.

Act IV. i. 21-3.

> PRIN. See, see, my beauty will be sav'd by merit.
> O heresy in fair, fit for these days,
> A giving hand, though foul, shall have fair praise.

Dover Wilson says : " This seems to be a direct allusion to the conversion of Henry IV. ' Merit ' refers to the Roman doctrine of justification by works; while the ' heresy in fair, fit for these days ' and the ' detested crimes ' of which ' glory grows guilty ' . . . point unmistakably to the ' abominable act,' as Elizabeth described it, by which Henry bought Paris at the price of a mass. Henry IV. received ' absolution ' from the Archbishop of Bourges and heard mass publicly on July 25, 1593. England received the news with consternation."

The Princess might base her stigmatizing of salvation by merit as heresy on Rom. iii. 28: " Therfore, we hold that a man is iustified by faith, without the deedes of the lawe." Also Rom. iv. 9, v. 1, xi. 6. To think of purchasing remission of sin by merit was denounced as blasphemy in Homily on Fasting.

Act IV. ii. 1, 2.

> NATH. . . . and done in the testimony of a good
>   conscience.

2 Cor. i. 12: " For our reioycing is this, the testimonie of our conscience."

Ibid. 36, 40. See Cain and Adam.

Ibid. 91.

> HOL. Pearl enough for a swine.

Matt. vii. 6: " neither cast yee your pearles before the swine." The phrase had become a proverb.

Ibid. 169-70.

> NATH. And thank you too: for society (saith the text)
>   is the happiness of life.

L, Matrimony: " duly considering the causes for which Matrimony was ordained. . . . Thirdly, . . . for the mutual society, help, and comfort "; also Gen. ii. 18.

Act IV. iii. 65-7.

> LONG. Thou being a goddess, I forswore not thee.
> My vow was earthly, thou a heavenly love;
> Thy grace being gain'd cures all disgrace in me.

Playing with the ideas contained in John iii. 31: " he that is of the earth, is earthly, and speaketh of the earth: he that commeth from heauen is aboue all " (*G* for " earthly " reads " of the earth," as also *R*); Rom. iii. 24: " (But are) iustified freely by his grace, through the redemption that is in Christ Iesu " (*R*, " Iustified gratis by his grace ").

Ibid. 161-2.

> BER. You found his mote; the king your mote did see;
> But I a beam do find in each of three.

Luke vi. 41: " And why seest thou the mote that is in thy brothers eye, but considerest not the beame that is in thine owne eye ?"

Ibid. 168. See Solomon.

Ibid. 222.

> BER. *That, like a rude and savage man of Inde.

Jer. xiii. 23: " May a man of Inde chaunge his skinne " (*G*, " blacke More "). See Chapter IV., pages 71-2.

Ibid. 246-53.

> BER. *O ! 'tis the sun that maketh all things shine.
> KING. By heaven, thy love is black as ebony.
> BER. Is ebony like her ? O wood divine !
> A wife of such wood were felicity.
> O, who can give an oath ? where is a book ?
> That I may swear beauty doth beauty lack,
> If that she learn not of her eye to look,
> No face is fair that is not full so black.

Song of Sol. i. 4, 5: " I am blacke (O ye daughters of Hierusalem) but yet fayre and well fauoured, like as the tents of the Cedarenes, and as the hangings of Solomon. Maruaile not at mee that I am so blacke, for why? the Sunne hath shined vpon mee." *B* is markedly nearer than *G*. See Chapter IV., page 72.

Ibid. 361-2.

BER. Let us once lose our oaths to find ourselves,
Or else we lose ourselves to keep our oaths.

This looks like a play on the idea contained in Matt. xvi. 25 :
" For whosoeuer wil saue his life, shal lose it: againe, whoso-
euer will lose his life for my sake, shall finde it." See also
All's Well, I. i. 145, where Parolles applies it to virginity.

Ibid. 363-5.

BER. *It is religion to be thus forsworn,
For charity itself fulfils the law
And who can sever love from charity ?

Rom. xiii. 10: " Charitie worketh no ill to his neighbour,
therefore the fulfilling of the law is charitie." (*B* is the
only Tudor version that ever read " charitie " here. *G*
reads: " therefore is loue the fulfilling of the Law.")
See also *ibid.* 127. Longaville's " thy love is far from
charity," which might be held to point more clearly to the
controversy as to " love " or " charity " as the translation
of ἀγάπη. *Cf.* also *Titus Adronicus*, IV. ii. 43, where the
controversy is made the subject of jest. See also *The
Merchant of Venice*, I. ii. 84. See Chapter I., pages 11-2, and
Chapter IV., pages 70-1.

Act V. i. 137-8, and *V. ii.* 538, etc. See Joshua and Judas
Maccabæus.

Act V. ii. 185-6.

KING. Say to her, we have measur'd many miles
To tread a measure with her on this grass.

Reminiscent of the stratagem practised by the Gibeonites
on Joshua (Josh. ix. 3-27). Dover Wilson says, " Musco-
vites were, of course, savages to the Elizabethans."

Ibid. 269.

ROS. *Well-liking wits they have: gross, gross: fat, fat.

Ps. xcii. 13: " And shall be fat and well-liking " (*G*,
" they shalbe fat and flourishing ").

Ibid. 292.

BOYET. *And leap for joy, though they are lame
with blows.

Luke vi. 23: " And leape ye for ioy " (*G*, " Reioyce yee
in that day, and be glad "; *R*, " Be glad in that day and

reioyce "); Isa. xxxv. 6: " Then shall the lame men leape as an Hart." See Chapter IV., pages 72-3.

Ibid. 323. See Adam and Eve.

Ibid. 340-1.

> KING. All hail, sweet madam, and fair time of day !
> PRIN. *" Fair " in " All Hail " is foul, as I conceive.

See Judas Iscariot and also Chapter VI.

Ibid. 372.

> ROS. I dare not call them fools.

Presumably because of Matt. v. 22: " whosoeuer shall say (thou) foole, shalbe in danger of hell fire."

Ibid. 597 *et seq.* See Judas Iscariot.

See also I. i. 54 (Matt. v. 37); I. i. 202 (Num. v. 13); I. i. 271-2 (1 Pet. iii. 7); III. i. 210-1 (Matt. xxvi. 41); IV. iii. 2, 3 (Ecclus. xiii. 1); IV. iii. 177-8 and V. ii. 346-7 (Num. xxx. 2); IV. iii. 257 (2 Cor. xi. 14). The name Holofernes is to be found in the Book of Judith.

ROMEO AND JULIET

1593-4. A corrupt form of the play issued in 1597. First authentic edition 1599. Reprints 1609 and undated. The 1623 text printed from 1609 edition. No Biblical proper names occur in the play.

Act II. ii. 112-5.

> JUL.   Do not swear at all;
> Or, if thou wilt, swear by thy gracious self,
> Which is the god of my idolatry,
> And I'll believe thee.

Juliet's request seems to be founded on Heb. vi. 13 : " For when God made the promise to Abraham, because he coulde sweare by no greater, he sware by himselfe."

Act II. iii. 3.

> FRIAR L. *And flecked darkness like a drunkard reels.

Does this owe anything to the figure in Isa. xxiv. 20: " The earth shall reele to and fro like a drunkard " ? (*G*, " A drunken man ").

Ibid. 27-30.

> FRIAR L. Two such opposed kings encamp them still
> In man as well as herbs, grace and rude will:
> And where the worser is predominant
> Full soon the canker death eats up that plant.

The idea of conflict in each man between two opposing forces, between the grace of the spirit and the rude will of the flesh, is emphasized in the Bible. Shakespeare elsewhere maintains a man's " better angel " (*Othello*, V. ii. 206), and his " ill angel " (*2 King Henry IV*, I. ii. 188), and the conflict between the two in Sonnet 144. Gal. v. 17, perhaps, best expresses the Friar's intention : " For the flesh lusteth contrary to the spirite, and the spirite contrary to the flesh: these are contrary one to the other, so that ye can not do what ye would." See also Rom. vi., where the kingships of grace and sin are more exactly paralleled, especially vi. 21 : " For the end of those things, is death."

Ibid. 86.

> ROM. Doth grace for grace.

See John i. 16 : " And of his fulnesse haue all we receiued, and grace for grace."

Act II. vi. 11-14.

> FRIAR L.   The sweetest honey
> Is loathsome in his own deliciousness
> And in the taste confounds the appetite.
> Therefore love moderately.

Cf. Prov. xxv. 15: " If thou findest hony, eate so much as is sufficient for thee: least thou be ouer full, and parbreake it out againe." See also Prov. xxvii. 7.

Act III. ii. 76.

> JUL. . . . wolvish-ravening lamb.

Cf. Matt. vii. 15.

Ibid. 108-11.

> JUL. Some word there was, worser than Tybalt's
>   death
> That murder'd me: I would forget it fain;
> But O ! it presses to my memory,
> Like damned guilty deeds to sinners' minds.

Cf. Ps. li. 3—*L, Morning Prayer :* " I do know mine owne wickedness, and my synne is alway against me." (In the Psalter: " For I acknowledge my faults: and my sin is ever before me.") See also *L, Communion, The General Confession :* " The remembrance of them is grievous unto us; The burden of them is intolerable."

Act III. iii. 128.

> FRIAR L. Killing that love which thou hast vow'd to
> cherish.

L, Matrimony : In plighting his troth the man vows " to love and to cherish " his wife.

Act III. v. 73-4.

> LADY CAP. . . . some grief shows much of love;
> But much of grief shows still some want of wit.

Cf. Ecclus. xxxviii. 17-23 : " make lamentation expediently, and be earnest in mourning, and vse lamentation as he is worthie, and that a day or two, lest thou bee euill spoken of: and then comfort thy selfe, because of the heauinesse. 18: For of heauinesse commeth death, the heauinesse of the heart breaketh strength. 21: thou shalt doe him no good, but hurt thy selfe. 23: Let the remembrance of the dead ceasse in his rest, & comfort thee againe ouer him, seeing his spirit is departed from him."

Act IV. i. 38.

> JUL. Or shall I come to you at evening Mass ?

This line has caused Ritson, Wordsworth and Fripp to make certain deductions as to Shakespeare's religion on the ground that he showed here an ignorance of Roman Practice. While, in the ordinary way in the Latin Church, Mass would not be celebrated in the evening before midnight, evening Mass in that Church is not unknown, and is a feature of the Oriental Rite. The point is one of discipline and not of doctrine. In this line " Mass " does not seem to imply " a celebration of the Eucharist," but simply a service. In Shakespeare's time, it is true, in England the term " Mass " was normally employed in its restricted sense, but it was quite possible that Shakespeare had come across the phrase " evening Mass " in its wider and older sense, and that he used it accordingly.

Ibid. 55.

>   JUL. God join'd my heart and Romeo's, thou our
>   hands.

L, Matrimony : " Then shall the Priest join their right
hands together, and say, Those whom God hath joined
together let no man put asunder."

Act IV. v. 49-54.

>   NURSE. O woe !   O woeful, woeful, woeful day !
>   Most lamentable day, most woeful day
>   That ever, ever, I did yet behold !
>   O day !   O day !   O day !   O hateful day !
>   Never was seen so black a day as this:
>   O woeful day !   O woeful day !

It is not unreasonable to suppose that for this howling of
the Nurse a hint was taken from Ezek. xxx. 2, 3 : " Thus
sayeth the Lorde God, Howle, woe worth this day: For the
day is neere, the day of the Lorde is at hand, the darke
day."

Ibid. 75-6.

>   FRIAR L. *O, in this love, you love your child so ill,
>   That you run mad, seeing that she is well.

Cf. the Shunamite's reply to Elisha's inquiry in 2 Kings
iv. 26 : " Is all well with thee, and with thy husband, and
with the ladde?   And she answered, All is well " (*G,* " Art
thou in health ? is thine husband in health ? & is the childe
in health ?   And she answered, We are in health "). See
also Act V. i. 14-16; *Macbeth,* IV. iii. 176; *Antony and Cleopatra,* II. v. 31-33. Less emphatically, but still unmistakably, the Shunamite's reply is alluded to in *2 King Henry IV.,*
V. ii. 3, and *The Winter's Tale,* V. i. 30.

Act V. iii. 229-30.

>   FRIAR L. *I will be brief, for my short date of breath
>   Is not so long as is a tedious tale.

Ps. xc. 9: " we bring our years to an end, as it were a tale
that is told " (*G,* " wee haue spent our yeeres as a
thought "). See also *King John,* III. iv. 108; *Macbeth,* V. v.
26, 27, and pages 77-8.

See also I. i. 20 (1 Pet. iii. 7); I. i. 71 *(Luke xxiii. 34 *G*);
III. ii. 67 (1 Cor. xv. 52, etc.); III. ii. 80-2 (2 Cor. xi. 14);
III. iii. 82 (Lam. iii. 15, etc.).

KING RICHARD II.

1594-5. First edition 1597. Reprinted 1598 (twice), 1608, 1615. Abdication scene first introduced in 1608 edition. Reprinted in 1623 Folio from 1615 edition. The Biblical interest of the play lies principally in Richard. In his prosperity he is gay, light-hearted and profane. As his mind darkens with grief he becomes more and more Scriptural, until finally his heaviness of soul overwhelms him. At the first stroke of misfortune his mind appears to occupy itself with Job. Both Norfolk and the Bishop of Carlisle, in proportion to the number of their lines, quote Scripture very largely. The play is almost entirely in verse.

Act I. i. 104. See Abel.

Ibid. 174-5.

K. RICH.   Lions make leopards tame.
NORF. *Yea, but not change his spots.

Jer. xiii. 23 *G* : " Can the blacke More change his skin? or the leopard his spots?" (*B,* " May a man of Inde chaunge his skinne, and the catte of the mountaine her spots?"). See Chapter IV., page 61.

Act I. ii. 8.

GAUNT. *Will rain hot vengeance on offenders' heads.

Gen. xix. 24 : " Then the Lord rained vpon Sodome and Gomorrhe brimstone and fire "; Jude 7 *G*: " As Sodome and Gomorrhe, and the cities about them . . . are set foorth for an ensample, and suffer the vengeance of eternall fire " (*B* and *R,* " paine "); Ps. cxl. 10: " Let hot burning coals fall upon them "; Ps. xi. 7: " Upon the ungodly he shall rain snares, fire and brimstone."

Ibid. 20.

DUCH. . . . his summer leaves all faded.

Cf. Isa. i. 30 *G* : " For ye shall be as an oke, whose leafe fadeth " (*B,* " As a tree whose leaues are fallen away ").

Ibid. 23-4.

DUCH. . . . *that self-mould that fashion'd thee
Made him a man.

Although the Duchess's " mould " is a shape and not earth, *cf.* Job xxxiii. 6: " I am euen as thou: for I am fashioned and made euen of the same moulde" (*G*, " Beholde, I am according to thy wish in Gods stead : I am also formed of the clay"). See also Job xxxi. 15 : "He that fashioned me in my mothers wombe, made he not him also ? were we not both shapen alike in our mothers bodies ?" (*G*, " He that hath made me in the wombe, hath hee not made him ? hath not hee alone facioned vs in the wombe?").

Ibid. 37-41.

> GAUNT. God's is the quarrel: for God's substitute,
> His deputy anointed in his sight,
> Hath caus'd his death; the which, if wrongfully,
> Let heaven revenge, for I may never lift
> An angry arm against his minister.

Cf. 1 Sam. xxiv. 6: " The Lord keepe me from doing that thing vnto my master the Lords anoynted, to lay mine hand vpon him, seeing he is the anoynted of the Lord." 1 Sam. xxvi. 9: " for who can laye his hande on the Lordes anoynted, and bee gyltlesse?" Deut. xxxii. 35, Ps. xciv. 1: " thou God, to whom vengeance belongeth, shew thyself." For the king as God's minister to execute his wrath see Rom. xiii. 4; also *Prayer for the Queen, L, Communion* : " So rule the heart of thy chosen servant Elizabeth our Queen and Governour, that she (knowing whose minister she is)."

Ibid. 43.

> GAUNT. *To God, the widow's champion and defence.

Ps. lxviii. 5: " He is a Father of the fatherless, and defendeth the cause of the widows " (*G*, " and a Iudge of the widowes "); Ps. cxlvi. 9: " he defendeth the fatherless and widow " (*G*, " he relieveth the fatherlesse and widow ").

Act I. iii. 101-2.

> MAR. . . . and God defend the right.
> BOLING. Strong as a tower in hope, I cry, Amen.

Ps. lxi. 3: " for thou hast been my hope, and a strong tower for me against the enemy."

Ibid. 202-3.

> NORF. *My name be blotted from the Book of Life,
> And I from heaven banish'd as from hence.

See Rev. iii. 5: " He that ouercommeth, shalbe thus clothed in white aray, and I wil not blot out his name out of the booke of life " (*G* and *R*, " put out "). The Authorised introduced the word " blot " into Exod. xxxii. 32, 33 and Ps. lxix. 29, although the reading there in *B* more literally represented the original.

Act II. i. 42. See Eden.

Ibid. 55-6.

> GAUNT. As is the Sepulchre in stubborn Jewry
> Of the world's ransom, blessed Mary's Son.

For Christ as a " ransom " see 1 Tim. ii. 6: " Who gaue himselfe, a raunsome for all "; Matt. xx. 28: " & to giue his life a ransome for many."

Act II. ii. 3-4.

> BUSHY. To lay aside life-harming heaviness,
> And entertain a cheerful disposition.

See Ecclus. xxx. 23: " as for sorowe and heauinesse, driue it farre from thee: for heauinesse hath slayne many a man, and bringeth no profit."

Ibid. 76.

> QUEEN. Uncle, for God's sake, speak comfortable
> words.

L, Communion : " Hear what comfortable words our Saviour Christ saith unto all that truly turn to him." Zech. i. 13 *G*: " And the Lorde answered the Angell that talked with me, with good wordes and comfortable wordes " (*B*, " So the Lorde gaue a louing & a comfortable answere "). See also " speake no discomfortable wordes " of Ecclus. xviii. 14. This is the more probable source of the Queen's remark. See Chapter IV., pages 62-3.

Act III. i. 5, 6.

> BOLING. . . . yet to wash your blood
> From off my hands here in the view of men.

See Pilate.

Ibid. 21.

> BOLING. Eating the bitter bread of banishment.

This use of bread is Biblical in kind. *Cf.* 1 Kings xxii. 27: " feede him with bread of affliction, and with water of trouble."

Act III. ii. 36.

> K. Rich. Discomfortable cousin !

" Discomfortable " in the sense of " causing depression " is very rare. It was adopted by Coverdale and was preserved both in the Bishops' and Genevan of Ecclus. xviii. 14: " whatsoeuer thou giuest, speake no discomfortable wordes." See Chapter IV., pages 62-3. In Tobit x. 4 *B*, " she wept with discomfortable teares," is not the same; its sense is " inconsolable."

Ibid. 36-46.

> K. Rich. . . . know'st thou not,
> That when the searching eye of heaven is hid
> Behind the globe, that lights the lower world,
> Then thieves and robbers range abroad unseen
> In murders and in outrage boldly here;
> But when from under this terrestrial ball
> He fires the proud tops of the eastern pines
> And darts his light through every guilty hole,
> Then murders, treasons, and detested sins,
> The cloak of night being pluck'd from off their backs,
> Stand bare and naked, trembling at themselves ?

Has the thought in this passage been suggested by Job xxiv. 13-17 ? " Those are they that flee from the light, they knewe not his wayes, nor continue in his pathes. 14. The murderer riseth earely, and killeth the poore and needy, and in the night is as a thiefe. 15. The eye of the adulterer waiteth for the darknesse, and sayeth, There shall no eye see me: and hideth his face. 16. In the darke they dig through houses, which they marked for themselues in the day time: they know not the light. 17. The morning is to them euen as the shadowe of death: if one knowe them (they are) in the terrours of the shadowe of death." See also Chapter II., pages 37-8.

Ibid. 54-7.

> K. Rich. Not all the water in the rough rude sea
> Can wash the balm off from an anointed king:
> The breath of worldly men cannot depose
> The Deputy elected by the Lord.

1 Sam. xxvi. 9, Rom. xiii. 4.

Ibid. 60-2.

> K. RICH. God for his Richard hath in heavenly pay
> A glorious angel: then, if angels fight,
> Weak men must fall, for heaven still guards the right.

Ps. xxxiv. 7: " The angel of the Lord tarrieth round about them that fear him: and delivereth them "; Matt. xxvi. 53: " Thinkest thou that I can not nowe pray to my father, and he shall cause to stand by me more then twelue legions of angels ?"

Ibid. 129.

> K. RICH. *O villains, vipers, damn'd without redemp-
> tion !

Matt. xxiii. 33: " Ye serpents, ye generation of vipers, how will yee escape the damnation of hell ?" (*R,* " iudgement of hel "). For " without redemption " see Deut. xx. 17: " But shalt destroy them without redemption " (*G,* " vtterly ").

Ibid. 132.   See Judas Iscariot.

Ibid. 162-3.

> K. RICH. Keeps Death his court, and there the antick
> sits
> Scoffing his state and grinning at his pomp.

Richard's thought is Biblical in cast though it is general rather than particular. Hence while his emotion is religious it is difficult to select texts having definite reference. But see Isa. xiv. 11: " Thy pompe and thy pride is layde downe into the pit, and so is the melody of thy instruments. Wormes be laid vnder thee, & wormes be thy couering."

Ibid. 167-8.

> K. RICH. As if this flesh which walls about our life
> Were brass impregnable.

For the unlikeness of flesh to brass see Job vi. 12: " Is my strength the strength of stones ? or is my flesh of brasse ?"

Ibid. 194-5.

> SCROOP. *Men judge by the complexion of the sky
> The state and inclination of the day.

Matt. xvi. 2, 3: " When it is euening, ye say, (It will be) faire weather: for the skie is red. And in the morning, (It wil bee) foule weather to day: for the skie is lowring redde " (*R* reads " element " for " skie ").

Act III. iii. 77-8.

> K. RICH. . . . show us the hand of God
> That hath dismiss'd us from our Stewardship.

See the Parable of the Unjust Steward, Luke xvi. 3 *et seq.*

Ibid. 85-7.

> K. RICH. Yet know, my master, God Omnipotent,
> Is mustering in his clouds on our behalf
> Armies of pestilence.

Is this in reminiscence of the destruction of Sennacherib's army (2 Kings xix. 35) ? That army was slain by an angel.

Act III. iv. 73, 75. See Adam, Eve.

Act IV. i. 99-100.

> BP. CAR. *And his pure soul unto his Captain Christ
> Under whose colours he had fought so long.

L, Baptism : " manfully to fight under his banner . . . and to continue Christ's faithful soldier and servant unto his life's end." Heb. ii. 10: " captaine of their saluation " (*G*, " Prince " and *R*, " author "). Matt ii. 6: " For out of thee shall there come a captaine, that shall governe my people Israel " (*G*, " the gouernour that shall feede ").

Ibid. 103-4, 144. See Abraham, Golgotha.

Ibid., 145-6.

> BP. CAR. O, if you raise this house against this house,
> It will the woefullest division prove.

Mark iii. 25: " And if a house bee diuided against it selfe, that house cannot continue." See also Luke xi. 17. The endowment of the Bishop with Scriptural quotation is deliberate. He had a reputation, according to Holinshed, for holiness. Hence Shakespeare makes him quote Scripture. Note the Scriptural expressions in his reference to Richard (lines 125-7).

> And shall the figure of God's majesty,
> His captain, steward, deputy elect,
> Anointed, crowned, planted many years.

Ibid. 169-71. See Judas Iscariot.

Ibid. 230-6.

>K. Rich. If thy offences were upon record,
>Would it not shame thee in so fair a troop
>To read a lecture of them ?   If thou wouldst
>There shouldst thou find one heinous article,
>Containing the deposing of a king
>And cracking the strong warrant of an oath,
>*Mark'd with a blot, damn'd in the Book of Heaven.

There are many passages in the Old Testament dealing with the sanctity of oaths (*e.g.,* Num. xxx. 2) too numerous to specify here.   There is evidence that Shakespeare read Ezek. xvi. (see *Julius Cæsar,* II. iv. 39-40, *Hamlet,* III. iii. 80); it is interesting, therefore, to turn to the next chapter and peruse verse 16 in connection with Richard's speech: " As truely as I liue, sayeth the Lorde God, he shall die at Babylon in the place where the king dwelleth that made him king, whose othe he hath despised, and whose couenant he hath broken."   As for " blot " and the " book of heaven," see Act I. iii. 202.

Concerning the sanctity of kings, see 1 Sam. xxvi. 9.

Ibid. 239-42.   See Pilate.

Ibid. 283-4, 287-8.

>K. Rich.   Was this the face
>That like the sun did make beholders wink ? . . .
>A brittle glory shineth in this face,
>As brittle as the glory is the face.

It has been asserted that this figure was probably suggested by the Transfiguration.   The analogy seems somewhat distant.

See Matt. xvii. 2: " And was transfigured before them, and his face did shine as the Sunne."

Act V. i. 24.

>K. Rich. Our holy lives must win a new world's crown.

See Jas. i. 12: " he shall receiue the crowne of life, which the Lorde hath promised to them that loue him "; 2 Tim. iv. 8: " a crowne of righteousnesse "; 1 Pet. v. 4: " an incorruptible crowne of glory."

Act V. iii. 31.

> AUM. My tongue cleave to my roof within my mouth.

Ps. cxxxvii. 6: " let my tongue cleave to the roof of my mouth." See also Job xxix. 10.

Ibid. 85.

> YORK. This fester'd joint cut off, the rest rest sound.

Cf. Matt xviii. 8: " If then thy hand or thy foote offend thee, cut them off, and cast (them) from thee."

Ibid. 102.

> DUCH. His words come from his mouth, ours from our
>   breast.

That is, the petition of the Duke is as in Matt. xv. 8: " This people draweth nigh vnto me with their mouth, and honoureth me with their lips: howbeit, their heart is farre from mee " (*R* omits " dravveth nigh vnto me with their mouth ").

Ibid. 103.

> DUCH. He prays but faintly.

Cf. Ecclus vii. 10: " Be not faint hearted when thou makest thy prayer."

Ibid. 104.

> DUCH. We pray with heart and soul and all beside.

See Deut. iv. 29: " If from thence thou shalt seeke the Lorde thy God, thou shalt finde him, if thou seeke him with all thy heart, & with all thy soule."

Ibid. 107-10.

> DUCH. His prayers are full of false hypocrisy;
>   Ours of true zeal and deep integrity.
>   Our prayers do out-pray his: then let them have
>   That mercy, which true prayer ought to have.

Probably the Parable of the Pharisee and the Publican was in mind. Unlike the Pharisee, the Publican prayed earnestly for mercy, and hence in Luke xviii. 14: " I tel you, this man departed (home) to his house iustified rather then the other." Richard was probably quoting from this chapter in V. v. 11-17.

Ibid. 146.

DUCH. Come, my old son; I pray God make thee new.

Cf. L, Baptism: " O Merciful God, grant that the Old Adam in this child may be so buried, that the new man may be raised up in him."

Act V. v. 11-17.

K. RICH.   The better sort,
As thoughts of things divine, are intermixt
With scruples and do set the word itself
Against the word:
*As thus, " Come, little ones," and then again,
" It is as hard to come as for a camel
To thread the postern of a small needle's eye."

Luke xviii. 16: " Suffer litle children to come vnto me " (*G*, " Suffer the babes to come vnto me " ; *R*, " Suffer children to come vnto me "). Also Matt. xix. 14, Mark x. 14 and *L, Baptism.*
Luke xviii. 25: " For it is easier for a Camel to goe thorow a needles eye," also Mark x. 25 and Matt. xix. 24. See Chapter V. Note that both these passages occur in the same chapter.

Ibid. 61-2.

K. RICH. This music mads me; let it sound no more.
For though it have holp madmen to their wits.

Possibly a reference to Saul. See 1 Sam. xvi. 15-23.

Ibid. 88.

K. RICH. Since pride must have a fall.

Prov. xvi. 18: " Pride goeth before destruction: and an high minde before the fall."

Act V. vi. 43. See Cain.

See also I. i. 114 (Prov. vi. 16, 17); I. i. 160 (Matt. v. 9); III. i. 34* (Ps. cxvi. 3); V. iii. 131 (Ephes. iv. 32).

A MIDSUMMER-NIGHT'S DREAM

1594-5. Printed in 1600 and reprinted in 1619. It was from the latter edition that the text in the Folio was printed. In a play of the kind Biblical quotations to any extent are not to be expected.

Act I. i. 65.

THES. *Either to die the death.

Matt. xv. 4: " let him die the death " (*R*, " dying let him dye").

It is interesting to note that the text in *Matthew* deals with conduct to parents as does Theseus here. However " die the death " occurs in the Old Testament in the Bishops' as well as in the New Testament so too much should not be made of the point. It is sufficient as a possibility of what may have floated across Shakespeare's mind.

Ibid. 74-5.

THES. Thrice blessed they, that master so their blood,
To undergo such maiden pilgrimage.

As well as Gen. xlvii. 9 see Ps. cxix. 54: " in the house of my pilgrimage." As for the blessed lot of celibacy see 1 Cor. vii. 1-26.

Act II. i. 173-4.   See Leviathan.

Ibid. 195.

HEL. You draw me, you hard-hearted Adamant.

Cf. Zech. vii. 12: " Yea they made their heartes as an Adamant stone."

Act III. ii. 260-1.

LYS.   vile thing let loose,
Or I will shake thee from me like a serpent.

Cf. the incident in Acts xxviii. 5, when Paul shook off the viper into the fire: " And he shooke off the Viper into the fire " (*G*, " the worme " ; *R*, " the beast ").

Act IV. i. 218-20.

BOTTOM. *The eye of man hath not heard, the ear of man hath not seen, man's hand is not able to taste, his tongue to conceive, nor his heart to report.

A parody of 1 Cor. ii. 9: " The eye hath not seene, and the eare hath not heard, neither haue entred into the heart of man " (G, " The things which eye hath not seene, neyther eare hath heard, neither came into mans heart ").

See also I. i. 152-3 (Matt. x. 38, xvi. 24).

THE MERCHANT OF VENICE

1595-6. First printed 1600 and reprinted in 1619. The 1623 Folio was printed from the first edition.   Probably owing to its melodramatic character of all Shakespeare's comedies this has been the most successful in the theatre.   From the point of view of Scriptural quotations it is the most important of all the plays, for in it Shakespeare affords evidence of having studied the Bible closely in his delineation of Shylock.   In the deal between Laban and Jacob he may be said to have used the Bible as he used Holinshed or North in other plays.   Apart from Shylock the play is by no means devoid of Scriptural interest.

NOTE ON SOME OF THE NAMES OF THE CHARACTERS.

Some of the names of the characters have a Biblical interest.   Obviously Shylock's name is not Biblical, although one writer did seek to identify it with Shiloh (Gen. xlix. 10), but he had had a wife called Leah, which as everybody knows was the name of Jacob's elder wife.

Tubal and Chus,* the former an active character and the latter merely mentioned, are alluded to by Jessica as Shylock's countrymen.   Both are names of Noah's grandsons. Tubal was the fifth son of Japheth (See Gen. x. 2).   Chus is the Bishops' form (also that of all the other versions except the Great Bible and Geneva) of Cush the eldest son of Ham (See Gen. x. 6).   Chus also occurs in Hakluyt in the narrative of George Best, " Cham and his blacke sonne Chus." As names of Hebrews, Shakespeare cannot be said to have been happy in his choice in either case.   See Chapter VI.

Attempts by Karl Elze and others have been made to identify Jessica with Lot's sister, Iscah (Gen. xi. 29), chiefly because of 'Ιεσχά in the Septuagint and Iesca in Matthews' and Taverner's Bibles (it is Iisca in the Great Bible and Iischa in the Bishops').   Karl Elze developed his theory.   As Elze said that in Hebrew Iscah signified a spy or looker out, he wanted to know if it had any reference to Shylock's warning to his daughter not to " thrust her head into the public

street to gaze on Christian fools." Another theory as to
the name Jessica is that Shakespeare invented it as a feminine form of Jesse. Any conclusion in the matter is impossible,
though it must be said Karl Elze's derivation is very uncon-
vincing.

Act I. i. 74-5.
> GRAT. You have too much respect upon the world:
> They lose it that do buy it with much care.

The thought here is obviously of the New Testament.
See 1 John ii. 15-7: " See that ye loue not the world, neither
the things that are in the world. . . . For all that is in the
world, as the lust of the flesh, and the lust of the eyes, and the
pride of life, is not of the father, but of the worlde. And
the world passeth away, and the lust thereof: but he that
fulfilleth the will of God, abideth for euer." Matt. xvi. 26:
" For what is a man profited if hee shal winne the whole
world, and lose his owne soule ?" (*R*, " and sustaine the
damage of his soule ?").

Ibid. 95-7.
> GRAT. O, my Antonio, I do know of these,
> That therefore only are reputed wise
> For saying nothing.

Job xiii. 5: " Would God ye kept your tongue, for then
might ye be taken for wise men " (*G*, " Oh, that you would
holde your tongue, that it might bee imputed to you for
wisedome !"). Prov. xvii. 28: "Yea, a very foole when he
holdeth his tongue, is counted wise."

Ibid. 97-9.
> GRAT.   when, I am very sure,
> If they should speak, would almost damn those ears
> Which, hearing them, would call their brothers fools.

Matt. v. 22: " whosoeuer shal say vnto his brother, (Racha,)
shalbe in danger of a counsel: but whosoeuer shall say
(thou) foole, shalbe in danger of hell fire."

Act I. ii. 13-21.
> PORTIA. If to do were as easy as to know what were good
> to do, chapels had been churches, and poor men's cottages
> princes' palaces. It is a good divine that follows his
> own instructions; I can easier teach twenty what were

good to be done, than be one of the twenty to follow mine own teaching. The brain may devise laws for the blood, but a hot temper leaps o'er a cold decree.

Although the disparity between precept and practice is well known, yet the observations in the New Testament are so pointed in the matter that it is difficult not to believe that Portia's remarks received inspiration from passages such as Rom. vii. 18-9: " For I knowe, that in me (that is to say in my flesh) dwelleth no good thing. For to will, is present with me: but I finde no meanes to perfourme that which is good. For the good that I would, do I not: but the euil which I woulde not, that doe I." Or Rom. ii. 21: " Thou therefore which teachest another, teachest thou not thy selfe ? Thou preachest a man shoulde not steale, yet stealest thou ?" See also Matt. xxvi. 41. Also Cf. Matt. xxiii. 3 for the censure of the Scribes and Pharisees as teachers who say and do not: " All therefore whatsoeuer they bid you obserue, that obserue and doe, but doe not ye after their workes: for they say, and do not."

Ibid. 82-8.

NERIS. What think you of the Scottish lord, his neighbour ?
PORTIA. *That he hath a neighbourly charity in him, for he borrowed a box of the ear of the Englishman, and swore he would pay him again when he was able: I think the Frenchman became his surety, and seal'd under for another.

The point of the joke lies in Rom. xiii. 10: " Charitie worketh no ill to his neighbour." See Chapter II., pages 22-3 and Chapter IV., page 71.

Act I. iii. 25.

SHY. . . . and then there is the peril of waters.

In respect of " the peril of waters," the example of 2 Cor. xi. 26 may be of interest: " In iourneying often, in perils of waters." In that verse " in perils " occurs no less than eight times.

Ibid. 34-6.

SHY. Yes, to smell pork: to eat of the habitation which your prophet the Nazarite conjured the devil into.

A reference to Luke viii. 33 in which Christ conjured the devils into the swine of the Gadarenes. See also Nazarite.

Ibid. 42.

> SHY. How like a fawning publican he looks !

Shylock meant to stigmatize Antonio as a creature of the ruling classes just as the Publican had been of the foreigner. Antonio bullied Jews, just as had the publicans.

Ibid. 72 *et seq.* See Jacob, also Abraham, Laban.

Ibid. 99-103.

> ANT. The devil can cite Scripture for his purpose.
> An evil soul producing holy witness
> Is like a villain with a smiling cheek,
> A goodly apple rotten at the heart.
> O, what a goodly outside falsehood hath !

For the devil citing Scripture see Matt. iv. 5 and Luke iv. 10. There is also the usual allusion to 2 Cor. xi. 13, 14, if we agree with some in reading " What a godly outside."

Act II. i. 1, 2.

> MOR. Mislike me not for my complexion,
> The shadowed livery of the burnisht sun.

Recalls Song of Sol. i. 5: " Maruaile not at mee that I am so blacke, for why ? the Sunne hath shined vpon mee " (*G*, " Regard ye me not because I am blacke: for the sunne hath looked vpon mee ").

Ibid. 29.

> MOR. Pluck the young sucking cubs from the she-
>   bear.

The she-bear robbed of her young as a symbol of ferocity is Biblical. See 2 Sam. xvii. 8.

Act II. ii. 71-2.

> GOBBO. *Marry, God forbid ! the boy was the very staff of
> my age, my very prop.

Cf. Tobit v. 23: " Now when they were gone, his mother began to weepe, and said, The staffe of our age hast thou taken away " (*G*, "staffe of our hand "). Also Tobit x. 4 *B*. See Chapter IV., page 73.

Act II. v. 36, 44. See Jacob, Hagar.

Act II. vi. 14-9. See Prodigal.

Act II. ix. 63.

ARRAGON (reading the scroll of the silver casket).
*The fire seven times tried this.

Cf. Ps. xii. 7: " even as the silver, which from the earth
is tried, and purified seven times in the fire " (*G*, "as the
siluer, tried in a fornace of earth, fined seuen folde ").

Act III. i. 92-3.

SHY. The curse never fell upon our Nation till now; I
never felt it till now.

Shylock, though a non-Christian, was credited with a
knowledge of the New Testament, see Act I. iii. 34, where
he refers to the devils and the swine of the Gadarenes. It
is, therefore, not unreasonable to suppose that he here refers
to Matt. xxvii. 25, where the Jews took upon themselves and
their children the guilt for the Crucifixion: " Then answered
all the people, and saide, His blood be on vs, and on our
children." Note "our Nation" and see Chapter V., pages 96-7.

Act III. ii. 57.

PORTIA. I stand for sacrifice.

Cf. L, Communion : " And here we offer and present unto
thee, O Lord, ourselves, our souls and bodies, to be a reasonable, holy, and lively sacrifice unto thee." See also Rom.
xii. 1 *G*, " that yee giue vp your bodies a liuing sacrifice "
(*B*, " quicke sacrifice ").

Ibid. 73-4.

BASS. So may the outward shows be least themselves:
The world is still deceiv'd with ornament.

The deceit of external ornament is not an uncommon
thought but it is decidedly emphasized in the Bible. Compare the question in 2 Cor. x. 7: " Looke ye on things after
the vtter appearance ?"

Ibid. 77-80, 99-101.

BASS.   In religion
What damned error, but some sober brow
Will bless it, and approve it with a text,
Hiding the grossness with fair ornament. . . .
                              in a word,
The seeming truth, which cunning times put on
To entrap the wisest.

Satan quoting Scripture in Matt. iv. 6 and Luke iv. 10, 11. Also 2 Cor. xi. 12-15. But the whole has such a resemblance to Matt. xxiv. 24, that it cannot be passed over: " For there shall arise false Christes, & false prophets, and shall shewe great signes, and wonders: in so much that (if it were possible) they shall deceiue the very elect."

Ibid. 88-99.

BASS.   Look on beauty,
And you shall see 'tis purchas'd by the weight, etc.

However strangely Bassanio's soliloquy may consort with his previous character, there is no doubt that it is a model of orthodoxy. About the whole there is a Biblical ring; Bassanio almost prays and meditates on Scriptural maxims, paraphrasing elaborately all he has ever heard. The sum total of these lines is that beauty is vanity and fairness is deceitful, a lure to entice the simple.

A parallel may be found in Prov. xxxi. 30: " As for fauour it is deceitfull, and beautie is a vaine thing."

There are numerous other passages that might also serve, but as *Proverbs* was sometimes perused by Shakespeare we may as well take it as another to illustrate the Biblical base of his observations.

Act III. iii. 6, 7.

SHY. Thou call'dst me dog before thou hadst a cause,
But, since I am a dog, beware my fangs.

See Chapter V., page 97.

Act III. v. 1, 2, 14, 15.

LAUNCE. *Yes, truly, for look you, the sins of the father are to be laid upon the children. . . .
JESS. So the sins of my mother should be visited upon me.

L, Catechism and *Communion, Second Commandment:* " and visit the sins of the fathers upon the children." (No Biblical version reads " sins "; *G* has " iniquitie "; Exod. xx. 5 *B,* " sinne.")

Ibid. 20-1.

JESS. *I shall be sav'd by my husband, he hath made me a Christian.

1 Cor. vii. 14: " the unbeleeuing wife is sanctified by the husbande." (*T* reads " to " for " by.")

Act IV. i. 36.

> SHY. And by our holy Sabaoth have I sworn.

This is the reading in the only authentic edition. It is supported in *King Richard III.* The point is dealt with in Chapter VI.

Ibid. 184-6.

> PORTIA. The quality of mercy is not strain'd,
> It droppeth as the gentle rain from heaven
> Upon the place beneath.

Cf. Ecclus. xxxv. 19: " O howe faire a thing is mercie in the time of anguishe and trouble ? it is like a cloude of raine that commeth in the time of drought." *Cf.* also Deut. xxxii. 2: " My doctrine shall drop as doeth the raine: and my speache shall flowe as doeth the dew, as the showre vpon the hearbes, and as the droppes vpon the grasse."

Ibid. 193-7.

> PORTIA. But mercy is above this sceptred sway,
> It is enthroned in the hearts of kings,
> It is an attribute to God himself;
> And earthly power doth then show likest God's
> When mercy seasons justice.

Ecclus. ii. 21: " For his mercie is as great as himselfe." *L, Communion :* " But thou art the same Lord, whose property is always to have mercy." See also Ps. ciii. 3, 4, 8, 10, 13, and Ps. cxxxvi.

Ibid. 198-200.

> PORTIA. Though justice be thy plea, consider this,
> That, in the course of justice, none of us
> Should see salvation.

L, Ps. cxliii. 2: " Enter not into iudgemente with thy seruaunts, O Lord, for no fleshe is righteous in thy syght " (quoted at *Morning Prayer*).

Ibid. 200-2.

> PORTIA.   We do pray for mercy,
> And that same prayer doth teach us all to render
> The deeds of mercy.

It is unfortunate that the Apocrypha is no longer an open book to the British people, and consequently Portia's remark addressed to a non-Christian like Shylock has caused some misapprehension. In Shakespeare's day the Old Testament Apocrypha was bound up with every complete Bible and Shakespeare evidently was acquainted with it (his two daughters had names to be found in it). If we turn to Ecclus. xxviii. 2-5 we shall find Portia's observation as to the prayer sufficiently justified:

" Forgiue thy neighbour the hurt that he hath done thee, and so shall thy sinnes be forgiuen thee also when thou prayest. A man that beareth hatred against another, howe dare he desire forgiuenesse of God? Hee that sheweth no mercie to a man which is like himselfe, howe dare hee aske forgiuenes of his sinnes? If he that is but flesh, beareth hatred, and keepeth it, who will entreate for his sinnes?"

As far as known, *Ecclesiasticus* provides the only direct parallel to the passage in *The Lord's Prayer*.

Ibid. 223-4 and 334, 297. See Daniel, Barrabas.

Act V. i. 61-2.

> LOREN. But in his motion like an Angel sings,
> Still quiring to the young-eyed Cherubins.

" Still quiring " means continually tuning in concert. *Cf. L, Morning Prayer,* the *Te Deum Laudamus:* " To thee all Angels cry aloud: the Heavens, and all the Powers therein. To thee Cherubin, and Seraphin: continually do cry." The *Te Deum* is always sung or said at *Morning Prayer,* except usually in Lent and sometimes in Advent.

Dover Wilson points out that mediæval tradition ascribed to the Cherubim miraculously keen sight, hence " young-eyed." See also *Troil. and Cress.,* III. ii. 72-3; *Hamlet,* IV. iii. 51; *Macbeth,* I. vii. 22-4.

Ibid. 91.

> PORTIA. So shines a good deed in a naughty world.

L, Communion, Offertory (Matt. v. 16): " Let your light so shine before men, that they may see your good works."

Ibid. 294-5.

LOREN. Fair ladies, you drop Manna in the way
Of starved people.

Exod. xvi. 15.

See also I. ii. 60 (Isa. xxxiii. 22); I. iii. 36-9 (Acts x. 28
and xi. 3); I. iii. 133-5 (Deut. xxiii. 20); III. v. 24-6
(Lev. xi. 7, 8, etc.); IV. i. 88 (Jas. ii. 13).

1 KING HENRY IV.

1595-6. Printed 1598. Reprinted 1599, 1604, 1608, 1613,
1622. Subject to excision of a number of profanities, the
1623 Folio printed from the 1613 edition. The play is notable
for the introduction of Falstaff, Shakespeare's great comic
creation. His comic character is heightened by his ready
Biblical quotation; his quotations are the aptest in the whole
of the plays. His use of the Bible not only discloses a well-
instructed youth, but also suggests an educated man.

Act I. i. 25-7.

K. HEN.   those blessed feet
Which fourteen hundred years ago were nail'd
For our advantage on the bitter cross.

L, Communion, Prayer of Consecration : " to suffer death upon
the cross for our redemption." The King's mood in this
scene is heavy with religious emotion. His reference in
lines 78-9 to the sin of envy is reminiscent of *The Litany*,
" from envy, hatred, and malice, and all uncharitableness,
Good Lord, deliver us."

Act I. ii. 99-100.

PRINCE. . . . *for wisdom cries out in the streets and
no man regards it.

Evidently this allusion to Prov. i. 20, 24 was considered profane, for in the 1623 Folio it was modified. 20: " Wisedome
cryeth without, & putteth forth her voyce in the streetes."
24: " Because I haue called, and yee refused, I haue stretched
out my hand, and no man regarded " (*G*, " and none
would regard "). See Chapter IV., pages 73-4.

Ibid. 104-6.

FAL. Before I knew thee, Hal, I knew nothing; and now am I, if a man should speak truly, little better than one of the wicked.

Falstaff first compares himself with Adam in a state of ignorance and then, it might appear, gives a deadly thrust. Compare the crucifixion of Christ between the two thieves and Mark xv. 28: " He was counted among the wicked " (*R*, " And vvith the vvicked he vvas reputed ").

Ibid. 114-5.

PRINCE. *I see a good amendment of life in thee.

See Chapter IV., page 61.

Ibid. 116-7.

FAL. Why, Hal, 'tis my vocation, Hal: 'tis no sin for a man to labour in his vocation.

Falstaff's reply is in the spirit of the *Catechism*: " to labour truly to get mine own living," and of 2 Thess. iii. 10 to which the Genevan (not the Tomson) attached a note: " Then by the worde of God none ought to liue idlely, but ought to giue himselfe to some vocation, to get his liuing by, and to doe good to others." *Cf.* also Homily against Idleness: " so every one . . . ought . . . in some kind of labour to exercise himself, according as the vocation, whereunto God hath called him, shall require." This Homily was probably quoted in *All's Well*, I. iii. 25.

Ibid. 119.

FAL. Oh, if men were to be saved by merit.

We may take it that Falstaff, like the Princess in *Love's Labour's Lost*, is referring to justification by faith and not by works. See Rom. iii. 28: " Therfore, we hold that a man is iustified by faith, without the deedes of the lawe." Salvation by merit was denounced in Homily on Fasting.

Ibid. 169-72.

FAL. Well, God give thee the spirit of persuasion, and him the ears of profiting, that what thou speakest may move, and what he hears may be believed.

Cf. Acts xxvi. 28: " Somewhat thou perswadest mee to be a Christian "; Matt. xiii. 23: " is he that heareth the word, and vnderstandeth it, which also beareth fruite, and bringeth foorth, some an hundred folde, some sixtie fold, some thirtie folde "; *L, Collect* said on any occasion, but especially at the close of a service : " Grant, we beseech thee, Almighty God, that the words, which we have heard this day with our outward ears, may through thy grace be so grafted inwardly in our hearts, that they may bring forth in us the fruit of good living."

Ibid. 239.

PRINCE. *Redeeming time.

See Eph. v. 16: " Redeeming the tyme, because the dayes are euill " (*T*, " season "); Col. iv. 5: " redeeming the time " (*T*, " and redeeme the season," *G*, " redeeme the time "). See Chapter IV., page 74.

Act I. iii. 125.

HOTS. And if the devil come and roar for them.

1 Pet. v. 8: " your aduersarie the deuil, as a roaring Lion."

Ibid. 239.

HOTS. Why, look you, I am whipp'd and scourg'd with rods.

Cf. the scourging of Christ, Mark xv. 15, and his being smitten on the head with a reed (xv. 19).

Act II. iv. 107.   See Adam.

Ibid. 253-4.

PRINCE. These lies are like their father that begets them.

For the devil as the father of lies see John viii. 44: " Ye are of your father the deuil, and the lustes of your father wil ye doe: he was a murderer from the beginning, & abode not in the trueth, because there is no trueth in him.   When he speaketh a lie, he speaketh of his owne: For he is a lier, and the father of it."

Ibid. 376.   See Lucifer.

Ibid. 460-2.

> FAL. This pitch, as ancient writers do report, doth defile:
> so doth the company thou keepest.

As this text is in Ecclus. xiii. 1, from the Apocrypha and
not from one of the Hebrew Canonical books, Carter attached
importance to the words " as ancient writers do report " and
contended that Shakespeare meant deliberately to distinguish
the Apocrypha from the Canon recognized as such by Hebrews. The Council of Trent included *Ecclesiasticus* within
the Canon. By *Article VI.* the Church of England excluded
it and traditional Puritan thought has approved this exclu-
sion. I fear Carter elsewhere bore witness against his contention here. According to him, Helena in *All's Well,*
II. i. included the *History of Susanna* in Holy Writ.

Ibid. 476-8.

> FAL. If then, the tree may be known by the fruit, as the
> fruit by the tree.

Luke vi. 44: " For euery tree is knowen by his owne
fruite."

Ibid. 526-8. See Pharaoh.

Act III. i. 13-5.

> GLEN.   at my nativity
> The front of heaven was full of fiery shapes,
> *Of burning cressets.

This figurative use of " cresset " is rare. It also occurs
in Ecclus. xlviii. 1: " Then stoode vp Elias the Prophete as
a fire, and his worde burnt like a cresset " (*G*, " a lampe ").

Act III. ii. 50-2.

> K. HEN. And then I stole all courtesy from heaven,
> And dress'd myself in such humility
> That I did pluck allegiance from men's hearts.

Cf. 2 Sam. xv. 5, 6: " And when any man came nigh to
him, & did him obeysance, he put forth his hand, and tooke
him to him, and kissed him. And on this maner did
Absalom to all Israel, that came to the king for iudgment:
so Absalom stale the hearts of the men of Israel." It might
be thought that " dress'd myself in such humility " was

suggested by " clothed with humility " of 1 Pet. v. 5. This is the Authorised reading and is quite unlike all Tudor versions.

Ibid. 70-3.

> K. HEN. That, being daily swallowed by men's eyes
> They surfeited with honey and began
> To loathe the taste of sweetness, whereof a little
> More than a little is by much too much.

Prov. xxv. 15-6: " If thou findest hony, eate so much as is sufficient for thee: least thou be ouer full, and parbreake it out againe. Withdrawe thy foote from thy neighbours house: least he be wearie of thee, and so hate thee."

Act III. iii. 13-14.

BARD. Sir John, you are so fretful, you cannot live long.

Cf. Ecclus. xxx. 23, 24: " as for sorowe and heauinesse, driue it farre from thee: for heauinesse hath slayne many a man, and bringeth no profit. Zeale and anger shorten the dayes of the life, carefulnes and sorow bring age before the time."

Ibid. 35-7. See Dives.

Ibid. 39-40.

FAL. By this fire, that's God's Angel.

See Exod. iii. 2: " And the Angel of the Lord appeared vnto him in a flame of fire out of the middes of a bush "; Heb. i. 7: " He maketh his angels spirits, and his ministers a flame of fire " (*G*, " He maketh the Spirits his messengers "). Also Ps. civ. 4. Omitted in Folio owing to its profanity.

Ibid. 90-1. See Prodigal.

Ibid. 167-8.

FAL. The King himself is to be feared as the lion.

Prov. xx. 2: " The feare of the king is as the roaring of a Lion."

Ibid. 187-8.

FAL. Thou seest I have more flesh than another man and therefore more frailty.

Cf. L, Prelude to Confirmation (as in former Prayer Books): " partly by the frailtie of their own flesh "; Matt. xxvi. 41; Mark xiv. 38: " the flesh is weake."

Act IV. ii. 27, 36-8.   See Lazarus, Prodigal.

Act IV. iii. 81-4.

> HOTS. Cries out upon abuses, seems to weep
> Over his country's wrongs; and by this face,
> This seeming brow of justice, did he win
> The hearts of all that he did angle for.

Cf. Henry's own confession (Act III. ii. 50-2 and 2 Sam. xv. 5, 6). See also 2 Sam. xv. 2, 3, 4: " And Absalom rose vp early, & stoode in the place of the entring in of the gate: and euery man that had any matter, and came to the king for iudgement, him did Absalom call vnto him, & said, Of what citie art thou ? He answered, Thy seruant is of one of the tribes of Israel. And Absalom said vnto him, See, thy matters are good and righteous, but there is no man (deputed) of the king to heare thee. Absalom said moreouer, Oh that I were made iudge in the lande, that euery man which hath any plea and matter in the law, might come to me, and that I might do him iustice ?"

Shakespeare connected Bolingbroke's conduct in *King Richard II.* with Absalom. See *King Richard II.,* I. iv. 23-8, which though less relative to 2 Sam. xv. 2-6 than the two passages in *1 King Henry IV.* is undoubtedly an echo of it.

See also II. iv. 310 (Matt. xxvi. 41); *ibid.* 497 (Gal. v. 4); III. iii. 27* (*L, Morning Prayer,* Matt. iii. 2, also Homily on Repentance); *ibid.* 42 (Matt. viii. 12).

2 KING HENRY IV.

1596-7. First printed 1600. The text in the 1623 Folio is independently printed—although closely related to the 1600 edition, it is not derived from it. This is the earliest play in which Genevan readings show a decided preponderance over Bishops'.

Act I. i. 47.

TRAV. *He seem'd in running to devour the way.

To speak of steeds devouring or swallowing ground covered is very frequent. In fact the phrase is second nature to one that owns or loves a horse. But see Job xxxix. 27 *G,* " He swalloweth the ground for fiercenesse and rage "

(*B, ibid.* 24: " Yet rusheth hee in fiercely, beating the ground ").

Ibid. 83.

Mor. But, for my lord, your son—

In this scene the arrival of the messengers is reminiscent of Ahimaaz and the Cushite, the messengers sent by Joab to acquaint David of the fate of his son's rebellion. See 2 Sam. xviii. 25 *et seq.*

Ibid. 157. See Cain.

Act I. ii. 7-8.

Fal. *this foolish compounded clay man.

Job xiii. 12: " and your bodies like the clay." Job xxxiii. 6 *G*: " I am also formed of the clay " (*B*, " moulde ").

Ibid. 38-41, 145. See Dives, Achitophel and Job.

Ibid. 179-80.

Ch. Jus. . . . you are as a candle, the better part burnt out.

See Job xviii. 6: " his candle shall be put out with him."

Ibid. 187-91.

Ch. Jus. You follow the young prince up and down, like his ill angel.
Fal. Not so, my lord ! your ill angel is light, but I hope he that looks upon me will take me without weighing.

A double play. According to 2 Cor. xi. 14 Satan appears as an " angell of light " and an angel, the coin, if bad, is light in weight.

Ibid. 218-19.

Fal. I am only old in judgment and understanding.

See Job xii. 12: " Among olde persons there is wisedome, and in age is vnderstanding " (*G*, " Among the ancient is wisedome, and in the length of dayes is vnderstanding "). See also 1 Cor. xiv. 20 *G*, " but in vnderstanding bee of a ripe age " (*B*, " perfect," and *R*, " in sense be perfect ").

Ibid. 223-6.

> FAL. I have check'd him for it, and the young lion repents:
> marry, not in ashes and sackcloth, but in new silk and
> old sack.

Matt. xi. 21, Luke x. 13: "they had a great while ago
repented, sitting in sackcloth and ashes."

Ibid. 256-7.

> CH. JUS. . . . you are too impatient to bear crosses.

A play on crossed coins and on Luke xiv. 27: "And
whosoeuer doth not beare his crosse."

Act I. iii. 41-62.

> L. BARD.   When we mean to build,
> We first survey the plot, etc.

Bardolph's speech here is obviously an application of the
Parable of the Builder as contained in Luke xiv. 28-30.
Usually Shakespeare condenses in his paraphrases of Parables. *Cf.* Gratiano's application of the Parable of the Prodigal
in *The Merchant of Venice,* or the Duke's of the Parable of
the Talents in *Measure for Measure.* Here Lord Bardolph
is prolix and repeats himself. The audience familiar with
the parable in question could follow each detail with interest, otherwise an argument of such length would have
wearied. Possibly on this account it was omitted in the
Quarto.

The companion Parable of the King making war is contained in the next verse of the same chapter (Luke xiv. 31).
Bardolph touches upon the theme of this Parable in lines
15-17. It was Shakespeare's object apparently to represent
this group of rebels as active in debate but slow in action.

Ibid. 89-90.

> ABP. YORK. An habitation giddy and unsure
> Hath he that buildeth on the vulgar heart.

Cf. Luke vi. 49: "But he that heareth, & doeth it not, is
like a man that without foundation built an house vpon the
earth: against which the flood did beate vehemently, and
it fell immediatly." The Archbishop, like the Bishop of
Carlisle in *King Richard II.,* had a reputation for learning
and piety. Hence in each case Shakespeare's use of Scriptural parallels.

Ibid. 94-99.

> ABP. YORK. And being now trimm'd in thine own
>   desires,
> Thou, beastly feeder, art so full of him,
> That thou provok'st thyself to cast him up.
> So, so, thou common dog, didst thou disgorge
> Thy glutton bosom of the royal Richard;
> And now thou wouldst eat thy dead vomit up.

2 Pet. ii. 22: " The dogge is turned to his owne vomite
againe." Also Prov. xxvi. 11. Compare *King Henry V.*,
III. vii. 71-3 for the verse in French from the Olivetan
version of 2 Pet.

Ibid. 103-4.

> ABP. YORK. Thou that threw'st dust upon his goodly
>   head
> When through proud London he came sighing on.

Cf. 2 Sam. xvi. 13: " And as Dauid and his men went by
the way, Semei went along on the hilles side ouer against
him, & cursed as he went, and threw stones at him, and
cast dust." *Cf. King Richard II.*, V. ii. 30-8, for the Duke of
York's description of Richard's humiliation in a passage
which Dryden admired exceedingly.

Act II. i. 161. See Prodigal.

Act II. ii. 26-8.

> PRINCE. *God knows whether those that bawl out the
> ruins of thy linen shall inherit his kingdom.

This was omitted from the Folio apparently because of
its profanity. The allusion is to Matt. xxv. 34: " Come ye
blessed of my father, inherite the kingdom, which hath ben
prepared for you from the foundation of the world " (*R*
reads " possesse " for " inherite," *T* " take the inheritance ").
This is another instance where Shakespeare may have quoted
either *B* or *G* but not *T*.

Ibid. 111-116.

> POINS. And how doth the martlemas, your master ?
> BARD. In bodily health, sir ?
> POINS. Marry, the immortal part needs a physician, but
>   that moves not him: though that be sick, it dies not.

Evidently in playful allusion to Matt. ix. 12: " They that
be whole, neede not a Physicion, but they that are sicke."

Ibid. 130.   See Japhet.

Act II. iv. 62-5.

> QUICK. . . . *you cannot one bear with another's con-
> firmities. . . . One must bear, and that must be you:
> you are the weaker vessel.

Rom. xv. 1 *G*: " We which are strong, ought to beare the
infirmities of the weake " (*B*, " the frailenesse " ; *R*, " susteine the infirmities of the vveake "). See page 65.

1 Pet. iii. 7 *G*: " giuing honour vnto the woman, as vnto
the weaker vessell " (*B*, " vnto the wife "; for " weaker vessel "
R reads " the vveaker feminine vessel ").

Ibid. 365-7.   See Lucifer.

Act III. ii. 40-3.

> SHALL. Certain: 'tis certain: very sure, very sure: Death,
> as the Psalmist saith, is certain to all: all shall die. How
> a good yoke of bullocks at Stamford fair ?

The Psalmist makes no such remark, although he alludes
frequently enough to the brevity of man's life. The allusion to the Psalmist was omitted in the Folio, doubtless
because the mention of the Psalmist in such ludicrous circumstances was considered profane. Shakespeare loved
to endow people like the Nurse in *Romeo and Juliet* and
Shallow in this with seeming profundity on man's mortality.
Carter calls attention to Ecclus. xxxviii. 25 which provides
an amusing comment on the colloquy between Shallow and
Silence:

" Howe can hee get wisedome that holdeth the plough,
and hee that hath pleasure in the goade and in driuing the
oxen, and is occupyed in their labours, and his talke is but
of the breeding of bullockes ?" Hazlitt derived great
pleasure from this chat between Shallow and Silence.

Ibid. 278-81.

> FAL. Will you tell me, Master Shallow, how to choose a
> man ? Care I for the limb, the thewes, the stature, bulk,
> and big assemblance of a man ? Give me the spirit,
> Master Shallow.

Cf. 1 Sam. xvi. 7, where David is preferred by God to
his brothers.

Act IV. i. 194-6, 204-9.

Mow. *We shall be winnow'd with so rough a wind
That even our corn shall seem as light as chaff
And good from bad find no partition.
ABP. YORK. . . . for full well he knows,
He cannot so precisely weed this land
As his misdoubts present occasion:
His foes are so enrooted with his friends
*That, plucking to unfix an enemy,
He doth unfasten so and shake a friend.

Cf. Matt. xiii. 29 *G*: " Nay, lest while yee goe about to
gather the tares, yee plucke vp also with them the wheate "
(*B* and *R*, " roote vp "; *L, Gospel, Fifth Sunday after Epiphany*
as *G*). See Chapter IV. In lines 215-6: " the king hath
wasted all his rods On late offenders ": Hastings seems to
desire to contribute his quota by a remark reminiscent of
Ps. lxxxix. 32: " I will visit their offences with the rod."
For the figure of being winnowed *cf.* Luke xxii. 31 *G*:
" Satan hath desired you, to winow you, as wheate "
(*B* and *R*, " sift "). The winnowing of the disciples may
have been in mind.

Act IV. ii. 10.

LANC. Turning the word to sword and life to death.

Cf. Eph. vi. 17: " the sword of the spirite, which is the
word of God." It should be noted that " word " and
" sword " are not an antithesis in *Ephesians*. See also *The
Merry Wives*, III. i. 44-5. See Chapter VI. See also Philip.
ii. 16: " Holding fast the worde of life."

Ibid. 27.

LANC. Under the counterfeited zeal of God.

Rom. x. 2: " that they haue a zeale of God." This reading
" zeal of God " was first introduced by the 1560 Genevan and
was adopted by both the Bishops' and the Rheims as well as
afterwards by the Authorised. It is therefore essentially
an Elizabethan reading.

Act IV. iii. 95-6.

FAL. nor a man cannot make him laugh: but that's no
marvel, he drinks no wine.

Cf. Ecclus. xxxi. 28: " wine measurably drunken, is a
reioycing of the soule and body: a measurable drinking, is

health to soule and body" (*G*, "Wine measurably drunken and in time, bringeth gladnesse and cheerefulnesse of minde)." See also *Othello*, II. iii. 299-300.

Act IV. iv. 35.

K. HEN. As flaws congealed in the spring of day.

For this use of "spring of day" meaning "dawn" *cf.* 1 Sam. ix. 26: "And when they arose early about the spring of the day, Samuel called Saul vpon the top of the house"; Hos. vi. 3: "he shal goe forth as the spring of the day, and come vnto vs as the rayne, and as the latter rayne vnto the earth" (*G* reads "the morning" instead of "the spring of the day"). It seems strange that Shakespeare never used Tindale's "day-spring from on high" that we find in *L, Benedictus.*

Ibid. 79-80.

K. HEN. 'Tis seldom when the bee doth leave her comb
In the dead carrion.

See Judg. xiv. 8: "he turned out of the way to see the carkeise of the Lion: and beholde, there was a swarme of Bees and hony in the carkeise of the Lion."

Act IV. v. 8.

CLAR. I am here, brother, full of heaviness.

Ps. lxix. 21: "I am full of heaviness." Phil. ii. 26: "and was full of heauinesse."

Ibid. 106.

K. HEN. Which thou hast whetted on thy stony heart.

A "stony heart" instead of a "fleshy heart" is Ezekiel's. See Ezekiel xxxvi. 26: "A newe heart also wil I giue you, and a newe spirit wil I put into you: as for that stony heart I wil take it out of your flesh, & giue you a fleshie heart."

Ibid. 182-4.

K. HEN.   God knows, my son,
By what by-paths and indirect crook'd ways
I met this crown.

Although doubtless the figure was common enough, still it is to be noted that it is also Biblical. See Prov. ii 14-15: "and delight in the wickednesse of the euill: Whose wayes are crooked, and they froward in their paths."

Act V. ii. 3.*

See *Romeo and Juliet*, IV. v. 75-6; *Macbeth*, IV. iii. 176; *Antony and Cleopatra*, II. v. 31 for allusion to the Shunamite's reply to Elisha.

Act V. iii. 102.   See Assyrians.

Ibid. 114.

SHALL. *I am, sir, under the king, in some authority.

Cf. Luke vii. 8 *G*: "For I likewise am a man set vnder authoritie" (*B*, "vnder power"; *R*, "subiect to authoritie").

See also II. ii. 52-3* (Job xxxiv. 36 *G*); II. iv. 254 (Ecclus. xxviii. 6); IV. iii. 16 (Eph. vi. 5).

THE MERRY WIVES OF WINDSOR

1596-7. First published in corrupt and imperfect form in 1602. Reprinted 1619. First authentic edition 1623. Tradition asserts that this bustling comedy, which acts well on the stage, was written in response to Elizabeth's command, and that it was completed in a fortnight. There are several indications of haste, most notably that the comedy is almost entirely in prose. The Scriptural quotations are of the same boisterous kind as found in the two parts of *King Henry IV*.

Act I. i. 152-5.

FAL. Pistol.

PISTOL. He hears with ears.

EVANS. The Tevil and his Tam! What phrase is this, "He hears with ear"?   Why, it is affectations.

This is a joke at the expense of the Parson, who does not recognize the familiar phrase from *L, Litany*: "O God, we have heard with our ears, and our fathers have declared unto us." The phrase "heard with our ears" occurs also in Ps. xliv.1, 2 Sam. xviii. 12, Ezek. xxiv. 26 *G*, and there is an echo of it in Luke viii. 8: "He that hath eares to heare."

Act I. iii. 36.

PISTOL. Young ravens must have food.

Ps. cxlvii. 9: "and feedeth the young ravens that call upon him."

13

Ibid. 56-9.

FAL. Now the report goes, she has all the rule of her husband's purse: he hath a legion of angels.

PISTOL. As many devils entertain.

The well-worn joke on angels the coins, " twelue legions of angels " (Matt. xxvi. 53) and the legion of devils (Luke viii. 30).

Act II. i. 20.   See Herod.

Ibid. 115-6.

PISTOL. *He wooes both high and low, both rich and poor, both young and old, one with another.

Ps. xlix. 2: " High and low, rich and poor: one with another " (*G*, " As wel low as hie, both rich and poore ").

Act II. iii. 7.   See Bible.

Act III. i. 42-3.

EVANS. Pless you from his mercy sake, all of you.

Cf. Ps. vi. 4: " O save me for thy mercy's sake."

Ibid. 44-5.

SHALL. What ?   The sword and the word ?   Do you study them both, Master Parson ?

Cf. Eph. vi. 17: " the sword of the spirite, which is the word of God." In *Ephesians* " sword " and " word " do not form an antithesis.   See *2 King Henry IV.*, IV. ii. 10 and Chapter VI.

Act IV. ii. 166-7.

EVANS. *Master Ford, you must pray, and not follow the imaginations of your own heart.

Jer. xiii. 10: " they folowe the wicked imaginations of their owne heart " (*G*, " stubburnnesse ").

Act IV. v. 8.   See Prodigal.

Act V. i. 23-5.

FAL. *I fear not Goliath with a weaver's beam, because I know, also, life is a shuttle.

See Goliath; Job vii. 6: " My dayes passe ouer more speedily then a weauers shuttle " (*G*, " shittle ").

Act V. v. 167-9.   See Job and Sathan.

NOTE.

Act II. i. 63-4.

MRS. FORD. . . . than the Hundredth Psalm to the tune of Greensleeves.

The Hundredth Psalm is the *Jubilate Deo omnis terra* (Vulgate, Psalm 99). Mrs. Ford is not referring here to the Prayer Book Psalter but to the Metrical Version by Hopkins. It is one of the psalms that have survived, and is still very well known under the title of " Old Hundredth." The first stanza is:

> All people that on earth do dwel,
>> Sing to the Lord with cheerfull voice:
> Him serue with feare, his praise foorth tell,
>> Come ye before him and reioice."

The tune was given in the book as well as the words, and it should be observed that the tune to which it was sung is the same as to-day.

Unlike Old Hundredth, Greensleeves was bright and lilting. Some Puritans were prone to sing their metrical psalms to inappropriate popular tunes (*cf. Winter's Tale,* IV. ii. 47-8: " but one Puritan amongst them, and he sings psalms to hornpipes ").

KING HENRY V.

1597-8. A corrupt version was published in 1600, and re-printed in 1602 and 1619. Sole authoritative text is that of the 1623 Folio.

Act I. i. 22.

CANTER. The King is full of grace, and fair regard.

John i. 14: " full of grace and trueth." *L, Gospel, Annunciation of the Virgin Mary,* Luke i. 28: " Haile ful of grace " (*B,* " Hayle (thou that art) in high fauour "; *G,* " Haile thou that art freely beloued "; *R* as *L*).

Ibid. 29. See Adam.

Act I. ii. 31-2.

KING. That what you speak is in your conscience wash'd
As pure as sin with Baptism.

Cf. Acts xxii. 16: " Arise, & be baptized, & wash away thy sinnes "; *L, Baptism :* " and by the Baptism of thy well beloved son Jesus Christ, didst sanctify the flood Jordan and all other waters, to the mystical washing away of sin." This differs slightly from the form of words now in use. The alteration was made in 1662.

Ibid. 99-100.

> CANTER. When the man dies, let the inheritance
> Descend unto the daughter.

Num. xxvii. 8. This quotation of the answer of Moses to the daughters of Zelophehad is from Holinshed, the principal source for the play. See *Numbers* in the list of Proper Names.

Act II. ii. 33.

> KING. *And shall forget the office of our hand.

Ps. cxxxvii. 5: " let my right hand forget her cunning " (*G*, " let my right hand forget to play ").

Ibid. 42.

> KING. *It was excess of wine that set him on.

Todd suggests comparison with 1 Pet. iv. 3: " in excesse of wines " (*G*, " drunkennesse ").

Ibid. 79-81.

> KING. The mercy that was quick in us but late,
> By your own counsel is suppress'd and kill'd:
> *You must not dare, for shame, to talk of mercy.

See Ecclus. xxviii. 4: " Hee that sheweth no mercie to a man which is like himselfe, howe dare hee aske forgiuenes of his sinnes ? " (*G* has " will " for " dare ").

Ibid. 124.   See Legion.

Act II. iii. 9-11, 41.   See Abraham, Babylon.

Act II. iv. 102.

> EXETER. *And bids you, in the bowels of the Lord.

Philem. 20: " comfort my bowels in the Lord "; Phil. i. 8: " in the bowels of Iesus Christ " (*G*, " heart roote "; *R* as *B*), etc.

Act III. ii. 24.

PISTOL. *Be merciful, great Duke, to men of mould !

Cf. Job xxxiii. 6: "for I am fashioned and made euen of the same moulde " (*G*, " I am also formed of the clay "). Also Tobit viii. 8: " Thou madest Adam of the moulde of the earth " (*G* omits " of the moulde of the earth ").

Ibid. 39-40.

BOY. For Nym, he hath heard that men of few words are the best men.

See Eccles. v. 1: " therefore let thy wordes be fewe."

Ibid. 126-7.

JAMY. By the Mass, ere these eyes of mine take themselves to slumber.

Ps. cxxxii. 4: " I will not suffer mine eyes to sleep, nor mine eyelids to slumber."

Act III. iii. 26-7, 41.   See Leviathan, Herod.

Act III. vi. 134-6.

MOUNT. England shall repent his folly, . . . and admire our sufferance.

The full implication of this may be gathered from 2 Cor. xi. 19: " For ye suffer fooles gladly, seeing yee your selues are wise."

Act III. vii. 71-2.

DAUPH. *Le chien est retourné à son propre vomissement et la truie lavée au bourbier.

2 Pet. ii. 22.   See Chapter IV., pages 86-7.

Act IV. i. 179-81.

KING. though they can outstrip men, they have no wings to fly from God.   War is his beadle, war is his vengeance.

For this thought of the ubiquity of God, compare 2 *K. Henry VI.*, V. ii. 73, Amos ix. 2 and Ps. cxxxix. 6, 7; especially *ibid.* 8: " If I take the wings of the morning." For war as God's means of vengeance, see Jeremiah on Babylon. Jer. li. 20: " Thou hast bene mine hammer and weapons of warre: for with thee haue I broken the people

in pieces, & with thee haue I destroyed kingdomes." *Cf.*
also Ezek. v. 13 and xiv. 21.

Ibid. 192-3.

KING. . . . *and dying so, death is to him advantage.

Phil. i. 21: " For Christ (is) to me life, and death is to me
aduantage " (*G*, " For Christ is to me both in life, and in
death aduantage." *R*, " For vnto me, to liue is Christ:
and to die is gaine "). See Chapter IV., page 75.

Ibid. 288-90.

KING. Can sleep so soundly as the wretched slave,
Who with a body fill'd and vacant mind
Gets him to rest, cramm'd with distressful bread.

Cf. Eccles. v. 11: " A labouring man sleepeth sweetely,
whether it be litle or much that he eateth" (*G*, " The
sleepe of him that trauaileth, is sweete, whether hee eate
litle or much ").

" Distressful bread " has attracted attention and attempts
have been made to identify it with " bread of tears " (Ps.
lxxx. 5) and " bread of sorow " (Ps. cxxvii. 2 *G*). I suggest
that it means no more than bread gained by distress or fatigue
of the body—*i.e.*, by the sweat of the brow.

Ibid. 291.

KING. Never sees horrid night, the child of hell.

Matt. xxiii. 15 may have suggested to Shakespeare this
phrase: " yee make him two folde more the childe of hell."

Act IV. iii. 34-6.

KING. Rather proclaim it, Westmoreland, through my
host
That he, which hath no stomach to this fight
Let him depart.

Cf. the action of Judas Maccabæus in removing the fearful
as related in 1 Macc. iii. 56. See *ibid.* v. 49: " Wherefore
Iudas commanded a proclamation to be made throughout
the host "; 2 Macc. xiv. 18: " & the bold stomackes that they
had to fight." See also incident recorded of Gideon's army
in Judg. vii. 3.

Act IV. vii. 66, 145. See Assyrian, Belzebub and Lucifer.

Act IV. viii. 111-3.

> KING.   O God ! thy arm was here:
> And not to us, but to thy arm alone
> Ascribe we all.

Ps. xliv. 3, 4: " For they gat not the land in possession through their own sword: neither was it their own arm that helped them; But thy right hand, and thine arm."

Ibid. 128.

> KING. *Let there be sung *Non nobis* and *Te Deum*.

See Chapter IV., pages 80-1.

Act V. ii. 41.

> BURG. Her vine, the merry cheerer of the heart.

Ps. civ. 15: " and wine that maketh glad the heart of man." Compare also the answer of the vine in Jotham's Parable of the trees, Judg. ix. 13. It is interesting to compare the tenour of Burgundy's speech, lines 33-67, with Isa. xxxii. 10-20.

Ibid. 214-5.

> KING. If ever thou be'st mine, Kate, as I have a saving faith within me tells me thou shalt.

Cf. Luke vii. 50: " Thy faith hath saued thee."

See also II. i. 122 (*L, Burial,* Job xiv. 1); II. ii. 114-7 (Matt. iv. 1-10, Luke iv. 1-12); *ibid.* 121-2 (1 Pet. v. 8); III. vi. 129-30 (Mark v. 39); IV. i. 192 (Matt. vii. 4).

MUCH ADO ABOUT NOTHING

1597-8. Printed in 1600, from which edition the 1623 Folio reprinted. There is nothing noteworthy about its Scriptural allusions. There is no character to whom Scriptural quotations are given more than to another.

Act I. i. 158-9.

> D. PED. I dare swear he is no hypocrite, but prays from his heart.

That is unlike the hypocrites of Matt. xv. 7 who honoured God with their lips but their hearts were far from him.

Act II. i. 41-52.

BEAT. I am not for him, therefore I will even take sixpence
in earnest of the bear-ward, and lead his apes into hell.
LEON. Well then, go you into hell?
BEAT. No, but to the gate: and there will the Devil meet
me, like an old cuckold with horns on his head, and say,
" Get you to heaven, Beatrice; get you to heaven: here's
no place for you maids." So deliver I up my apes and
away to St. Peter for the heavens: he shows me where the
bachelors sit.

Leading apes in hell was the penalty for old maids. Beatrice refutes this, relying apparently on Rev. xiv. 4: " These
are they which were not defiled with women, for they are
virgins," as being among the company of the Lamb. See
also St. Peter.

Ibid. 63-7.

BEAT. Not till God make men of some other metal than
earth. Would it not grieve a woman to be overmaster'd
with a piece of valiant dust? to make an account of her
life to a clod of wayward marl?

An obvious reference to Gen. ii. 7. It should be noted,
however, that woman was not created out of dust, hence the
contrast hinted at by Beatrice.

Ibid. 67-9.

BEAT. Adam's sons are my brethren: and truly I hold it
a sin to match in my kindred.

In allusion to the Table of Kindred and Affinity contained
in the Book of Common Prayer.

Ibid. 261. See Adam.

Ibid. 332-4.

BEAT. *Thus goes every one to the world but I, and I
am sunburnt.

See Chapter II., pages 29-30.

Act II. iii. 248-50.

BENED. . . . happy are they that hear their detractions,
and can put them to mending.

Cf. Ecclus. xx. 4: " O how good a thing is it, a man that
is reprooued, to shew openly his repentance." Prov. ix. 8:
" rebuke a wise man, and he will loue thee."

Act III. iii. 141-3. See Pharaoh, Bel.

Act III. iv. 30.

MARG. *Is not marriage honourable in a beggar ?

L, Matrimony : " holy Matrimony; which is an honourable estate . . . and is commended of Saint Paul to be honourable among all men." Heb. xiii. 4 *G*: " Marriage is honourable among all " (*B*, " Wedlocke ").

Ibid. 59-60.

MARG. but God send every one their heart's desire.

We have become so accustomed to the phrase " heart's desire " that we never think of its Biblical occurrence. Exactly in the sense used by Margaret it occurs in Ps. xxxvii. 4: " Delight thou in the Lord: and he shall give thee thy heart's desire." Also Ps. xx. 4: " Grant thee thy heart's desire: and fulfill all thy mind " (*G*, " according to thine heart "). *Cf.* also Ezek. xxiv. 21 *G*.

Act V. i. 171.

D. PED. " Nay," said I, " he hath the tongues."

This phrase to denote ability to speak several languages is frequent in the New Testament. See Acts x. 46: " they heard them speake with tongues "; Acts xix. 6: " and they spake with tongues "; 1 Cor. xiii. 1: " Though I speake with the tongues of men, and of angels."

Ibid. 185-6.

CLAUDIO. All, all; and, moreover, God saw him when he was hid in the garden.
See Adam. An allusion to Gen. iii. 8.

Ibid. 257.

D. PED. *Runs not this speech like iron through your blood ?

Evidently based upon Ps. cv. 18, which, following a mistake in the Vulgate, reads: " the iron entered into his soul " (*G*, " and he was layd in yrons "). See page 78.

See also II. iii. 212-4 (Matt. v. 39, Eph. vi. 5, Phil. ii. 12); III. iii. 61 (Ecclus. xiii. 1); *ibid.* 73 (*L*, *Nunc Dimittis*, Luke ii. 29); IV. i. 12-4, 23-6 (*L*, *Matrimony*).

JULIUS CÆSAR

1598-9. First published 1623. As might be expected, when North's *Plutarch* is the source, Scriptural allusion is small.

Act II. ii. 26-7

CÆSAR.   What can be avoided
Whose end is purpos'd by the mighty gods ?

A common thought, but see Isa. xliii. 13 *G*: " before the day was, I am, and there is none that can deliuer out of mine hand: I will doe it, and who shall let it ?" (*B*, " I doe the worke, and who shal be able to let it ?").

Ibid. 33.

CÆSAR. *The valiant never taste of death but once.

" Taste of death " is a curious phrase occurring in the Gospels. See Luke ix. 27: " there be some standing here, which shall in no wise taste of death." See also Matt. xvi. 28, Mark ix. 1, John viii. 52. " Taste of death " follows the Greek texts; " taste death," as in the Wicliffite and Rheims, follows the Latin Vulgate. *B* is the only Elizabethan version to follow the Greek literally in Heb. ii. 9. *Cf. King Henry V.*, II. ii. 178-80: " to your death; The taste whereof, God of his mercy give you Patience to endure." See page 28.

Act II. iv. 39-40.

PORTIA.   Ay me ! How weak a thing
The heart of woman is !

Todd calls attention for words and thought to Ezek. xvi. 30: " How weake is thine heart, sayeth the Lord God, seeing thou doest all these, (euen) the woorkes of a presumptuous whorish woman."

Act III. ii. 233-4.

ANT.   that should move
The stones of Rome to rise and mutiny.

Doubtless in allusion to the figure of the stones crying out. See Luke xix. 40.

Act IV. i. 50-1.

OCT. *And some that smile have in their hearts, I fear,
Millions of mischiefs.

Ps. xxviii. 3: " which speak friendly to their neighbours, but imagine mischief in their hearts " (*G*, " which speake friendly to their neighbours, when malice is in their hearts ").

Act IV. iii. 85.

CASSIUS. *A friend should bear his friend's infirmities.

Rom. xv. 1 *G*: " We which are strong, ought to beare the infirmities of the weake " (*B*, " frailenesse "; *R*, " susteine the infirmities ").

Act V. v. 41-2.

BRUTUS.   my bones would rest
That have but labour'd to attain this hour.

Cf. Job iii. 17: " There must the wicked ceasse from their tyranny, and there such as laboured valiantly, be at rest."

See also I. ii. 151 (Gen. vi. *et seq.*); III. i. 232* (Luke xxiii. 24 *G*); V. v. 20 (John ii. 4).

AS YOU LIKE IT

1598-9. First printed 1623. Excepting possibly old Adam, there is no one person in the play to whom Scriptural quotation might be said properly to belong, not even Jaques. Many quote the Bible and none overmuch, and nearly all quotations are much as might have been found in every-day speech.

Act I. i. 40-2, *Act II. i.* 5. See Prodigal. See Adam.

Act II. i. 49-57.

1ST LORD.   then being there alone,
Left and abandoned of his velvet friend,
" 'Tis right," quoth he, " thus misery doth part
The flux of company ": anon, a careless herd,
Full of the pasture, jumps along by him
And never stays to greet him. " Ay," quoth Jaques,
" Sweep on you fat and greasy citizens;
'Tis just the fashion; wherefore do you look
Upon that poor and broken bankrupt there ?"

This might have been rejected had there not been evidence elsewhere that Shakespeare knew Ecclus. xiii. 22: " when the poore falleth, his acquaintance forsake him." (This more exactly enforces the first four lines than *G*, " when the poore falleth, his friendes driue him away.") *Ibid.* 21: " so doeth the rich abhorre the poore." Compare also the conduct of the Priest and the Levite in the Parable of the Good Samaritan (Luke x. 30-2).

This theme of *Ecclesiasticus* recurs in *Hamlet, Troilus and Cressida, Timon of Athens* and *King Henry VIII.*

Act II. iii. 43-5.

> ADAM. Take that, and he, that doth the ravens feed,
> Yea, providently caters for the sparrow,
> Be comfort to my age.

Luke xii. 24: " Consider the rauens, for they neither sowe nor reape, which neither haue storehouse nor barne, & (notwithstanding) God feedeth them "; Luke xii. 6: " Are not fiue sparrowes sold for two farthings, and not one of them is forgotten before God ?" Note that both these quotations are from the same chapter.

It is evident that Shakespeare intended Adam as a pious Bible-reading old man, and his lines 5-15 might very justly be considered to have a Biblical background such as Ps. xxxvii. 33: " The ungodly seeth the righteous: and seeketh occasion to slay him "; the envy Joseph excited among his brethren (see the Bishops' note on Gen. xxxvii. 8: " Gods graces to the godly, are an occasion that the wicked hate them," and compare it with: " Know you not, master, to some kind of men Their graces serve them but as enemies ?"); Cain's murder of Abel with the question in 1 John iii. 12: " And wherfore slew he him ? because his owne workes were euil, and his brothers righteous."

Act II. iv. 81-3.

> CORIN. My master is of churlish disposition
> And little recks to find the way to heaven
> By doing deeds of hospitality.

See Rom. xii. 13: " Distributing to the necessitie of saints, giuen to hospitalitie." But it seems to have been the churlishness of Nabal that was in Shakespeare's mind; see 1 Sam. xxv. 2 *et seq.* See Chapter II., page 29.

Act II. v. 61. See Egypt.

Act II. vii. 64-5.

>DUKE S. Most mischievous foul sin, in chiding sin:
>For thou thyself hast been a libertine.

Shakespeare repeatedly alludes to Rom. ii. 22 *et seq.*, even as early as *2 Henry VI.* where King Henry reproved Cardinal Beaufort. Rom. ii. 22: " Thou that sayest a man shoulde not commit adulterie, breakest thou wedlocke ?"

Act III. ii. 124.

>TOUCH. *Truly, the tree yields bad fruit.

Matt. vii. 18: " A good tree cannot bring foorth bad fruit " (*G*, " euill fruite "; *R*, " yeld euil fruites ").

Ibid. 381-2.

>ROS. I will not cast away my physic, but on those that are sick.

Cf. Matt. ix. 12: " They that be whole, neede not a Physicion, but they that are sicke."

Act III. iv. 7-9. See Judas Iscariot.

Act III. v. 90.

>PHE. Thou hast my love, is not that neighbourly ?

L, Catechism: " My duty towards my Neighbour, is to love him as myself."

Act IV. i. 135-7, 140-2, 144.

>CEL. Will you, Orlando, have to wife this Rosalind ?
>ORL. I will. . . .
>ROS. Then you must say, I take thee, Rosalind, for wife.
>ORL. I take thee, Rosalind, for wife.
>ROS. . . . But I do take thee, Orlando, for my husband.

Rosalind and Orlando have practised the betrothal part of the service and not the actual wedding. See *Twelfth Night,* V. i. 160-3.

Act V. iii. 4, 5.

> AUDREY. I hope it is no dishonest desire, to desire to
> be a woman of the world ?

See Chapter II., page 29.   This adaptation of Luke
xx. 34 here provides an argument that, although the song
is not of Shakespeare's authorship, the scene is.

Ibid. 30.

> SONG. How that a life was but a flower.

Ps. ciii. 15: " The days of man are but as grass: for he
flourisheth as a flower of the field."   The song from which
the line is taken is most improbably of Shakespeare's authorship.   See *Times Literary Supplement*, Jan. 5th and 12th, 1933.

Act V. iv. 35-8.

> JAQUES. *There is sure another flood toward, and these
> couples are coming to the Ark.   Here comes a pair of
> very strange beasts, which in all tongues are call'd fools.

Gen. vii. 2 *G*: " Of euery cleane beast, thou shalt take to
thee by seuens, the male and his female: but of vncleane
beasts by couples, the male and his female " (*B*, " but of
vncleane cattel, two, the male and his female "). See
Chapter IV., page 66.   Both *B* and *G* in their notes
interpreted " the seven " to mean three pairs for breed and
the seventh for sacrifice.

See also II. iv. 5, 6 (1 Pet. iii. 5); *ibid.* 12-4 (Luke xiv. 27);
III. ii. 138-41* (Gen. xlvii. 9, Ps. cxix. 54, Ps. xxxix. 6);
III. iii. 71-8, 92-3 (*L, Matrimony*).

ALL'S WELL THAT ENDS WELL

1599-1600.   First published in 1623.   The Clown is the
principal exponent of Scriptural quotation.

Act I. i. 65-6.

> LAFEU. Moderate lamentation is the right of the dead,
> excessive grief the enemy to the living.

See Ecclus. xxxviii. 17, 20-2: " make lamentation expediently, and be earnest in mourning, and vse lamentation as

he is worthie, and that a day or two, lest thou bee euill spoken of: and then comfort thy selfe, because of the heauinesse. 20. Take no heauinesse to heart, driue it away, and remember the last things. Forget it not, for there is no turning againe, thou shalt doe him no good, but hurt thy selfe. Remember his iudgement, thine also shall be likewise: vnto mee yesterday, vnto thee to day."

Ibid. 105-7.

> HEL.   to sit and draw
> His arched brows, his hawking eye, his curls,
> In our heart's table.

The figure, "the heart's table," is Biblical. See Jer. xvii. 1: "written in the table of your heartes" (*G*, "grauen"), and Prov. iii. 3 *G*: "write them vpon the table of thine heart" (*B*, "tables").

Ibid. 144-5.

> PAR. Virginity, by being once lost, may be ten times found: by being ever kept, it is ever lost.

A play on Matt. x. 39: "He that findeth his life, shall lose it: and he that loseth his life for my sake, shal finde it." See also Matt. xvi. 25, Mark viii. 35, Luke ix. 24, xvii. 33. *Cf.* also John xii. 24, 25: "if it die, it bringeth forth much fruite. He that loueth his life, shal lose it: & he that hateth his life in this worlde, shal keepe it vnto life eternall." Similar play on the idea contained in the verse was made by Berowne in *Love's Labour's Lost*, IV., iii. 361-2, though with less daring.

Ibid. 159-60.

> PAR. . . . made of self-love, which is the most inhibited sin in the Canon.

Citing from Deut. vi. 4, 5 and Lev. xix. 18, in Mark xii. 29-33 and in other passages one is commanded first to love God with all one's might, secondly to love one's neighbour as oneself. The same is emphasized in *L, Catechism*. This duty of loving God and one's neighbour has been traditionally interpreted as condemning self-indulgence or self-love.

Act I. iii. 18-9.

CLOWN. No, madam, 'tis not so well that I am poor, though many of the rich are damn'd.

Mark x. 23: "How hardly shall they that haue riches, enter into the kingdome of God!" But the reference is really to Dives and Lazarus (Luke xvi. 22, 23).

Ibid. 19-21.

CLOWN. . . . but, if I may have your ladyship's good will to go to the world, Isbel the woman and I will do as we may.

See Chapter II., page 29.

Ibid. 25-8.

CLOWN. Service is no heritage, and I think I shall never have the blessing of God, till I have issue o' my body: for they say, barnes are blessings.

Ps. cxxvii. 4: "Lo, children and the fruit of the womb: are an heritage and gift that cometh of the Lord." Ps. cxxviii. 3-5: "Thy wife shall be as the fruitful vine: upon the walls of thine house. Thy children like the olive-branches: round about thy table. Lo, thus shall the man be blessed: that feareth the Lord." Also: "forgetting how service is no heritage" (Homily against Idleness). This remark in the Homily was specially addressed to "serving men."

Ibid. 29-32.

COUNT. Tell me thy reason why thou wilt marry.
CLOWN. My poor body, madam, requires it, I am driven on by the flesh.

1 Cor. vii. 9: "But if they cannot abstaine, let them marry: for it is better to marry then to burne."

Ibid. 35-40.

CLOWN. Faith, madam, I have other holy reasons, such as they are.
COUNT. May the world know them?
CLOWN. I have been, madam, a wicked creature, as you and all flesh and blood are, and, indeed, I do marry that I may repent.

The Countess, as one of the children of this world given in marriage, hopes she may be permitted to know the Clown's holy reasons. For the Clown's reply see *L, Baptism*: " forasmuch as all men are conceived and born in sin "; and 1 Cor. vii. 14: " For the vnbeleeuing husband is sanctified by the wife " (*T*, " sanctified to the wife," which is not what the Clown intends). Evidently 1 Cor. vii. 14, which contains St. Paul's views on marriage, as read in church, is in the Clown's mind.

Ibid. 50-5.

> CLOWN. . . . he, that comforts my wife, is the cherisher of my flesh and blood: he, that cherishes my flesh and blood, loves my flesh and blood: he, that loves my flesh and blood, is my friend: ergo, he, that kisses my wife, is my friend.

Playing on Eph. v. 28, 29: " So ought men to loue their wiues as their owne bodies: he that loueth his wife, loueth himselfe. For no man euer yet hated his owne flesh: but nourisheth and cherisheth it." Substantially in this form the passage was read in *L, Matrimony*.

Ibid. 97-101.

> CLOWN. That man should be at woman's command, and yet no hurt done ! Though honesty be no Puritan, yet it will do no hurt: it will wear the surplice of humility over the black gown of a big heart.

According to Titus ii. 5, wives should be obedient to their own husbands, and by *L, Matrimony*, the woman undertakes to obey the man. Inferentially, the Clown contends, it is not natural that a man should have to obey a woman. But honesty does not stand on form; it is peaceable and harmless and will don the surplice of conformity and obedience so as to conceal the black gown of nonconformity and disobedience.

In Shakespeare's time the Puritan clergy objected to the white surplice and preferred to wear black gowns, which came in time to be known as Geneva gowns. Something of the prejudice survived until recently, and there were at the beginning of the twentieth century in the Church of England a few clergy who before preaching doffed the surplice and donned a black gown instead.

14

Act II. i. 139-40.

> HEL. He, that of greatest works is finisher,
> Oft does them by the weakest minister.

Cf. 1 Cor. i. 27: " God hath chosen the weake things of the worlde, to confound the things which are mightie." Also compare the slaying of Sisera by Jael and Goliath by David. Lafeu in II. iii. 40 repeats the theme: " If a most weak and debile minister, great power."

Ibid. 141-2.

> HEL. So Holy Writ in babes hath judgment shown,
> When Judges have been babes.

Susanna 45: " For when she was led foorth to death, the Lorde raised vp the spirite of a young childe, whose name was Daniel."

Ibid. 142-3.

> HEL.   great floods have flown
> From simple sources.

A reference to the striking of the rock by Moses at Horeb, Exod. xvii. 6, and again in Kadesh, Num. xx. 11.

Ibid. 143-4.

> HEL.   and great seas have dried
> When miracles have by the great'st been denied.

An allusion to the crossing of the Red Sea by the Israelites on dry land (see Exod. xiv. 21, etc.) and the incredulity of the people. Helen's speech should be compared with Ps. cxiv. (*In Exitu Israel de Aegypto*).

Act III. ii. 89-91.

> COUNT. A very tainted fellow, and full of wickedness,
> My son corrupts a well-derived nature
> With his inducement.

Cf. 1 Cor. xv. 33: " Euill wordes corrupt good maners " (*G,* " speakings ").

Act IV. iv. 23-4.

> HEL. When saucy trusting of the cozen'd thoughts
> Defiles the pitchy night.

This is an instance of Shakespeare's quick association of words. He had played every variation on Ecclus. xiii. 1:

"Who so toucheth pitche, shall be difiled withall"; here he actually uses the idea the other way about and it is the pitch that is defiled.

Act IV. v. 21. See Nabuchadnezar.

Ibid. 45-6.

CLOWN. *The black prince, sir: alias, the prince of darkness: alias, the devil.

Eph. vi. 12 *G*: " and against the worldly gouernors, the princes of the darkenesse of this worlde" (*B* omits "princes" and *R* has "rectors of the vvorld of this darkenes"). Bishop Warburton stigmatized the Clown's talk as "impious trash." *Cf. King Lear*, III. iv. 147: "The prince of darkness is a gentleman." The term was in regular use; see Tomson's Preface and Bacon's *Unity in Religion*.

Ibid. 50-3.

CLOWN. I am a woodland fellow, sir, that always loved a great fire, and the master I speak of ever keeps a good fire, but sure, he is the prince of the world.

Matt. xxv. 41: " the euerlasting fire, which is prepared for the deuil and his angels"; John xii. 31: " Nowe shal the prince of this world be cast out"; John xiv. 30: "for the prince of this worlde commeth."

Ibid. 54-9.

CLOWN. *I am for the house with the narrow gate, which I take to be too little for pomp to enter: some that humble themselves may, but the many will be too chill and tender and they'll be for the flow'ry way that leads to the broad gate and the great fire.

Matt. vii. 13: " Enter yee in at the straite gate, for wide is the gate, and broad is the way that leadeth to destruction, and many there be which goe in thereat" (*R*, "Enter ye by the narrovv gate: because brode is the gate"; *R* is the nearest to Shakespeare here).
Matt. xviii. 4: " Whosoeuer therefore shall humble himselfe as this litle childe, the same is the greatest in the kingdome of heauen." For " the flowery way" *cf.* Wisd. ii. 7-9 *G*: " Let vs fill our selues with costly wine and oyntments, and let not the floure of life passe by vs. Let vs crowne our

selues with rose buds afore they be withered. Let vs all
bee partakers of our wantonnesse " (*B* substantially in agreement).

See also II. i. 152-5 (Ecclus. xxxix. 19, 20 and Judges
vii. 2); II. iii. 244* (Ps. xviii. 4, cxvi. 3); II. v. 54 (Rom.
xii. 21).

HAMLET

1600-1. Printed in an imperfect and corrupt form in 1603.
First authentic edition 1604-5, of which a reprint was made in
1611. Folio text of 1623 was not printed from the 1604
Quarto but from a manuscript. Some think that the 1604-5
edition (usually called the 2nd Quarto) was directly printed
from Shakespeare's own manuscript, and that the Folio
version was derived from a manuscript copy of Shakespeare's
manuscript, and that it was from an adaptation of this copy
the 1st Quarto (1603) was in part derived.

Hamlet is the longest of all Shakespeare's plays: it has nearly
twice as many lines as *The Tempest*. Quotation from the Bible,
as well as from Juvenal, and reflection thereupon, help to
emphasize the Prince's scholarly and contemplative character.
The vein of Scriptural allusion is a development of that set in
All's Well. We are away from the gay allusion of Berowne or
the boisterous use of the Falstaff Plays.

Act I. ii. 90-6, 101.

KING.   and the survivor bound
In filial obligation for some term
To do obsequious sorrow; but to persever
In obstinate condolement is a course
Of impious stubbornness; 'tis unmanly grief;
It shows a will most incorrect to heaven,
A heart unfortified, or mind impatient,
    . . . Fie ! 'tis a fault to Heaven.

Observance of mourning for the dead depends on national
and local custom and not on any Scriptural injunction. At
the same time there is a resemblance so close to Ecclus.
xxxviii. 17-23 (see *Romeo and Juliet*, III. v. 73) as to suggest
that it is not accidental. See also Ecclus. xli. 3, 4 *G*: " Feare
not the iudgement of death: remember them that haue beene
before thee, and that come after: this is the ordinance of the
Lord ouer all flesh. And why wouldest thou be against the
pleasure of the most High ? whether it be tenne, or an hun-

dreth, or a thousand yeeres, there is no defence for life against the graue " (*B*, " Whether it be tenne, an hundred, or a thousande yeeres, death asketh not how long one hath liued "). " It shows a will most incorrect to heaven, A heart unfortified, or mind impatient " might be taken as a paraphrase of " And why wouldest thou be against the pleasure of the most High ?"

Ibid. 131-2.

HAM. Or that the Everlasting had not fix'd
His Canon 'gainst self-slaughter.

See Chapter VI. Refer to the List of Proper Names under " God " for " Everlasting."

Ibid. 133-4.

HAM. How weary, stale, flat and unprofitable
Seem to me all the uses of this world !

It is almost impossible to believe that this thought has not been inspired by Eccles. i. 14 *G*: " I haue considered all the works that are done vnder the sunne: and beholde, all is vanitie, and vexation of the spirite " (*B*, " Thus haue I considered all these thinges that come to passe vnder the sunne: and loe, they are all but vanitie and vexation of minde ").

Ibid. 244.

HAM. . . . *though hell itself should gape.

Cf. Isa. v. 14: " Therefore gapeth hell " (*G*, " hath inlarged it selfe ").

Act I. iii. 47-51.

OPH. Do not, as some ungracious pastors do,
Show me the steep and thorny way to heaven,
Whiles like a puff'd and reckless libertine
Himself the primrose path of dalliance treads
And recks not his own rede.

Cf. Matt. xxiii. 2, 3, 4: " The Scribes & the Pharisees sate in Moses seate: All therefore whatsoeuer they bid you obserue, that obserue and doe, but doe not ye after their workes: for they say, and do not. Yea, they binde together heauie burdens, and grieuous to be borne, and lay them on mens shoulders, but they themselues wil not moue them with (one) of their fingers." For the "steep and thorny way to heaven" *cf.* Matt. vii. 14: "Because straite is the gate, and narowe is the way which leadeth vnto life."

Ibid. 72.

POL. For the apparel oft proclaims the man.

The maxims of Polonius are in several instances quotations from *Euphues*; some bear resemblance to Lord Burleigh's Ten Precepts. The audience would recognize the source. One maxim is not unlike Ecclus. xix. 28: "A mans garment, laughter, and going, declare what he is."

Act I. iv. 39.

HAM. Angels and ministers of grace.

See Heb. i. 7: "He maketh his angels spirits, and his ministers a flame of fire," and Ps. civ. 4.

Act I. v. 92.

HAM. O all you host of heaven !

So the gods of the heathen are named by St. Stephen, Acts vii. 42: "and gaue them vp to worship the hoste of heauen."

Act II. ii. 323-8.

HAM. What piece of work is a man, how noble in reason, how infinite in faculties, in form and moving, how express and admirable, in action, how like an angel, in apprehension, how like a god, the beauty of the world, the paragon of animals !

Cf. Ps. viii. 4-6: "What is man, that thou art mindful of him : and the son of man, that thou visitest him ? Thou madest him lower than the angels: to crown him with glory and worship. Thou makest him to have dominion of the works of thy hands: and thou hast put all things in subjection under his feet." I have adopted Dover Wilson's suggestion as to punctuation of Hamlet's lines.

Ibid. 328-9.

HAM. And yet, to me, what is this quintessence of dust ?

For this and "man delights not me," *cf.* Eccles. iii. 18-20 *G*: "I considered in mine heart the state of the children of men that God had purged them: yet to see to, they are in themselues as beastes. For the condition of the children of men, and the condition of beastes are euen as one condition vnto them. As the one dyeth, so dyeth the other: for they haue all one breath, and there is no excellencie of man aboue the beast: for all is vanitie. All goe to one place, and all was of the dust, and all shall returne to the dust."

Ibid. 635-7.

HAM. The spirit that I have seen
May be a devil: and the devil hath power
T'assume a pleasing shape.

Another reference to 2 Cor. xi. 14. In the sixteenth century the controversy was whether ghosts were devils or were the souls of those in Purgatory. The former view was maintained in the Genevan Bible which, at " and Saul knewe that it was Samuel " (1 Sam. xxviii. 14), had this note: " To his imagination, albeit it was Satan, who to blinde his eyes tooke vpon him the forme of Samuel, as he can doe of an Angel of light." It is this belief that explains the perplexity of Hamlet and his indecision. The Bishops' adopted the Genevan note.

Act III. i. 78-80.

HAM. *But that the dread of something after death,
The undiscover'd country from whose bourne
No traveller returns.

Cf. Job x. 21-2: " Before I goe (thither from whence) I shall not turne againe, euen to the lande of darkenesse and shadowe of death: Yea a lande as darke as darkenesse it selfe, and into the shadowe of death where is none order, but the light (is there) as darkenesse." Job xvi. 22: " the way that I must goe is at hand, from whence I shal not turne againe." For the *G* of Job x. 21-2, see Chapter IV., pages 66-7. Also see Wisd. ii. 1: " in the death of a man there is no remedy, neither is there any man knowen to haue returned from the graue."

Hamlet had talked with a traveller from the " undiscover'd country." Dover Wilson explains the discrepancy as due to Hamlet's distrust of the Ghost (see II. ii. 635-7).

Act III. ii. 16. See Herod.

Ibid. 68-70.

> HAM. Since my dear soul was mistress of her choice
> And could of men distinguish her election
> *S'hath seal'd thee for herself.

For this figure of " sealing " *cf.* Ephes. iv. 30: " And grieue not the holy spirit of God, by whome ye are sealed vnto the day of redemption " (*R*, " and contristate not the holy Spirit of God: in vvhich you are signed vnto the day of redemption ").

Ibid. 265-6.

> OPH. Still better and worse.
> HAM. So you mistake your husbands.

The good Quarto reads " mistake your husbands " and this reading is substantially confirmed by the Folio. The corrupt Quarto of 1603 reads " must take " and it has been largely followed. Hamlet, in the sense of " so you commit the error of taking husbands," intends a cynical reference to *L, Matrimony*: " I N. take thee M. to my wedded husband, to have and to hold from this day forward, for better for worse." Ophelia stands for her whole sex.

Ibid. 355-6.

> HAM. And do still, by these pickers and stealers.

L, Catechism: " To keep my hands from picking and stealing." Dover Wilson suggests that the reference was intended to recall what follows: " and my tongue from evil speaking, lying and slandering." These were faults he imputed to his interlocutors.

Act III. iii. 37-8.

> KING. It hath the primal eldest curse upon't,
> A brother's murder !

In obvious reference to Cain's murder of Abel.

Ibid. 45-6.

> KING. Is there not rain enough in the sweet heavens
> To wash it white as snow ?

Ps. li. 7: " thou shalt wash me, and I shall be whiter than snow "; Isa. i. 18: " though your sinnes be as red as scarlet, they shall be as white as snowe."

Ibid. 51-6.

> KING.   But, oh, what form of prayer
> Can serve my turn ?   Forgive me my foul murder.
> That cannot be since I am still possess'd
> Of those effects for which I did the murder—
> My crown, mine own ambition and my queen.
> May one be pardon'd and retain th'offence ?

The whole of the King's soliloquy,—the incorruptibility of God's judgment, the demand for restitution, etc., is strongly paralleled in the Bible.

For the above, *cf.* Ecclus. xxxiv. 26-7: " He that washeth himselfe because of a dead bodie, and then toucheth the dead againe, what doeth his washing ?   So is it with a man that fasteth for his sinnes, and doth them againe: who will heare his prayer, or what doeth his fasting helpe him ?"   For a further consideration of this soliloquy of the King's see Chapter III., pages 53-4.

Ibid. 80.

> HAM. *A' took my father grossly, full of bread.

Ezek. xvi. 49 *G*: " Behold, this was the iniquitie of thy sister Sodom, Pride, fulnesse of bread, and abundance of idlenesse " (*B*, " fulnesse of meate ").

Act III. iv. 15.

> HAM. You are the Queen, your husband's brother's
>   wife.

The point lies in *L, The Table of Kindred and Affinity*: " A woman may not marry with her Husband's Brother."   It should be remembered that Elizabeth's legitimacy depended on the illegality of her father's marriage with his brother's widow.   The audience would thus sympathize with Hamlet's strong feelings.

Ibid. 34-5.

> HAM. Leave wringing of your hands.   Peace ! sit you
>   down,
> And let me wring your heart.

Cf. Joel ii. 13 *L*, Quoted at *Morning Prayer*: " Rente your heartes, and not your garmentes."

Ibid. 82.

> HAM. O shame, where is thy blush?

See Chapter II., page 33.

Ibid. 125-6.

> HAM. His form and cause conjoin'd, preaching to stones,
> Would make them capable.

Cf. the stones crying out in Luke xix. 40.

Act IV. ii. 5, 6.

> ROSEN. What have you done, my lord, with the dead body?
> HAM. Compounded it with dust, whereto 'tis kin.

Cf. Eccles. iii. 20 and *L, Burial*: " earth to earth, ashes to ashes, dust to dust."

Ibid. 24-6.

> ROSEN. I understand you not, my lord.
> HAM. I am glad of it: a knavish speech sleeps in a foolish ear.

Cf. Ecclus. xxii. 10: " Whoso telleth a foole of wisedome, is euen as a man which speaketh to one that is a sleepe, when hee hath tolde his tale, hee saith, What is the matter?"

Ibid. 30-2.

> HAM. *The king is a thing—
> GUILD. A thing, my lord?
> HAM. Of nothing.

" A thing of nothing " is not uncommon but see Ps. cxliv. 4: " Man is like a thing of nought " (*G*, " Man is like to vanitie "). Dover Wilson suggests that with the words following, " his time passeth away like a shadow," it is intended to indicate that the King's days are numbered.

Act IV. iii. 17-8.

> KING. Now, Hamlet, where's Polonius?
> HAM. At supper.

Cf. 2 King Henry VI., V. i. 214. Hamlet here, as the next line but one shows, is playing on the word " supper." In Rev. xix. 9: " Happie are they which are called vnto the supper of the Lambes marriage." When asked again, " Where is Polonius ?" he answers, " In heaven."

Act IV. v. 130-2.

> LAER. To hell, allegiance ! vows to the blackest devil !
> Conscience and grace to the profoundest pit !
> I dare damnation.

Cf. the " bottomlesse pit " of Rev. ix. 1 *et seq.*

Act V. i. 34, 40, 83. See Adam, Cain.

Ibid. 136.

> HAM. . . . 'tis for the dead, not for the quick.

Cf. L, Morning Prayer, Apostles' Creed: " he shall come to judge the quick and the dead." Also *Communion, Nicene Creed.*

Ibid. 248-52.

> DOCTOR. Her obsequies have been as far enlarg'd
> As we have warranty: her death was doubtful: etc.

See Chapter IV., pages 84-6.

Ibid. 262-4.

> LAER. . . . I tell thee, churlish priest,
> A minist'ring angel shall my sister be,
> When thou liest howling.

Laertes was trying to carry on the rite and then began to revile the Doctor for not taking up his part and in terms reminiscent of Christ's remark (also addressed to priests) in Matt. xxi. 31: " I say vnto you, that the Publicanes and the harlots go into the kingdome of God before you." For " When thou liest howling " *cf.* Matt. viii. 12: " there shall bee weeping and gnashing of teeth," among those cast out into outer darkness.

Ibid. 280-1.

> LAER. The devil take thy soul.
> HAM. Thou pray'st not well.

Some have assumed that this is a reference to Matt. v. 44. to pray for them that have hurt us, but it would seem rather to be that Hamlet reproves Laertes for praying to the devil.

Act V. ii. 9-11.

> HAM.   and that should learn us
> There's a divinity that shapes our ends,
> Rough-hew them how we will.

It is improbable that any passage of Scripture was in mind but see Prov. xvi. 9: " A man deuiseth a way in his heart: but it is the Lord that ordereth his goings." Hamlet's meaning is, Divine skill makes good our botches.

Ibid. 40.

> HAM. As love between them like the palm might
>   flourish.

Ps. xcii. 11: " The righteous shall flourish like a palm-tree."

Ibid. 232-3.

> HAM. . . . *there is special providence in the fall
>   of a sparrow.

Matt. x. 29 *G*: " Are not two sparrowes sold for a farthing, and one of them shall not fall on the ground without your Father?" (*R* substantially as *G*; *B*, " light on the ground ").

Ibid. 232, 233-7.

> HAM. . . . we defy augury; . . . If it be, 'tis not to come; if
> it be not to come, it will be now; if it be not now, yet it
> will come; the readiness is all; since no man of ought he
> leaves knows, what is't to leave betimes ?

Subject to alteration in punctuation, this is the reading of the 1604 Quarto. The Folio reads, " the readinesse is all, since no man ha's ought of what he leaues. What is't to leaue betimes?" If we accept the Folio reading, then 1 Tim. vi. 7 (read in the *Burial Service*) would apply: " We brought nothing into this world, neither may we cary anything out of this worlde." But I do not accept the Folio reading. I do not think it is in accord with what Hamlet has just been saying. Hamlet had a foreboding (ll. 222-3), but now he would despise all augury. What was to be was predestined; the fall of a sparrow was not accidental; our predestined fate would overtake us one time or another; if not now, then it was to come. To be prepared for any contingency was all we could do. Since then, in this life we did not know what a single day might bring forth, whether the event was to be fortunate or calamitous, what worse off were we in death of which we knew just as much as what the future in life had in store for us ? Why then should we fear to die our inevitable death sooner than later ? Hamlet's mood is first pessimistic and then fatalist, full of that omen which on the stage precedes catastrophe, and which keys up excitement in the audience. A theatrical device that never fails.

For " what is't to leave betimes?" perhaps Ecclus. xli. 4 *B* may be of interest: " Whether it be tenne, an hundred, or a thousande yeeres, death asketh not how long one hath liued."

Ibid. 372.

HAM. The rest is silence.

Carter says this has often been adduced as proof of unbelief in immortality. The term is a well-known Biblical one. See Ps. cxv. 17: " The dead praise not thee, O Lord: neither all they that go down into silence." 2 Esdras vii. 32: " those that dwell therein in silence."

See also I. i. 112 (Matt. vii. 3); II. ii. 559-63 (*L, Morning Prayer*, Ps. cxliii. 2, Ps. cxxx. 3); III. ii. 216-7 (Ecclus. xiii. 22); IV. iii. 55 (*L, Matrimony*, Eph. v. 31); V. i. 80 (Wisd. ii. 2).

TWELFTH NIGHT

1601-2. Evidently revised about 1605. First printed 1623. The Biblical allusions are all in the spirit of comedy. It is the first of a trio of plays wherein a certain sanctimonious type is mocked by a repetition of shibboleths in ridiculous circumstances.

Act I. iii. 2-3.

TOBY. I am sure care's an enemy to life.

Cf. Ecclus. xxx. 24: " Zeale and anger shorten the dayes of the life, carefulnes and sorow bring age before the time."

Act I. v. 14-6.

CLOWN. Well, God give them wisdom that have it: and those that are fools, let them use their talents.

An application of the Parable of the Talents, Matt. xxv. 28-9: " Take therefore the talent from him, and giue it vnto him which hath ten talents. For vnto euery one that hath, shalbe giuen."

Ibid. 30. See Eve.

Ibid. 35-7.

> CLOWN. Those wits, that think they have thee, do very oft prove fools: and I, that am sure I lack thee, may pass for a wise man.

Cf. 1 Cor. iii. 18: " If any man among you seeme (to himselfe) to be wise in this world, let him become a foole, that he may be wise."

Ibid. 135-6.

> TOBY. Let him be the devil an he will, I care not: " Give me Faith," say I.

That is, no matter if it is the devil that has appeared at the gate in the shape of the visitor, he (Sir Toby) relies for protection on faith and not on works. If any text can be said to have been in mind, Eph. vi. 16 will do as well as any: " Aboue all, taking the shield of fayth, wherewith ye may quench all the fierie dartes of the wicked."

Compare the pious sentiments of the intoxicated Cassio in *Othello*, II. iii. 106 *et seq.*, and see Chapter III., page 51.

Ibid. 227-8.

> VIOLA. . . . my words are as full of peace as matter.

For the phrase " full of matter " *cf.* Job xxxii. 18: " For I am ful of matter."

Act II. ii. 32-3.

> VIOLA. Alas ! our frailty is the cause, not we,
> For such as we are made of, such we be.

Cf. L, Collect (24th Sunday after Trinity): " that through thy bountiful goodness we may all be delivered from the bands of those şins, which by our frailty we have committed." *Cf.* also The Prelude to *Confirmation*, that formerly existed: " that partly by the frailtie of their own flesh."

Act II. iv. 38-9.

> DUKE.   whose fair flower,
> Being once display'd, doth fall that very hour.

Cf. Jas. i. 11: " For (as) the Sunne hath risen with heate, and the grasse hath withered, and his floure hath fallen away, and the beautie of the fashion of it hath perished."

Act II. v. 47.   See Jezabel.

Ibid. 207.

TOBY. *Wilt thou set thy foot o' my neck ?

As a token of complete subjugation this is so prominently associated with Joshua and the five kings that it is very probable the incident recorded in Josh. x. 24 was in mind: *G,* "And when they had brought out those kings vnto Ioshua, Ioshua called for al the men of Israel, and saide vnto the chiefe of the men of warre, which went with him, Come neere, set your feete vpon the necks " (*B,* "put").

Ibid. 212-4.

TOBY. Why, thou hast put him in such a dream, that when the image of it leaves him, he must run mad.

Cf. Ps. lxxiii. 19: " Yea, even like as a dream when one awaketh: so shalt thou make their image to vanish out of the city."

Act III. ii. 18-9, *III. iv.* 96-8.   See Noah.   See Legion.

Act III. iv. 109-11.

TOBY. What, man ! defy the devil; consider, he's an enemy to mankind.

See Jas. iv. 7: " resist the deuill, and he will flee from you "; 1 Pet. v. 8: " your aduersarie the deuil."   No useful purpose would be served by itemizing all the allusions to the devil in this baiting of Malvolio.   Obviously the narrative in Mark v. is principally in Maria's mind, though it is just possible Ecclus. xxi. 27: " When the vngodly curseth the blasphemer, he curseth his owne soule," may have been pointed at.   In a scene full of such high spirits orderly quotation would be impossible.

Ibid. 132.   See Sathan.

Act IV. ii. 21.

CLOWN. Peace in this prison !

Feste is here imitating the Priest who, in *L, Visitation of the Sick,* was directed on entering the sick person's house to say, " Peace be to this house."   Hence the commendation by Sir Toby.   Evidently in lines 26, 29, 30, Matt. xvii. 15 was in mind.

Ibid. 49.   See Egypt.

Act V. i. 11-19.

> ORSINO.   how doest thou, my good fellow?
> CLOWN. Truly, sir, the better for my foes, and the
>   worse for my friends.
> ORSINO. Just the contrary: the better for thy friends.
> CLOWN. No, sir, the worse.
> ORSINO. How can that be?
> CLOWN. *Marry, sir, they praise me,

Luke vi. 26: " Woe vnto you when men shal prayse you:
for so did their fathers to the false prophets " (*G*, " speake
well of you "; *R*, " blesse you "). See pages 68 and 75.

Ibid. 160-3.

> PRIEST. A contract of eternal bond of love
> Confirm'd by mutual joinder of your hands,
> Attested by the holy close of lips,
> Strengthen'd by interchangement of your rings.

These lines should be carefully noted.   It will be observed
from *L, Matrimony* that Sebastian and Olivia were wedded
and not merely betrothed, as might have been expected from
Act IV. iii. 26.   Hence Olivia's addressing Cesario as " Husband."   It is the " mutual joinder of the hands " that is
very important.   In the betrothal the joinder of hands is
not mutual, in the sense that both equally and at one and
the same time do not take hold of each other's right hand.
Note the words " attested " and " strengthen'd " which thus
explain the introduction of features that do not belong to
the rite.

Ibid. 294.   See Belzebub.

Ibid. 401, 3, 5.

> SONG. When that I was and a little tiny boy,
> A foolish thing was but a toy,
> But when I came to man's estate.

Were the opening lines of the song inspired by the striking
passage in 1 Cor. xiii. 11: " When I was a childe, I spake as
a childe, I vnderstoode as a childe, I imagined as a childe: but
as soone as I was a man, I put away childishnesse "?   (The

resemblance of *G* is more marked: " I thought as a childe: but when I became a man, I put away childish things." Perhaps the resemblance of *R* is greater still : " Vvhen I vvas a litle one, I spake as a litle one, I vnderstood as a litle one, I thought as a litle one. But vvhen I vvas made a man, I did avvay the things that belonged to a litle one.")

See also I. v. 80* (2 Sam. xxii. 5, Ps. xviii. 3 *B*); *ibid.* 271-2 (Ecclus. x. 7, 14, 18); II. ii. 28-9 (2 Cor. xi. 14).

TROILUS AND CRESSIDA

1602-3. First printed in 1609, and there were two issues of the edition. Again printed in 1623 in the Folio. Both editions are good, but the exact relationship between them is a matter of some controversy still undetermined. The early stage history of the play is wrapped in some mystery, and whether presented at all in the public theatre is not absolutely certain. It may have had no more than private audiences. Scriptural quotations in quantity are not to be expected, but, such as they are, they are not without interest.

Act I. iii. 31.

NESTOR. *With due observance of thy godlike seat.

In the Bishops' " seat " is continually used instead of " throne " for the Deity. See Matt. v. 34: " for it is Gods seat " (*G* and *R*, " throne "), and Matt. xxiii. 22: " the seate of God " (*G* and *R*, " throne ").

Ibid. 241-2.

ÆNEAS. The worthiness of praise distains his worth,
If that the prais'd himself bring the praise forth.

These two lines are quoted here because, on account of the thought contained, they and lines like them are frequently represented as Biblical. There are at least three English proverbs to the same effect, and saws of the kind must have existed ever since a tongue could toll the praise of its owner and another tongue could add its tart comment. See again Act II. iii. 166-9. Compare Prov. xxvii. 2: " Let another man prayse thee, and not thine owne mouth, yea, other folkes, & not thine owne lippes."

15

Act II. ii. 56-7.

HECTOR.   'Tis mad idolatry
To make the service greater than the god.

Cf. Matt. xxiii. 19 *G*: " Ye fooles and blinde, whether
is greater, the offering, or the altar which sanctifieth the
offering?" (*B* and *R* substitute " gift " for " offering.")

Ibid. 81-3.

TROIL.   Why, she is a pearl
Whose price hath launch'd above a thousand ships
And turn'd crown'd kings to merchants.

The " pearl of great price " of Matt. xiii. 45-6 was a
favourite metaphor of Shakespeare's time. The Gospel
text is, " Againe, the kingdome of heauen is like vnto a
marchant man, seeking goodly pearles: Which when he had
found one precious pearle, went and solde all that he had,
and bought it."

Ibid. 172.

HECTOR. Have ears more deaf than adders to the
        voice.

Ps. lviii. 4-5: " even like the deaf adder that stoppeth her
ears; Which refuseth to hear the voice of the charmer:
charm he never so wisely."

Act III. i. 1-8, 13-16.

PAND. Friend, you, pray you, a word. Do not you follow
the young Lord Paris?
SERV. Ay, sir, when he goes before me.
PAND. You depend upon him, I mean?
SERV. Sir, I do depend upon the Lord.
PAND. You depend upon a noble gentleman; I must needs
praise him.
SERV. The Lord be praised. . . .
SERV. I hope I shall know your honour better?
PAND. I do desire it.
SERV. You are in the state of grace?

This servant is, as anybody can understand, playing on
the cant phrases of fervent devotees, and the point would
lose nothing in gesture and tone of voice. " You are in the
state of grace " after " I do desire it " (taken by the Servant

to be a desire that his honour might be better) addressed to
the disreputable Pandarus would gain by the reply, " Grace !
not so, friend: honour and lordship are my titles." The
ridicule of the cant phrases of zealots in *Twelfth Night*,
I. v. 135-6 and *Othello*, II. iii. 106 should be compared with
this passage here. See Chapter III., page 51.

Ibid. 148.

    PAND. . . . *is love a generation of vipers ?

    Matt. iii. 7, xii. 34, xxiii. 33, Luke iii. 7. This last reads:
" O generation of vipers, who hath forewarned you to flee
from the wrath to come ?" (*B* has " generation " in all
except Matt. xii. 34; *G*, " generations " in all except Matt.
xxiii. 33; and *R*, " brood " or " broodes.")

Act III. iii. 153-5.

    ULYS.   Take the instant way,
    For honour travels in a straight so narrow,
    Where one but goes abreast.

    Apparently in reminiscence of Matt. vii. 14: " Because
straite is the gate, and narowe is the way which leadeth vnto
life."

    The Quarto and Folio reading " straight " is retained here
instead of " strait " usually adopted by editors. The meaning in my opinion is governed by the word " instant " in
the line before, which means quickest, and therefore I take
our line to imply that honour travels in a straight path so
narrow, etc.

Act IV. i. 75-6.

    PARIS. Fair Diomed, you do as chapmen do
    Dispraise the thing that you desire to buy.

    Cf. Prov. xx. 14: " It is naught, it is naught (sayeth he
that buyeth) but when he commeth to his owne house,
then he boasteth of his (peniworth)."

Act IV. ii. 103-6.

    CRESS.   I have forgot my father;
    I know no touch of consanguinity:
    No kin, no love, no blood, no soul so near me
    As the sweet Troilus.

    In obvious elaboration of Matt. xix. 5: " For this cause
shall a man leaue his father and his mother, and shall be

knit to his wife: and they twaine shall be one flesh." But see also 1 Esdras iv. 21: " Yea, hee ieopardeth his life with his wife, and remembreth neither father nor mother, nor countrey."

Act IV. iv. 80.

>   TROIL. *Alas ! a kind of godly jealousy.

2 Cor. xi. 2: " For I am ielous ouer you with godly ielousie " (*R,* " for I emulate you vvith the emulation of God ").

Act V. ii. 65.

>   TROIL. ☉ beauty, where is thy faith ?

Cf. Luke viii. 25: " And he sayde vnto them, Where is your faith ?"

See also III. iii. 70-8 (Ecclus. xiii. 22).

OTHELLO

>   1603-4. First printed 1622. The Folio edition in 1623 was printed from a manuscript and not from the previous edition. The 1623 edition is generally held to be the premier edition, although the Quarto is quite a good text. A large proportion of the Biblical allusions proceed from the mouth of Iago.

Act I. ii. 9-10.

>   IAGO. That, with the little godliness I have,
>   *I did full hard forbear him.

Col. iii. 13: " Forbearing one another " (*R,* " supporting "). Also Eph. iv. 2 *B.*

Act II. i. 64-5.

>   CASS. And in th'essential vesture of creation
>   Does tire the ingener.

It is impossible to make a tolerable reading of these difficult lines. Obviously the intention is to represent Desdemona as the top of creation. This has led one commentator to deduce that in speaking of the vesture of creation Shakespeare had in mind Ps. cii. 26-7: " They shall perish, but thou shalt endure: they all shall wax old as doth a garment; And as a vesture shalt thou change them, and they shall be changed."

Act II. iii. 75.

IAGO. *Man's life's but a span.

Ps. xxxix. 6: " Behold, thou hast made my days as it were a span long " (*G*, " as an hand bredth ").

Ibid. 106-8.

CASS. Well, God's above all; and there be souls must be saved, and there be souls must not be saved.

This is the interpretation placed by extreme Calvinists on Rom. ix. 18: " So hath he mercie on whom he will, and whom he will he hardeneth." (See *Measure for Measure*, I. ii. 131-2.) Compare the intoxicated Sir Toby's " 'Give me faith,' say I," *Twelfth Night*, I. v. 136.

Ibid. 110-15.

CASS. For mine own part—no offence to the General, nor any man of quality,—I hope to be saved.
IAGO. And so do I too, lieutenant.
CASS. Ay, but, by your leave, not before me: the lieutenant is to be saved before the ancient.

" I hope to be saved " was originally derived from Rom. viii. 24: " For we are saued by hope." See Chapter III. page 50.

Ibid. 299-300.

CASS. It hath pleas'd the devil drunkenness to give place to the devil wrath.

Cf. Eph. iv. 27: " Neither giue place to the deuil." Ecclus. xxxi. 29-30 *G*: " But wine drunken with excesse, maketh bitternesse of minde with brawlings and scoldings. Drunkennesse encreaseth the courage of a foole, till he offende: it diminisheth his strength and maketh wounds." Drunkenness ànd wrath were two of the Seven Deadly Sins and as such figured in the Moralities. The whole of Cassio's apostrophe on drunkenness finds a close parallel in Ecclus. xxxi. 25-31.

Ibid. 315-6.

IAGO. Come, come: good wine is a good familiar creature, if it be well us'd.

This observation depends on no particular warrant, but it is interesting to compare it with Ecclus. xxxi. 28: " Wine was made from the beginning to make men glad, and not for drunkennes: wine measurably drunken, is a reioycing of the soule and body: a measurable drinking, is health to soule and body."

Ibid. 351-3.

> IAGO.   And then for her
> To win the Moor, were't to renounce his Baptism,
> *All seals and symbols of redeemed sin.

This is a statement of the Anglican doctrine of the Remission of Sins and the gift of the Spirit through Baptism; the mention of "seals" and "symbols" is important. *Cf.* Eph. iv. 30: "And grieue not the holy spirit of God, by whome ye are sealed vnto the day of redemption" (*R*, "And contristate not the holy Spirit of God: in vvhich you are signed vnto the day of redemption").

Act III. i. 48-9.

> EMIL. That he you hurt is of great fame in Cyprus,
> And great affinity.

That is "he is of powerful kindred." "Affinity" is frequently used in the Bible to denote connections by marriage, though less in the Authorised than in its predecessors. Shakespeare only uses the noun this once. *Cf.* both *B* and *G*, Ruth ii. 20: "The man is nigh vnto vs, and of our affinitie." The Authorised reads "of our next kinsmen."

Act III. iii. 155-6.

> IAGO. Good name in man and woman, dear my lord,
> Is the immediate jewel of their souls.

Cf. Prov. xxii. 1: "A good name is more to be desired then great riches"; Ecclus. xli. 12: "Labour to get thee a good name: for that shal continue surer by thee then a thousand great treasures of golde" (*G* omits "good"). The probability that Iago is quoting Scripture is increased by his confessed policy to "suggest at first with heavenly shows." *Cf.* "Is not that treasure, which before all other is most regarded of honest persons, the good fame and name of man and woman, lost through whoredom?" (Homily against Adultery, Part II.).

Ibid. 203-4.

IAGO. their best conscience
Is not to leave't undone, but kept unknown.

Cf. L, Morning Prayer: "We have left undone those things which we ought to have done."

Ibid. 382-4.

OTH. Thou shouldst be honest.
IAGO. I should be wise: for honesty's a fool
And loses that it works for.

See the Parable of the Unjust Steward, Luke xvi. 8: "And the Lorde commended the vniust Stewarde, because he had done wisely." The Unjust Steward symbolized the servant that was wise though dishonest.

Act IV. ii. 14-5.

EMIL. If any wretch have put this in your head,
Let heaven requite it with the serpent's curse.

That is that the wretch should receive the curse meted out to the serpent. See Gen. iii. 14: "Because thou hast done this, thou art cursed aboue all cattell, and aboue euery beast of the fielde: vpon thy belly shalt thou goe, and dust shalt thou eate all the dayes of thy life."

Ibid. 46-52.

OTH. Had it pleas'd Heaven
To try me with affliction, had he rain'd
All kinds of sores and shames on my bare head:
Steep'd me in poverty to the very lips,
Given to captivity, me, and my utmost hopes,
I should have found in some place of my soul
A drop of patience.

A comparison with Job whose sons were killed, his cattle captured, his wealth all lost, and his body all covered with boils and sores, and who yet retained patience.

Ibid. 58-61.

OTH. *The fountain from the which my current runs
Or else dries up: to be discarded thence !
Or keep it as a cistern for foul toads
To knot and gender in.

Prov. v. 15-8 *G*. See Chapter IV., pages 67-8.

Ibid. 81-4.

> DES.   No, as I am a Christian.
> If to preserve this vessel for my lord
> From any other foul unlawful touch
> Be not to be a strumpet, I am none.

 1 Thess. iv. 3-4: " that yee should absteine from fornication: That euery one of you should know how to possesse
his vessell in holinesse and honour."

Ibid. 90-1.   See Peter.

Ibid. 152-3.

> DES. If ere my will did trespass 'gainst his love,
> Either in discourse of thought, or actual deed.

See Chapter II., pages 34-5.

Act V. ii. 46.

> OTH. *Peace, and be still !

Mark iv. 39. Carter thought this reading was confined
to Tindale and Geneva; he was misled by the " English
Hexapla." " Peace, and be still " was the normal reading
of all Tudor versions, including the Great Bible and the
Bishops', before the appearance of the Rheims. The
Authorised copied the Rheims reading.

Ibid. 130.

> OTH. She turn'd to folly, and she was a whore.

This identification of " folly " with " whore " is Biblical.
See Deut. xxii. 21: " because she hath wrought follie in
Israel, to play the whore."

Ibid. 132.

> OTH. She was false as water.

The treachery of water is old, as old as Gen. xlix. 4, where
Jacob speaks of Reuben as " Vnstable as water " (*G*, " light
as water ").

Ibid. 345-7.   See Judean.

Ibid. 346-7.

OTH.   threw a pearl away
Richer than all his tribe.

An allusion to the Pearl of Great Price of Matt. xiii. 45-6.
See Chapter V., pages 92-3 n.

See also I. i. 155* (Ps. xviii. 4); II. iii. 359-62 (Matt. iv.,
Luke iv.); *ibid.* 369 (Ecclus. xiii. 1); V. ii. 194 (*L, Matrimony*, Eph. v. 24).

MEASURE FOR MEASURE

1604-5. First printed 1623. The Biblical interest of the
play is large. It is the only play of Shakespeare's with a title
based on Scripture. Exception was taken by Dr. Johnson to
the views on death expressed by the Duke in the habit of a
friar (see Act III. i.). Others have centred on Angelo and
have attempted to identify him as a Puritan, which, in the
historical sense of the term, he was not. It is one of the
seven plays in which the name of God is not mentioned,
although it is evident in several places that the name of God
did stand in the original. A remarkable feature of the play,
having regard to the large Scriptural interest, is the absence of
any Biblical proper name.

NOTE.—The title of the play is the popular adaptation of
Matt. vii. 2: " and with what measure yee mete, it shalbe
measured to you againe."

Act I. i. 29-40, 43.

The Duke in his opening speech makes an application of
The Parable of the Talents. As in the Parable, the Duke is
about to go on a journey and he summons his servants to
him and commits his powers to them. See Matt. xxv. 15
et seq.

15: " And vnto one he gaue fiue talents, to an other two,
& to another one, to euery man after his abilitie, and straight-
way tooke his iourney." 27: "& then at my comming
shoulde I haue receiued mine owne with vantage."

Act I. ii. 4-6.

1 GENT. Heaven grant us its peace, but not the King of
Hungary's.
2 GENT. Amen.

Cf. L, Litany: " Grant us thy peace."

Ibid. 25-8.

> 1 GENT. I think, or in any religion.
> LUCIO. Ay, why not? Grace is grace, despite of all
> controversy. As for example: Thou thyself art a wicked
> villain, despite of all grace.

Cf. Rom. xi. 6: " If it bee of grace, then is it not nowe of
workes: for then grace is no more grace."

Ibid. 131-2.

> CLAUD. *The words of heaven: on whom it will, it
> will:
> On whom it will not, so: yet still, 'tis just.

Rom. ix. 15 *G*: " I will haue mercie on him, to whom I
will shewe mercie: and will haue compassion on him, on
whom I will haue compassion." (*B* is less emphatic: " I
will shewe mercie, to whom so euer I shew mercie: and will
haue compassion, on whom so euer I haue compassion,"
though in Exod. xxxiii. 19 it reads as does the Genevan here
in *Romans*.) See also verse 18 for "will not": *Othello*,
II. iii. 106-8.
St. Paul is quoting God, as in Exod. xxxiii. 19; Claudio
referred first to the demi-god Authority and that reminded
him of the words of God himself.

Act I. iii. 52-3.

> DUKE. . . . or that his appetite
> Is more to bread than stone.

The contrast of bread with stone is due to Matt. vii. 9:
" What man is there of you, if his sonne aske bread, wil he
giue him a stone?"

Act II. ii. 29-33.

> ISAB. There is a vice, that most I do abhor,
> And most desire should meet the blow of justice:
> For which I would not plead, but that I must;
> For which I must not plead, but that I am
> At war, 'twixt will and will not.

This passage gave Johnson some difficulty which a reference to Rom. vii. might have resolved. St. Paul laments
that owing to his carnal nature he does that of which he does
not approve, and that which is against his will (verse 15), so

that in verse 23 he is " rebelling against the lawe of my mind "
(*R*, " repugning "). Isabella means she is disinclined to
plead but that she is compelled by natural ties; yet her plead-
ing is forbidden by principle, but that the law of her affections conflicts with the law of her mind and inclination.

Ibid. 73-5.

> Isab. Why, all the souls that were, were forfeit once:
> And he that might the vantage best have took
> Found out the remedy.

Bp. Warburton characterized the first line as false divinity,
he would have had " are " for " were." Henley's reply
was that in this instance the player was the better divine.
Isabella means that all were forfeit before the Redemption
upon the Cross. *Cf. L, Communion:* " to suffer death upon
the cross for our redemption."

Ibid. 75-7.

> Isab.   How would you be,
> If he, which is the top of judgment, should
> But judge you as you are ?

Cf. Ezek. vii. 27: " I will doe vnto them after their owne
wayes, according to their owne iudgements will I iudge
them: and they shall know that I am the Lord." Ps. cxliii. 2,
quoted *L, Morning Prayer:* " Enter not into iudgemente with
thy seruaunts, O Lord, for no fleshe is righteous in thy syght."
Also Rom. iii. 20: " Because that by the deedes of the lawe,
there shall no flesh bee iustified in his sight."

Ibid. 79.

> Isab. Like man new made.

Cf. L, Baptism : " that the new man may be raised up in
him." It was strange that Bp. Warburton and Dr. Johnson
should have overlooked the man made new by Baptism when
explaining the phrase.

Ibid. 117-22.

> Isab.   but man, proud man,
> Drest in a little brief authority,
> Most ignorant of what he's most assur'd,
> His glassy essence, like an angry ape,
> Plays such fantastic tricks before high heaven,
> As makes the angels weep.

Grotius says that the Rabbis taught that the angels wept because of men's sins. For the opposite figure of joy in the presence of the angels of God, see Luke xv. 10.

Ibid. 136-41.

> ISAB.   Go to your bosom:
> Knock there, and ask your heart, what it doth know
> That's like my brother's fault: if it confess
> A natural guiltiness, such as is his,
> Let it not sound a thought upon your tongue
> Against my brother's life.

Cf. the appeal to the conscience of those accusing the woman taken in adultery: John viii. 3-11.

Ibid. 157-9.

> ISAB. *Heaven keep your honour safe.
> ANGEL.   Amen:
> For I am going that way to temptation,
> Where prayers cross.

It would not have been necessary to notice this, had not the passage puzzled Johnson and emendation was actually proposed. "Lead us not into temptation" of the Lord's Prayer is crossed by Angelo's desire to see Isabella on the morrow and thus encounter temptation anew. As to Isabella's valediction, *cf.* Eph. ii. 8: "For by grace are ye made safe "(*G*, "are yee saued"; also *R*, subst. as *G*).

Ibid. 170-2.

> ANGEL.   Having waste ground enough,
> Shall we desire to raze the sanctuary,
> And pitch our evils there?

See Chapter II., pages 31-3, and *King Henry VIII.*, II. i. 66-7.

Act II. iii. 3-5.

> DUKE. *Bound by my charity, and my blest order,
> I come to visit the afflicted spirits
> Here in the prison.

Cf. "preached vnto the spirits that were in prison," I Pet. iii. 19 (*R*, "preached to them also that vvere in prison ").

Ibid. 19-20.

> DUKE. Repent you, fair one, of the sin you carry ?
> JUL. I do, and bear the shame most patiently.

Cf. Ps. xciv. 13. " That thou mayest give him patience in time of adversity " (*G*, " That thou mayest giue him rest from the dayes of euill ").

Ibid. 30-4.

> DUKE. 'Tis meet so, daughter, but lest you do repent
> As that the sin hath brought you to this shame,
> Which sorrow is always toward ourselves, not heaven,
> Showing we would not spare heaven, as we love it,
> But as we stand in fear.

The thought here may have been suggested by 2 Cor. vii. 10: " For godly sorowe causeth repentance vnto saluation, not to be repented of: but the sorowe of the worlde causeth death." Isa. xxix. 14: " For as much as this people, when they be in trouble, do honour me with their mouth, & with their lips, but their hart is farre from me, and the feare which they haue vnto me, proceedeth of a commandement that is taught of men." (*G* omits " when they be in trouble " and otherwise differs somewhat but not materially.)

Act II. iv. 4-7.

> ANGEL.   Heaven in my mouth,
> As if I did but only chew his name:
> And in my heart, the strong and swelling evil
> Of my conception.

It is very evident that " Heaven " has been substituted for " God " and that Shakespeare originally wrote " God in my mouth." See Isa. xxix. 14 *ante,* Matt. xv. 8: " This people draweth nigh vnto me with their mouth, and honoureth me with their lips: howbeit, their heart is farre from mee."

Ibid. 122.

> ANGEL. *We are all frail.

Ecclus. viii. 5: " but remember that wee are fraile euery one " (*G*, " all worthy blame ").

Act III. i. 2-4.

> CLAUDIO. *The miserable have no other medicine
> But only hope:
> I have hope to live, and am prepar'd to die.

Cf. Job v. 16 *G*: " So that the poore hath his hope "
(*B*, " He is the hope of the poore "); Job xvii. 13 *G*: " Though
I hope, yet the graue shall be mine house " (*B*, " Though
I tary neuer so much "). Note the Duke (ll. 16-7) alludes to
the next verse.

Ibid. 6-8.

> DUKE.   Reason thus with life:
> If I do lose thee, I do lose a thing
> That none but fools would keep.

Cf. John xii. 25: " He that loueth his life, shal lose it: & he
that hateth his life in this worlde, shal keepe it vnto life
eternall."

Ibid. 16-7.

> DUKE. For thou dost fear the soft and tender fork
> Of a poor worm.

Cf. Job xvii. 14: " I sayd to corruption, Thou art my father:
and to the wormes, You are my mother, and my sister."

Ibid. 17-9.

> DUKE.   *Thy best of rest is sleep
> And that thou oft provok'st: yet grossly fear'st
> Thy death, which is no more.

Job xiv. 12 *G*: " So man sleepeth and riseth not: for he
shall not wake againe, nor be raised from his sleepe till the
heauen be no more."
Dr. Johnson characterized " Thy death, which is no more,"
as " in the friar is impious, in the reasoner is foolish, and in
the poet trite and vulgar." Johnson forgot that as sovereign
the Duke knew, as did the audience, that Claudio would not
be executed. Claudio's opening remark strongly suggested
Job, so it was not unnatural for the Duke also to quote from
Job. The whole tone of the Duke's remarks is enforced by
Ecclus. xli. 3: " Be not thou afraid of death, remember
them that haue bene before thee, & that come after thee."

Ibid. 25.

DUKE. If thou art rich, thou'rt poor.

Rev. iii. 17: " Because thou sayest, I am rich, & increased with goods, and haue neede of nothing: and knowest not how that thou art wretched, and miserable, & poore, and blind, and naked."

Ibid. 26-8.

DUKE. For like an ass, whose back with ingots bows,
Thou bear'st thy heavy riches but a journey
And death unloads thee.

L, Burial, 1 Tim. vi. 6: " We brought nothing into this world, neither may we cary anything out of this worlde." Ps. xlix. 17: " For he shall carry nothing away with him when he dieth: neither shall his pomp follow him."

Ibid. 42-3.

CLAUD. To sue to live, I find I seek to die,
And, seeking death, find life.

See Matt. xvi. 25: " For whosoeuer wil saue his life, shal lose it: againe, whosoeuer will lose his life for my sake, shall finde it." Also Matt. x. 39, etc.

Act III. ii. 191-3.

LUCIO. The Duke yet would have dark deeds darkly answered. He would never bring them to light.

Cf. Luke xii. 3: " Therfore, what so euer ye haue spoken in darknesse, shalbe heard in the light."

Ibid. 283-4.

DUKE. He, who the sword of Heaven will bear,
Should be as holy, as severe.

See Rom. xiii. 4: " for he beareth not the sword in vaine: For hee is the minister of God, reuenger of wrath on him that doeth euill."

Ibid. 293-4.

DUKE. O, what may man within him hide,
Though angel on the outward side ?

A common thought, but see the comparison of the Scribes and Pharisees with painted sepulchres: " which in deede appeare beautifull outward, but are within ful of dead (mens) bones, and of all filthinesse" (Matt. xxiii. 27). This comparison of Angelo seemed almost to have been in Isabella's mind in Act III. i. 90-1.

Act IV. ii. 1-5.

>PROV. Come hither, sirrah. Can you cut off a man's head?
>CLOWN. *If the man be a bachelor, sir, I can: but if he be a married man, he's his wife's head, and I can never cut off a woman's head.

A reference to Eph. v. 23 *G*: "For the husband is the wiues head" (*B*, "head of the wife"; *R*, "head of the woman"). 1 Cor. xi. 3: "the man is the womans head."

Ibid. 69-70.

>CLAUD. *As fast lock'd up in sleep, as guiltless labour,
>When it lies starkly in the traveller's bones.

Eccles. v. 11 *G*, 1595 and 1598 roman letter quarto editions: "The sleepe of him that trauelleth, is sweete" (*G* 1560 and all black letter editions, "trauaileth"; *G* roman letter 1576, 1587, 1590, etc., "traueileth"; *B*, "A labouring man sleepeth sweetely"). See Chapter IV., page 69.

Act IV. iv. 36-7.

>ANGEL. Alack, when once our grace we have forgot,
>Nothing goes right; we would, and we would not.

Cf. Rom. vii. 15, 16: "for what I would, that doe I not. . . . If I doe nowe that which I would not"; Gal. v. 17, *L, Epistle, 14th Sunday after Trinity*: "For the fleshe lusteth contrary to the spirite, and the spirite contrary to the fleshe; these are contrary one to the other, so that ye cannot doe what soeuer ye would."

Act V. i. 45-6.

>ISAB.   for truth is truth
>To th' end of reck'ning.

See 1 Esdras iv. 38: "As for the trueth it endureth, and is alway strong, it liueth, and conquereth for euermore world without ende."

See also I. ii. 6-17 (*L, Catechism*, Exod. xx. 13); III. i. 81-3 (Rev. xxi. 9, Ecclus. xli. 2); *ibid.* 214-5 (Prov. xxviii. 1); V. i. 109-13 (Rom. ii. 1-3); *ibid.* 398-9 (Ecclus. xli. 2); *ibid.* 410-12 (Exod. xxi. 24-5, Matt. vii. 2).

KING LEAR

1605-6. First printed in 1608. Reprinted in 1619. Printed in 1623 Folio from manuscript, and from 1608 Quarto.

Act I. i. 93-4.

> CORD.   I cannot heave
> My heart into my mouth.

There is something of Cordelia's meaning in Ecclus. xxi. 26: " The heart of fooles is in their mouth: but the mouth of the wise is in his heart."

Ibid. 253.

> FRANCE. Fairest Cordelia, that art most rich being poor.

Cf. 2 Cor. vi. 10: " as poore, and yet making many rich: as hauing nothing, and yet possessing all thinges " (*R*, " as needie, but enriching many ").

Ibid. 284-5.

> CORD. Who covers faults, at last with shame derides:
> Well may you prosper !

Cf. Prov. xxviii. 13: " He that hideth his sinnes, shal not prosper " (Authorised, " covereth ").

Act I. ii. 119-25.

> GLOUC. . . . brothers divide; in cities, mutinies; in countries, discord; in palaces, treason; and the bond crack'd 'twixt son and father. This villain of mine comes under the prediction; there's son against father; the King falls from bias of nature; there's father against child.

Evidently with reference to Mark xiii. 8-12: " For there shall nation rise against nation, and kingdome against kingdome . . . these are the beginnings of sorowes. 12 The brother shall betray the brother to death, & the father the sonne: and the children shall rise against their fathers and mothers, & shal put them to death." See also Mic. vii. 6 (*King Richard III.*, V. iv. 37-9).

Act I. iv. 17.

> KENT. . . . to fear judgment.

This phrase has caused some difficulty. " Judgment " is used in the Biblical sense. *Cf.* Ps. i. 6: " Therefore the

16

ungodly shall not be able to stand in the judgment "; Jer.
viii. 7 G: " my people knoweth not the iudgement of the
Lord " (B, " the time of the punishment "). Kent means
that he fears God.

Act II. iv. 68-9.

>   FOOL. We'll set thee to school to an ant, to teach thee
>   there's no labouring i' th' winter.

It is interesting to note that in the famous passage in
Prov. vi. 6-8, in none of the popular contemporary versions
occurred the term " ant." In G it was " pismire," and in
C and B it was " Emmet." In the Authorised it is " ant."
In B it reads: " Go to the Emmet, thou sluggard, consider
her wayes, and learne to be wise. . . . Yet in the sommer
she prouideth her meate, and gathereth her foode together
in the haruest." This might be another example of Shakespeare's possible influence on the Authorised.

Act III. iv. 79-82.

>   EDGAR. . . . obey thy parents; keep thy words justly; swear
>   not; commit not with man's sworn spouse; set not thy
>   sweet heart on proud array.

Edgar in his feigned madness quotes a number of Biblical
injunctions.
Eph. vi. 1: " Children, obey your parents "; Deut.
xxiii. 23: " But that which is once gone out of thy lips, thou
must keepe, and doe "; Matt. v. 34: " Sweare not at al ";
Catechism: " Thou shalt not commit adultery "; 1 Tim. ii. 9:
" Likewise also the women, that they aray themselues in
comely apparell, with shamefastnesse and discreete beha-
uiour, not in braided heare, either golde, or pearles, or
costly aray " (G, " and modestie, not with broyded haire,
or golde, or pearles, or costly apparell "; R, " gorgeous
apparel ").

Ibid. 105-6.

>   LEAR. *Is man no more than this ? Consider him
>   well.

Cf. Heb. ii. 6 G: " What is man, that thou shouldest
be mindefull of him ! or the sonne of man that thou wouldest
consider him !" (B and R, " visitest ").

Act III. vi. 84-6.

> LEAR. . . . only I do not like the fashion of your garments:
> you will say they are Persian; but let them be chang'd.

See Chapter II., page 31.

Act IV. vi. 101-3.

> LEAR. *To say " ay " and " no " to every thing that I
> said ! " Ay " and " No " too was no good divinity.

That " Ay " and " No " is not good divinity is made clear
in 2 Cor. i. 18-9: " Yea God is faithfull, for our preaching
to you, was not yea, and nay.   For Gods sonne Iesus Christ
. . . was not yea and nay, but in him it was yea." (*G* reads
" word " for " preaching "; instead of " yea " and " nay," *R*
has " It is " and " It is not.")

Ibid. 112-4.

> LEAR.   What was thy cause ?
> Adultery ?
> Thou shalt not die.   Die for adultery ?   No.

Doubtless in allusion to the penalty prescribed for adultery
in Lev. xx. 10, also John viii. 5.

Ibid. 183-8.

> LEAR.   we came crying hither,
> Thou know'st, the first time that we smell the air,
> We wawl and cry.   I will preach to thee: mark.
> GLOUC. Alack, alack the day !
> LEAR. When we are born, we cry that we are come
> To this great stage of fools.

Cf. Wisd. vii. 3: " And when I was borne, I receiued like
ayre as other men, and fell vpon the earth which is of
like nature, crying & weeping at the first as all other doe.
6. All men then haue one entrance vnto life, and one
going out in like maner."

Act V. iii. 16-7.

> LEAR. *And take upon's the mystery of things
> As if we were God's spies.

Cf. Dan. ii. 29: " so hee that is the opener of mysteries,
telleth thee what is for to come."   In each case " mystery "
means a knowledge of events to come. *Cf.* also Ps. cxxxix. 2-3:

" and spiest out all my ways. For lo, there is not a word in my tongue: but thou, O Lord, knowest it altogether." (*G* differs widely.)

Ibid. 172-5.

> EDGAR. The gods are just, and of our pleasant vices
> Make instruments to plague us:
> The dark and vicious place where thee he got
> Cost him his eyes.

The idea that by means of our vices we are punished by God is Biblical. See Wisd. xii. 23: " Wherefore, whereas men haue liued dissolutely and vnrighteously, thou hast punished them sore with their owne abominations." Wisd. xi. 16: " wherwithal a man sinneth, by the same also shal he be punished." Jer. ii. 19: " Thine owne wickednesse shall reprooue thee . . . that thou mayest know and vnderstand how euil and hurtfull a thing it is that thou hast forsaken the Lord thy God, and hast not feared me."

Ibid. 265-6.

> KENT. Is this the promis'd end ?
> EDGAR. Or image of that horror ?

This might be taken to be in allusion to Matt. xxiv. 6-13: " It will come to passe, that yee shal heare of warres, and rumors of warres . . . but the end is not yet. . . . 8. All these are the beginning of sorowes. 9. Then shall they put you to trouble, and shal kill you." See 1 Pet. iv. 7: " The end of al things is at hand."

See also I. i. 100 (*L, Catechism*); IV. ii. 50-1 (Matt. v. 39, Luke vi. 29).

MACBETH

1605-6. First printed 1623. It is very evident that the play has been considerably abridged, so that, with the exception of the *Comedy of Errors*, it is the shortest of the plays in the Folio. Macbeth, like Angelo, is another instance of the struggle between " we would and we would not," a Pauline theme on which the Friar in *Romeo and Juliet* moralized.

Act I. ii. 41.   See Golgotha.

Act I. iv. 28-9.

> DUNC. I have begun to plant thee and will labour
> To make thee full of growing.

The comparison of man to trees planted is now common in our speech (*e.g.*, "The Plantation of Virginia," "The Plantation of Ulster," etc.), but it is also very frequent in the Bible. See Jer. xii. 2: "Thou plantest them, they take roote, they growe, and bring foorth fruite"; Jer. xi. 17: "For the Lorde of hostes that planted thee"; Ps. xcii. 12-3: "Such as are planted in the house of the Lord . . . and shall be fat and well-liking," etc.

Act I. vii. 1-2.

> MACB. If it were done, when 'tis done, then 'twere well
> It were done quickly.

It is possible that John xiii. 27: "That thou doest, doe quickly," may have been in mind, but it is doubtful, although it should be noted Macbeth was contemplating a betrayal.

Act II. ii. 68.

> L. MACB. A little water clears us of this deed.

Cf. the ceremonial of washing hands in testimony of innocence (Deut. xxi. 6) and Pilate's washing his hands (Matt. xxvii. 24).

Act II. iii. 5.   See Belzebub.

Ibid. 22-3.

> PORTER. . . . that go the primrose way to th' everlasting bonfire.

The idea that the road to hell is broad, easy and pleasant is Biblical (*cf.* Matt. vii. 13), but perhaps the best parallel of the Porter's remarks is in Wisd. ii. 6-8, for which see *All's Well*, IV. v. 54-59.

Ibid. 73-5.

> MACD. Most sacrilegious murder hath broke ope
> The Lord's anointed Temple, and stole thence
> The life o' th' building.

Two Biblical ideas: the King as the Lord's Anointed (2 Sam. i. 16) and the human body as a Temple (1 Cor. iii. 17 and vi. 19).

Ibid. 137.

> BANQ. In the great hand of God I stand.

Ps. xviii. 35: " thy right hand also shall hold me up."

Act III. i. 68-9.

> MACB.   and mine eternal jewel
> Given to the common enemy of man.

" Mine eternal jewel " means " my immortal soul," and
the " common enemy of man " is, of course, the devil, the
" aduersarie " (1 Pet. v. 8), the " Dragon " (Rev. xii. 9:
" And the great Dragon, that olde Serpent, called the deuil
& Satanas, was cast out, which deceiueth al the world ").
For the loss of the soul see Mark viii. 36: " For what shall it
profit a man, if hee shall winne all the worlde, and lose his
owne soule ?"

Ibid. 98-9.

> MACB. According to the gift which bounteous nature
> Hath in him clos'd.

See Eph. iv. 7: " according to the measure of the gift,"
and the Parable of the Talents, Matt. xxv. 15.

Act IV. i. 133-4.

> MACB.   Let this pernicious hour
> Stand aye accursed in the calendar !

Cf. Job iii. 5-6: " But let it be stained with darkenesse
and the shadowe of death, let the (dim) cloude fall vpon it,
which may make it terrible, as a most bitter day. Let the
darke storme ouercome that night, and let it not be ioyned
vnto the dayes of the yeere, nor counted in the number of
the moneths."

Act IV. ii. 12.

> L. MACD. All is the fear and nothing is the love.

Cf. 1 John iv. 18: " There is no feare in loue, but perfect
loue casteth out feare: for feare hath painefulnesse. Hee
that feareth, is not perfect in loue."

Act IV. iii. 22. See Lucifer.

Ibid. 111.

> MACD. Died every day she liv'd.

1 Cor. xv. 31: " I die dayly."

Ibid. 236-7.

MALC.   Macbeth
*Is ripe for shaking.

Not at all an unusual figure, but *cf.* Nah. iii. 12 *G*: " All
thy strong cities shall be like figge trees with the first ripe figs:
for if they bee shaken, they fall into the mouth of the eater "
(*B*, " stirred ").

Act V. v. 16-8.

SEYTON. The queen, my lord, is dead.
MACB. She should have died hereafter;
There would have been a time for such a word.

The last line gave Dr. Johnson much trouble and he proposed to read " world " for " word." To me it looks as
though " word " is an allusion to Eccles. iii. 2: " a time to be
borne, and a time to die." The " word " Macbeth refers
to is " die." At that present there was no appointed time
to die; then there was far too much to do even to think of
such a thing, when everything was loaded with anxiety. A
fitter time was hereafter.

It should be noted that there was not in Shakespeare's
time all the distinction between " word " and " thing " or
" deed " as now exists. See Luke i. 37: " For with God
shall no worde be vnpossible," which was rendered by *G*
(copied by the Authorised though rejected by the Revised):
" For with God shall nothing be vnpossible." *G* followed
Tindale and the Great Bible, *R* the more accurate *B. Cf.
Hamlet*, IV. v. 104-5:

Antiquity forgot, custom not known,
The ratifiers and props of every word,

where " every word " is used in the sense of " every thing."

Ibid. 23.

MACB. The way to dusty death.

Ps. xxii. 15: " and thou shalt bring me into the dust of
death " (*L*, *Burial*, " dust to dust ").

Ibid. 23.

MACB. Out, out, brief candle !

Job xviii. 6: " and his candle shall be put out with him."

Ibid. 24.

MACB. Life's but a walking shadow.

Ps. xxxix. 7: " For man walketh in a vain shadow."
See also Job viii. 9: " (For wee are but of yesterday, and consider not that our daies vpon earth are but a shadowe)."

Ibid. 26-7.

> MACB. *(speaking of life).* It is a tale
> Told by an idiot.

Ps. xc. 9: " we bring our years to an end, as it were a tale
that is told " (*G,* " wee haue spent our yeeres as a thought ").

See also II. iv. 40-1 (Matt. v. 44, etc.); III. i. 88-91
(Luke vi. 28 *G*); III. ii. 4-5 (Ps. cvi. 15); III. iv. 122
(Gen. ix. 6); IV. iii. 159 (John i. 14); *ibid.* 176-9* (2 Kings
iv. 26 *B*); V. vii. 11 (*L, Burial,* Job xiv. 1).

TIMON OF ATHENS

1606-7. First published in 1623. The stage history of this
very interesting tragedy is somewhat obscure; in fact, it is not
certain that the play was ever completed. The two graces
contained in the play—one by Apemantus in verse (in I. ii.
64-73), and one by Timon in prose (III. vi. 79-96)—are of
interest.

Act I. i. 50-1.

> POET. But flies an eagle flight, bold and forth on,
> Leaving no tract behind.

There is nothing particularly Biblical in this figure, but
it is remotely possible that the thought may have been suggested by Wisd. v. 11: " as a birde that flieth thorowe in the
aire, & no man can see any token where she is flowen, but
onely heareth the noise of her wings, beating the light
wind, parting the aire through the vehemencie of her going,
and flieth on shaking her wings, whereas afterward no token
of her way can be found."

Act I. ii. 10-11.

> TIMON.   and there's none
> Can truly say he gives, if he receives.

This sounds like an echo of Luke vi. 34: " And if ye lend
to them of whome ye hope to receiue, what thanke haue

ye?" Also Acts xx. 35: "It is more blessed to giue, then to receiue."

Ibid. 48-51.

> APEM. There's much example for't; the fellow that
> Sits next him, now parts bread with him, pledges
> The breath of him in a divided draught,
> Is the readiest man to kill him; 't 'as been proved.

The example that will occur almost to everybody will be Judas Iscariot.

Act II. ii. 77-80.

> PAGE. How dost thou, Apemantus?
> APEM. Would I had a rod in my mouth, that I might answer thee profitably.

Probably an application of Prov. xxvi. 3-4: "Vnto the horse belongeth a whip, to the asse a bridle, & a rod to the fooles backe. Giue not the foole an answere after his foolishnesse, least thou become like vnto him."

Act III. ii. 73-4.

> 1ST STRAN.   Who can call him
> His friend that dips in the same dish?

An allusion to Judas, see Matt. xxvi. 23.

Act III. vi. 69.

> SEC. LORD. This is the old man still.

A reference to the unregenerated man in *L, Baptism*: "may crucify the old man," also Eph. iv. 22.

Act IV. i. 25-8.

> TIMON.   Lust and liberty
> Creep in the minds and marrows of our youth,
> *That 'gainst the stream of virtue they may strive,
> And drown themselves in riot.

It is interesting that we have in the Bishops' of Ecclus. iv. 28 the identification of striving against the stream with going contrary to the precepts of virtue: "And striue thou not against the stream: but for righteousnesse take paines with all thy soule, and for the trueth striue thou vnto death" (*G* omits altogether "striue thou not against the stream").

Act V. i. 13-5.

PAINT. . . . you shall see him a palm in Athens again, and flourish with the highest.

Ps. xcii. 12: " The righteous shall flourish like a palm tree." Obviously the palm tree as a symbol of prosperity was not native to the English and we may safely assume the debt to the Psalter in this case. See also *Hamlet*, V. ii. 40.

Ibid. 170-1.

1ST SEN. *Who, like a boar too savage, doth root up His country's peace.

Ps. lxxx. 13: " The wild boar out of the wood doth root it up " (*G*, " hath destroyed it ").

See also I. ii. 233-4 (Ecclus. xiii. 1); III. v. 90 (Gen. ix. 6); IV. ii. 10-5 (Ecclus. xiii. 22); IV. iii. 173-5* (Luke vi. 26 *G*).

ANTONY AND CLEOPATRA

1607-8. First printed in 1623. The source is North's *Plutarch*. Its Scriptural interest is small.

Act I. i. 17.

ANT. Then must thou needs find out new heaven, new earth.

Cf. 2 Pet. iii. 13: " Neuertheles, we according to his promise, loke for a new heauen, and a new earth " (*G*," heauens "); also Rev. xxi. 1: " And I sawe a newe heauen, and a newe earth "; also Isa. lxv. 17.

Ibid. 35.

ANT. Kingdoms are clay.

For a comparison of the weakness in kingdoms to clay see Dan. ii. 42: " And (as) the toes of the feete (were) part of iron and part of clay: (so) shall the kingdome be part strong, and part broken."

Ibid. 35-7.

ANT.   our dungy earth alike Feeds beast as man; the nobleness of life Is to do thus.

It is possible that in this disparagement of affairs of state in favour of enjoyment there was a reminiscence of Eccles. iii. " Dungy earth " suggests the contemptuous " dung of the earth " of Ps. lxxxiii. 10. (*Cf.* also " of the whole dungy earth," *Winter's Tale*, II. i. 156.) For the rest *cf.* excerpts from Eccles. iii.

iii. 12: " So I perceiued that in those thinges there is nothing better for a man, then to be merry." . . . 18: " I communed with mine owne heart also concerning the children of men, how God hath chosen them, and yet letteth them appeare as though they were beastes." 19: " For it happeneth vnto men, as it doeth vnto beastes, euen one condition vnto them both: as the one dieth, so dieth the other: yea, they haue both one maner of breath: so that in this, a man hath no preeminence aboue a beast."

For Antony's desire to give himself up to pleasure see finally iii. 22 as in *G*: " Therefore I see that there is nothing better then that a man should reioyce in his affaires, because that is his portion. For who shall bring him to see what shall be after him ?"

Act I. ii. 30.   See Herod.

Act II. i. 5-8.

> MENE.   We ignorant of ourselves
> Beg often our own harms, which the wise powers
> Deny us for our good: so find we profit
> By losing of our prayers.

The thought is not uncommon but see Rom. viii. 26 *G*: " Likewise the spirit also helpeth our infirmities: for wee know not what to pray as we ought " (*B*, " For we knowe not what to desire as we ought "; *R* subst. as *G*).

Act III. iii. 3-6, *xi.* 127.   See Herod, Basan.

Act IV. xiii. 33.

> CLEOP. Our strength is all gone into heaviness.

Cleopatra plays upon " heaviness " as " weight " and " heaviness " as " sorrow." *Cf.* Ecclus. xxxviii. 18: " the heauinesse of the heart breaketh strength."

Act V. i. 15-7.

> CÆSAR.   *The round world
> Should have shook lions into civil streets,
> And citizens to their dens.

Perhaps the meaning is made clearer by reference to Ps. xciii. 2: " He hath made the round world so sure: that it cannot be moved " (*G* omits " round "). See Chapter IV., page 79.

See also II. v. 31-3* (2 Kings iv. 26 *B*).

CORIOLANUS

1608-9. First printed 1623. Although it follows North's Plutarch remarkably closely, of all the Plutarch plays it is the most interesting from our present point of view. There is a strong suggestion that before its composition Shakespeare read *Isaiah* in the Genevan version.

Act I. iii. 17-8.

> VOLUM. *I sprang not more in joy at first hearing he was a man-child.

This recalls Luke i. 44: " For loe, assoone as the voyce of thy salutation sounded in mine eares, the babe sprang in my wombe for ioy " (*R*, " did leape ").

Act II. i. 6-7.

> SIC. Nature teaches beasts to know their friends.

Cf. Isa. i. 3: " The oxe hath knowen his owner, and the asse his masters cribbe."

Ibid. 210.

> MEN. *The faults of fools but folly.

Cf. Prov. xiv. 24 *G*: " the follie of fooles is foolishnesse " (*B*, " the ignorance of fooles is very foolishnesse "). Note that the Authorised is nearer to Shakespeare than even *G*: " the foolishness of fools is folly."

Ibid. 276-7.

Sic.   will be his fire
To kindle their dry stubble.

For a comparison of the populace with " stubble " see
Isa. v. 24-5 *G*: " Therefore as the flame of fire deuoureth
the stubble, and as the chaffe is consumed of the flame: . . .
Therefore is the wrath of the Lord kindled against his people "
(*B*, " Therefore like as fire licketh vp the strawe, and as the
flame consumeth the stubble ").

Act II. iii. 96-7.

1st. Cit. *You have been a scourge to her enemies, you
have been a rod to her friends.

Cf. Ps. lxxxix. 32: " I will visit their offences with the
rod, and their sin with scourges " (*G*, " Then will I visite
their transgression with the rod, & their iniquitie with
strokes "); 1 Kings xii. 11: " my father hath chastised you
with roddes, but I will correct you with scourges " (also
G subst.).

Act III. i. 68-70.

Cor.   we nourish 'gainst our senate
The cockle of rebellion, insolence, sedition,
Which we ourselves have ploughed for, sow'd and
     scatter'd.

Cf. Hos. x. 13: " For you haue plowed vngodlines, you
haue reaped iniquitie."

Ibid. 79-81.

Brut.   You speak o' th' people,
As if you were a god to punish, not
A man of their infirmity.

" Infirmity," in the sense of " frailty," as applied to mankind is Biblical. *Cf.* Rom. vi. 19: " I speake after the maner
of men, because of the infirmitie of your flesh."

Ibid. 256-7.

Men.   His heart's his mouth:
What his breast forges, that his tongue must vent.

Menenius deplores his friend's impetuous folly in terms
reminiscent of Ecclus. xxi. 26: " The heart of fooles is in
their mouth: but the mouth of the wise is in his heart."

Act IV. i. 29-31.

> COR.   though I go alone
> Like to a lonely dragon, that his fen
> Makes fear'd, and talk'd of more than seen.

It has been suggested that Shakespeare took this figure from Job xxx. 29: " I am a brother of dragons, and a fellow of Estriches." *G* renders it: " I am a brother to the dragons, and a companion to the ostriches," and attaches a note in explanation: " I am like the wilde beasts that desire most solitarie places." But it is also likely that *Isaiah* suggested the thought. Dragons in *Isaiah* symbolize solitude. See Isa. xxxiv. 11-3: " for God shal spread out the lyne of desolation vpon it, and the stones of emptinesse. . . . Thornes shal grow in their palaces, nettles & thistles in their strong holds, that the dragons may haue their pleasure therein, & that they may be a court for Estriches." See also Isa. xiii. 20-22.

Act V. iii. 27.

> COR.   *Or those doves' eyes.

See Song of Sol. iv. i: " thou hast Doues eyes " (*G*, " thine eyes are like the doues "). Also i. 11. See page 28.

Ibid. 46.

> COR. . . . by the jealous Queen of Heaven.

The " queen of heauen " is mentioned in Jer. vii. 18 and Jer. xliv. 17, 18, 19, 25 (reference probably to Ishtar).

Act V. iv. 25-8.

> MEN. *He wants nothing of a god but eternity and a heaven to throne in.
> SIC. Yes, mercy, if you report him truly.

For these attributes of the Deity *cf.* Isa. lvii. 15 *G*: " For thus sayth hee, that is hie and excellent, hee that inhabiteth the eternitie, whose Name is the Holy one " (*B*, " euerlastingnes "); Isa. lxvi. 1 *G*: " Thus sayth the Lord, The heauen is my throne " (*B*, " seate "); *L, Communion :* " But thou art the same Lord, whose property is always to have mercy."

Ibid. 53-4.

> 2ND. MESS. *The trumpets, sackbuts, psalteries and
> fifes,
> Tabors and cymbals.

Cf. Dan. iii. 5 *G*: " That when ye heare the sounde of the
cornet, trumpet, harpe, sackebut, psalterie, dulcimer, and
all instruments of musicke, yee fall downe " (*B* reads
" Shawme " for " sackebut "); also *cf.* 1 Chron. xiii. 8:
" And Dauid and all Israel, played before the (arke of) God
with all their might, with singing, and Harps, Psalteries,
and Timbrels, and Cymbales, and Trumpets " (*G* reads
" violes " for " Psalteries ").

Act V. v. 152-4.

> AUF.   Though in this city he
> *Hath widowed and unchilded many a one
> Which to this hour bewail the injury.

Were it not for the suggestion that Shakespeare read
Isaiah before writing *Coriolanus*, no notice would have been
taken of this " Hath widowed and unchilded many a one."
As it is we have to remember that among the calamities of
war with which Babylon was threatened were these two
things.

See Isa. xlvii. 9 *G*: " But these two things shal come to
thee suddenly on one day, the losse of children, and widow-
hoode, they shall come vpon thee in their perfection " (*B*,
" widowehoode and desolation ").

If the inspiration came to Shakespeare from this source,
it is interesting to see how he dealt with it. We have single
words to denote deprivation of parents, " orphaned," or
loss of husband, " widowed," but none to represent " loss
of children." Shakespeare solved the problem by the word
" unchilded." *Cf.* Edgar's, " He childed as I father'd "
(*King Lear*, III. vi. 119).

See also II. iii. 36 (1 Cor. x. 25); V. iii. 139-40 (Matt.
v. 39).

CYMBELINE

1609-10. First published in 1623. The play's Scriptural
interest is not large.

Act II. iii. 102-3.

>Imog.   *One of your great knowing
>Should learn, being taught, forbearance.

Eph. iv. 2: " forbearing one another " (*G* and *R*, " supporting "). Also Col. iii. 13 *B* and *G*.

Act III. iii. 60-1.

>Bel.   Then was I as a tree
>Whose boughs did bend with fruit.

The comparison of a righteous man to a tree laden with
fruit is frequent in the Bible. See Ps. i. 3: " And he shall
be like a tree planted by the waterside: that will bring
forth his fruit in due season "; Jer. xvii. 8 *G*: " For hee shall
be as a tree that is planted by the water, which spreadeth
out her roots by the riuer, & shall not feele when the heate
commeth, but her leafe shalbe greene, and shall not care
for the yeere of drought, neither shall cease from yeelding
fruit."

Ibid. 91-2.

>Bel.   say, Thus mine enemy fell
>*And thus I set my foot on's neck.

Cf. Twelfth Night, II. v. 207 and Josh. x. 24 *G*.

Act III. iv. 78-80.

>Imog.   Against self-slaughter
>There is a prohibition so divine
>That cravens my weak hand.

See Chapter VI., pages 102-3.

Ibid. 121.

>Pisan. But if I were as wise as honest.

It is said that the servant who was wiser than honest was
the Unjust Steward in Luke xvi. 8: " And the Lorde commended the vniust Stewarde, because he had done wisely ";
cf. Iago in *Othello,* III. iii. 382-4.

Ibid. 127-8.

> PISAN. I'll give but notice you are dead, and send
>   him
> Some bloody sign of it.

Is this suggested by the device practised by Joseph's brethren? Gen. xxxvii. 31-2: "And they tooke Iosephs coate, and killed a kidde, and dipped the coate in the blood. And they sent the partie coloured coate, and caused it to be brought vnto their father, and said, This haue we found, see whether it be thy sonnes coat, or no."

Act III. vi. 1.

> IMOG. I see a man's life is a tedious one.

Evidently in playful allusion to the well-known Wisd. ii. 1: " Our life is short & tedious."

Act IV. ii. 4-5.

> IMOG. But clay and clay differs in dignity,
> Whose dust is both alike.

Cf. Rom. ix. 21: " Hath not the Potter power ouer the clay, euen of the same lumpe to make one vessell vnto honour, and another vnto dishonour ?"

Ibid. 260-1.

> GUID. Thou thy worldly task hast done,
> *Home art gone and ta'en thy wages.

Comparison of our life to a task appointed to a hired labourer to whom wages will be paid is after the Parable of the Labourers, Matt. xx. 1-16. See also 1 Cor. iii. 8 *G*: " euery man shall receiue his wages, according to his labour " (*B* and *R*, " rewarde ").

Ibid. 264-5.

> ARV. Fear no more the frown o' th' great:
> Thou art past the tyrant's stroke.

Reminiscent of Job's apostrophe on death. *Cf.* Job iii. 17-9: " There must the wicked ceasse from their tyranny, and there such as laboured valiantly, be at rest. There the prisoners rest together, they heare no more the voyce of the oppressour: There are small and great, and the seruant (is) free from his master."

Act V. iv. 101.

> JUP. Whom best I love, I cross.

An obvious paraphrase of Heb. xii. 6: " For whome the Lord loueth, he chastneth." Also Prov. iii. 12.

Ibid. 188-90.

> GAOLER. . . . *and how you shall speed in your journey's end, I think you'll never return to tell one.
> See also lines 180-1:
> GAOLER. . . '. for, look you, sir, you know not which way you shall go.

A not uncommon observation as to death, but *cf.* Job xvi. 22 *G*: " and I shall go the way, whence I shall not re-turne " (*B*, " turne againe "). *Cf. Hamlet*, III. i. 78-80.

Act V. v. 454-5.

> SOOTH. The lofty cedar, royal Cymbeline,
> Personates thee.

For the cedar as the symbol of royal greatness, see Ezek. xxxi. 3: " Beholde, Assur is a Cedar in Libanon, with faire branches, & with thicke shadowing boughes of a high stature, and his toppe was among the thicke boughs."

See also II. iii. 116-7 (Eph. vi. 1).

THE WINTER'S TALE

> 1610-11. It was first printed in 1623, for which edition there appears to have been some delay in procuring the copy. The play acts extremely well, although it is rarely performed owing to the fact that it contains no sustained part suitable to a prominent actor. The Scriptural allusions, if few, are not without interest.

Act I. ii. 45-51.

> POL. I may not, verily.
> HER. Verily?
> You put me off with limber vows: but I,
> Though you would seek t'unsphere the stars with
>   oaths,
> Should yet say, Sir, no going: Verily,
> You shall not go; a lady's " Verily " is
> As potent as a lord's.

" Verily, verily " (*R*, " Amen, Amen ") is a notable phrase in *St. John's Gospel* as an asseveration. " Thus did our Saviour Christ swear divers times, sayihg, Verily, verily " (Homily against Swearing and Perjury).

Act I. ii. 111-2.

> LEON. *my heart dances,
> But not for joy: not joy.

The audience expected " joy " and Leontes is at pains to dissipate the idea. See Ps. xxviii. 8: " therefore my heart danceth for joy " (*G*, " therefore mine heart shall reioyce ").

Ibid. 417-9.

> POLIX. Oh then, my best blood turn
> To an infected jelly, and my name
> Be yok'd with his, that did betray the Best.

See Judas Iscariot.

Act II. iii. 184-6.

> ANTIG. Come on, poor babe,
> Some powerful spirit instruct the kites and ravens
> To be thy nurses.

In possible reminiscence of Elijah being fed by the ravens at God's instruction. See 1 Kings xvii. 4-6.

Act III. iii. 124-5.

> CLOWN. If the sins of your youth are forgiven you.

Job xx. 11 *G*: " His bones are full of the sinne of his youth " (*B*, " From his youth his bones are full of sinnes "). Ps. xxv. 6: " O remember not the sins and offences of my youth."

Act IV. ii. 30-1.

> AUT. For the life to come, I sleep out the thought of it.

Cf. L, Communion, Nicene Creed : " And the life of the world to come."

Ibid. 104. See Prodigal.

Act IV. iii. 457-9.

> PERD. *The self-same sun, that shines upon his court,
> Hides not his visage from our cottage, but
> Looks on alike.

Cf. Ecclus. xlii. 16 *G*: " The sunne that shineth, looketh vpon all things " (*B*, " The Sunne ouerlooketh all things with his shine"). Ps. xix. 6: " and there is nothing hid from the heat thereof."

Ibid. 491.

FLOR.* Let Nature crush the sides o' th' earth together.

Cf. Jer. vi. 22 *G*. See pages 27, 28, 68, 69.

Ibid. 774-5.

AUT. How blessed are we, that are not simple men !
Yet Nature might have made me as these are.

Probably the Parable of the Pharisee and Publican was sufficiently familiar to the audience to make this assumption of superiority by Autolycus amusing. *Cf.* Luke xviii. 11: " God, I thanke thee, that I am not as other men are."

Act V. i. 3-6.

CLEOM.   indeed, paid down
More penitence than done trespass. At the last
*Do, as the heavens have done, forget your evil:
With them, forgive yourself.

See Chapter IV., pages 81-2, and *Two Gentlemen of Verona*, V. iv. 79-81. See also *L, Visitation of the Sick*: " O most merciful God, which . . . dost so put away the sins of those which truly repent, that thou rememberest them no more."

Act V. iii. 37-8.

LEON.   Does not the stone rebuke me,
For being more stone than it ?

Although the delightful conceit is the real inspiration of " does not the stone rebuke me," yet the figure of the stone rebuking from the wall is not unknown in the Bible and its repetition here may be of interest.

Hab. ii. 10-11: " Thou hast consulted shame to thine owne house, by destroying many people, and hast sinned against thine owne soule. For the stone shall crie out of the wall."

See also I. ii. 132-3 (Gen. xlix. 4 *B*); IV. Chorus, 24 (2 Pet. iii. 18); V. i. 30* (2 Kings iv. 26 *B*); V. ii. 54-5* (Luke vi. 23 *B*); *ibid.* 174* (*L, Morning Prayer*, Matt. iii. 2).

THE TEMPEST

1611-12. Not published until 1623. It is one of the shorter plays. It clearly was divided into five acts, and otherwise in its observance of the Unities follows what are called classical rules. Prospero is not one of the scholar princes well versed in the Bible; his form of learning is magic. Scriptural interest is small.

Act I. ii. 217.

ARIEL. *Not a hair perish'd.

If we were to assume that the shipwreck in which St. Paul was concerned (Acts xxvii. 34) was in Shakespeare's mind, then we would have an instance in which we could prefer *R* as the source: " for there shal not an heare of the head perish of any of you " (*B*, " for there shall not an heare fall from the head of any of you," with which *G* agrees). That this is not clear, see Luke xxi. 18: " And there shall in no case one haire of your head perish." The phrase was one frequently heard.

Ibid. 218-9.

ARIEL. On their sustaining garments not a blemish,
But fresher than before.

The vessel on which the King's friends were is stated to have been " all afire " and Carter suggests that the incident of Shadrach, Meshach, and Abednego was recalled by Shakespeare. See Dan. iii. 27 *G*: " not an haire of their head was burnt, neither were their coates changed, nor any smell of fire came vpon them " (*B*, " the very haire of their head was not burnt, and their clothes vnchanged, yea there was no smel of fire felt vpon them "). Notice that the non-perdition of the hair was also a matter for comment.

Ibid. 334-6.

CALIB.   and teach me how
*To name the bigger Light, and how the less
That burn by day and night.

Cf. Gen. i. 16 *G*: " God then made two great lightes: the greater light to rule the day, and the lesse light to rule the night " (*B*, " a great light to rule the day ").

Ibid. 406.

>   MIRAN. What is't ? a spirit ?

Was this ejaculation of Miranda's suggested by that of the disciples when they saw Christ walking on the water ?

See Matt. xiv. 26: " And when the disciples saw him walking on the sea, they were troubled, saying, that it is a spirit " (*R*, " saying, That it is a ghost "). The possibility can only be regarded as very remote.

Act II. i. 42-3.

>   ADR. . . . *subtle, tender and delicate temperance.

Except in compliment, " Tender and delicate " is not the usual order of these two adjectives. *Cf.* " delicate and tender prince " (*Hamlet*, IV. iv. 48). " Tender and delicate " according to the Genevan Version was the complimentary title of Babylon.

See Isa. xlvii. 1 *G*: " thou shalt no more be called, Tender and delicate " (*B*, " Tender and pleasant "). *Cf.* also Deut. xxviii. 56: " the woman that is so tender and delicate " (*G*, " tender and deintie ").

Ibid. 160.

>   GONZ. *No use of metal, corn, or wine, or oil.

See Chapter IV., page 80.

Act II. ii. 12-4.

>   CALIB.   sometime am I
>   *All wound with adders, who with cloven tongues
>   Do hiss me into madness.

Todd remarks upon " cloven tongues " which is to be found in Acts ii. 3: " And there appeared vnto them clouen tongues, like as they had bene of fire " (*R*, " parted tongues ").

Ibid. 61-2.

>   STEPH. *Do you put tricks upon's with savages and men of Inde ?

See *Love's Labour's Lost*, IV. iii. 222 and Jer. xiii. 23 *B*.

Act III. ii. 70-1.

> CALIB. Yea, yea, my lord, I'll yield him thee asleep,
> Where thou mayst knock a nail into his head.

There cannot be much doubt that this is in allusion to Jael's killing of Sisera. See Judg. iv. 21.

Act III. iii. 102-3. See Legion.

Act IV. i. 157-8.

> PROS. *and our little life
> Is rounded with a sleep.

Cf. Job xiv. 10-12 *G*, and *Measure for Measure*, III. i. 17-9.

Ibid. 263-4.

> PROS. more pinch-spotted make them,
> *Than pard, or cat o' mountain.

This may be a reference to the spotted creature named in Coverdale and preserved in the Bishops' of Jer. xiii. 23: " May a man of Inde chaunge his skinne, and the catte of the mountaine her spots ?" See also *Merry Wives*, II. ii. 28.

Act V. i. 48-9.

> PROS. Graves at my command
> Have wak'd their sleepers, op'd, and let 'em forth.

Cf. Matt. xxvii. 52: " And graues were opened, and many bodyes of saintes which slept, arose."

Note on the Name Ariel.—Wheresoever Shakespeare derived the name Ariel (the etymology of which is doubtful), it is indisputably a Biblical name. As applied to Jerusalem it occurs in the Bishops' of Isa. xxix. 1, 2, 8. There is no sound reason why the suggestion of the name to Shakespeare should not have come from the Bible. In the Genevan Version of *Isaiah*, which Shakespeare evidently read in his later days, Ariel does not occur in the text, but at Isa. xxix. 1 there is this conspicuous note: " The Ebrew word Ariel signifieth the Lyon of God, and signifieth the Altar, because the Altar seemed to deuoure the sacrifice that was offered to God, as Ezek. 43. 16." That Ariel is a Biblical name is not to imply that Shakespeare's conception of this airy spirit was Biblical. Clearly Ariel is independent of any Biblical model.

KING HENRY VIII.

1612-13. The latest of all the plays in the Folio. It is said to be identical with *All is True*, which was a new play in course of performance when the Globe Theatre was burnt in 1613. First printed in 1623. Its quotations from the Psalter are only surpassed in number by *2 King Henry VI*.

Act I. i. 89-92.

BUCK.   Every man,
After the hideous storm that follow'd, was
A thing inspir'd and, not consulting, broke
Into a general prophecy.

Evidently after the example of Acts xix. 6: " the holy Ghost came on them and they spake with tongues, and prophecied." Also see Saul in 1 Sam. x. 6: " And the spirite of the Lord will come vpon thee also, and thou shalt prophecie with them, and shalt be turned into another man "; also verses 11-12.

Ibid. 140-1.

NORF. Heat not a furnace for your foe so hot
That it do singe yourself.

In allusion to the furnace heated at Nebuchadnezzar's command for Abednego and his two companions. See Dan. iii. 22: " Therfore because the kings commandement was straite, & the furnace was exceeding hot, the men that put in Sidrach, Misach, and Abednego, the flame of the fire destroyed them."

Ibid. 223-4.

BUCK. *My life is spann'd already;
I am the shadow of poor Buckingham.

Ps. xxxix. 6-7: " Behold, thou hast made my days as it were a span long. . . . For man walketh in a vain shadow " (G, " Beholde, thou hast made my dayes as an hand bredth ").

Act I. iii. 60-2.

SANDS. Sparing would show a worse sin than ill
    doctrine:
Men of his way should be most liberal:
They are set here for examples.

Wolsey as a bishop was required to be hospitable. See
1 Tim. iii. 2: " A Bishop therefore must be blamelesse, the
husbande of one wife, watching, sober, comely apparelled,
a louer of hospitalitie."

Act II. i. 32-3.

    1ST. GENT.   he was stirr'd
    With such an agony, he sweat extremely.

Cf. L, Litany: " By thine Agony and bloody Sweat . . .
Good Lord, deliver us." See also Luke xxii. 44: " And he
was in an agonie, and hee prayed more earnestly, and his
sweat was like droppes of blood."

Ibid. 66-8.

    BUCK. Yet let 'em look they glory not in mischief;
    Nor build their evils on the graves of great men:
    For then, my guiltless blood must cry against 'em.

See *Measure for Measure,* II. ii. 170-2 and Chapter II.,
pages 31-3. *Cf.* Gen. iv. 10: " the voyce of thy brothers blood
crieth vnto me out of the ground."

Ibid. 77-8.

    BUCK. Make of your prayers one sweet sacrifice
    And lift my soul to heaven.

Cf. Ps. cxli. 2: " Let my prayer be set forth in thy sight as
the incense: and let the lifting up of my hands be an evening
sacrifice."

Ibid. 128-30.

    BUCK.   *when they once perceive
    The least rub in your fortunes, fall away
    Like water from ye.

For the phrase " fall away like water " see Ps. lviii. 6:
" let them fall away like water that runneth apace " (*G,* " Let
them melt like the waters "). For the sense of the passage
see also Ecclus. xiii. 22.

Act II. ii. 48-50.

    NORF.   All men's honours
    Lie like one lump before him, to be fashion'd
    Into what pitch he please.

Wolsey's policy was to reduce the nobles to impotence and to make them creatures of the Executive. Hence the Scriptural comparison. See Rom. ix. 21: "Hath not the Potter power ouer the clay, euen of the same lumpe to make one vessell vnto honour, and another vnto dishonour?" See also Wisd. xv. 7 (the passage which probably suggested that in *Romans*): "For the potter tempereth soft earth, laboureth it, and giueth it the fashion, of what so euer vessell serueth for our vse: and of the selfe same clay hee maketh both the vessels that serue for cleane vses, and also such as serue to the contrary: whereunto euery vessel serueth, the potter himselfe being the iudge."

Act II. iv. 105-7.

> Q. KATH.   *Y'are meek and humble-mouth'd:
> You sign your place and calling, in full seeming
> With meekness and humility.

See Eph. iv. 2 *G*: "With all humblenesse of minde, and meekenesse, with long suffering" (*B*, "With all lowlinesse and meekenesse"; *R*, "al humilitie and mildenes").

Act III. i. 106.

> Q. KATH. A woman lost among ye, laugh'd at, scorn'd?

"Laughed to scorn" is a frequent phrase in the Bible, *cf.* Ps. ii. 4. *G* gives a reading for 2 Kings xix. 21 close to the circumstances of the Queen: "O virgin, daughter of Zion, he hath despised thee, & laughed thee to scorne" (*B* agrees with Authorised). Job xii. 4, etc.

Ibid. 113-4.

> Q. KATH.   Woe upon ye
> And all such false professors!

See Luke xi. 44: "Woe vnto you Scribes & Pharisees hypocrites." See also Matt. xxiii. 13-6, especially verse 15 *G*, which reads: "to make one of your profession" (*B* and *R*, "one proselyte").

Ibid. 150-1.

> Q. KATH.   Like the lily
> That once was mistress of the field, and flourish'd.

Cf. Matt. vi. 28: " Learne of the Lilies of the fielde, howe they growe: they wearie not (themselues) with labour, neither (do they) spinne." 29: " And yet I say vnto you, that euen Solomon in all his royaltie, was not araied like one of these." *Cf.* also Ps. ciii. 15: " for he flourisheth as a flower of the field."

Act III. ii. 101-2.

WOLSEY.   that she should lie i' th' bosom of
Our hard rul'd king.

For a wife " to lie in the bosom " see the case of King David in his old age, 1 Kings i. 2: " Let there bee sought for my lord the king a yong virgin, to stand before the king, and to cherish him, and let her lye in thy bosome, that my lord the king may get heate."

Ibid. 244-5.

WOLSEY. Follow your envious courses, men of malice,
You have Christian warrant for 'em.

In probable allusion to the delivering of Christ to Pilate. See Matt. xxvii. 18: " For he knewe that for enuie they had deliuered him."

Ibid. 366-7.

WOLSEY. Vain pomp and glory of this world, I hate ye:
I feel my heart new open'd.

See *L, Baptism*: " Dost thou forsake the devil and all his works, the vain pomp and glory of the world?" Note the propriety of " heart new open'd " in connection with Baptism.

Ibid. 367-8.

WOLSEY.   O, how wretched
Is that poor man that hangs on princes' favours !

Ps. cxlvi. 2: " O put not your trust in princes, nor in any child of man: for there is no help in them." Ps. cxviii. 9: " It is better to trust in the Lord: than to put any confidence in princes."

Ibid. 372-3. See Lucifer.

Ibid. 456-8.

> WOLSEY. Had I but serv'd my God with half the zeal
> I serv'd my king, he would not in mine age
> Have left me naked to mine enemies.

Cf. Ps. lxxi. 8-9, 16: " Cast me not away in the time of age: forsake me not when my strength faileth me. For mine enemies speak against me. . . . Forsake me not, O God, in mine old age, when I am gray-headed." Ps. xxxvii. 23-5: " The Lord ordereth a good man's going: and maketh his way acceptable to himself. Though he fall, he shall not be cast away: for the Lord upholdeth him with his hand . . . yet saw I never the righteous forsaken." Also see Ps. cxviii. 9 quoted lines 367-8.

Act IV. ii. 172-3.

> KATH.   although unqueen'd, yet like
> A queen, and daughter to a king, inter me.

In 2 Kings ix. 34 it is recorded that after Jezebel had been thrown down and Jehu had trodden on her, the latter, when he had eaten and drunk and was presumably in a quieter mood, remembered she was a king's daughter and as such, entitled to interment—" and bury her, for she is a kings daughter."

Act V. i. 110-1.

> CRAN. And am right glad to catch this good occasion
> *Most throughly to be winnowed.

This figure may have been suggested by Luke xxii. 31 *G:* " Simon, Simon, behold, Satan hath desired you, to winow you, as wheate " (*B* and *R,* " sift "). Note that the Biblical figure is applied in the plural, whereas Cranmer's is in the singular. *Cf. 2 King Henry IV.,* IV. i. 194-6.

Act V. iii. 38.

> CRAN. *I speak it with a single heart, my lords.

Gen. xx. 5: " with a single heart, and innocent handes haue I done this " (*G,* " with an vpright minde, and innocent hands haue I done this ").

Ibid. 104-5.

>SUFF. When we first put this dangerous stone a-rolling
>'Twould fall upon ourselves.

Prov. xxvi. 27: " Who so diggeth vp a pit, shal fal therin: and he that rolleth vp a stone, it will returne vpon him."

Ibid. 113.

>CROM. Ye blew the fire that burns ye.

See not only Dan. iii. 22 (I. i. 140-1) but also Ecclus. xxviii. 12: " If thou blowe the sparke, it shal burne."

Act V. iv. 23, and *V. v.* 24-6. See Samson, Saba.

Act V. v. 34-6.

>CRAN. In her days every man shall eat in safety
>Under his own vine what he plants; and sing
>The merry songs of peace to all his neighbours.

See 1 Kings iv. 20-5: " And Iuda and Israel were many, (euen) as the sand of the sea in number, eating, drinking, and making merie." 25: " And Iuda and Israel dwelt without feare, euery man vnder his vine, and vnder his fig tree . . . all the dayes of Solomon." See also Mic. iv. 4 *G*: " But they shall sit euery man vnder his vine, and vnder his figge tree, and none shal make them afraide" (*B*, " vnder his vineyard ").

See also I. ii. 142-3* (1 Cor. xiii. 1, 4, 5 *B*2); III. i. 165-6 (Matt. v. 9); III. ii. 442-3 (Gen. i. 26); *ibid.* 444 (Luke vi. 27); IV. ii. 32-3* (1 Cor. xiii. 1 *B*2).

CHAPTER VIII

REMARKS ON SHAKESPEARE'S BIBLICAL PROPER NAMES

IT has often been remarked that the Biblical names actually mentioned in the course of the plays are comparatively few. Omitting names such as Paul, used in asseveration, the name of the Deity, names of characters such as Tubal, Chus and Leah in *The Merchant of Venice*, Ariel in *The Tempest*, and terms such as Israel, Hebrew, Jew, Psalmist, Paradise, Sabbath and the doubtful Persian, but including Leviathan, Dives, Lazarus and Prodigal, there are 55 Biblical proper names in the plays of the First Folio.

Mention by name on the stage may be taken as a reflection of popular knowledge, for it would be highly disastrous to make a point dependent on a name unfamiliar to the audience. The names, therefore, comprised in our list should be regarded as a guide to the Biblical knowledge possessed by Shakespeare's audience rather than as an indication of Shakespeare's own Biblical knowledge. They were names that could safely be mentioned without any risk of bewildering the spectators.

Two distinct attitudes to these proper names have been adopted. Simple though the names may be, Biblical scholars, as a rule, have been impressed by Shakespeare's use of them and an indubitably great scholar like Ginsburg went out of his way to applaud him. On the other hand, those who have not been Biblical scholars have been prone to express themselves contemptuously and have been inclined to stigmatize the Biblical knowledge therein displayed as on the level of that to be expected in any " grammar-school " boy.

This disparity in valuation is perhaps easily explicable. The names of Alexander, Hannibal and Julius Cæsar are vaguely familiar to everybody, yet it is possible to imagine circumstances in which the simple mention of any of those men might evoke the delight of learned historians, where he that was unlearned in such matters would despise it and pass it by. The difference would be due to the fact that the learned perceived something in the context that was hidden from the unlearned, the point was richer because of his deeper knowledge.

It is not the mere mention of Biblical proper names by Shakespeare that so much attracts the delighted attention of Biblical scholars as the way and the circumstances in which they are mentioned. They are thrilled by the comparison of Joan of Arc with the invincible Deborah, for whom even the stars in their courses fought and to whom all classes rallied. They are enthusiastic about Shylock's "What says that fool of Hagar's offspring?" Shylock's narrative of the deal between Laban and Jacob drew from Ginsburg eloquent eulogy. He wrote: " Every item in this remarkable dialogue exhibits Shakespeare as one of the most original interpreters of the Bible. Jacob is selected because he was not only preferred by God himself to his brother Esau, but because his additional name was Israel,—the name from which Shylock and his race obtained the appellation *Israelites*. The paraphrase ' the eanlings which were streak'd and pied ' is Shakespeare's own, and beautifully reflects the sense of the original. The reply which he puts into the mouth of Anthonio, that it was God's wonderful interposition, and must not be adduced as justifying foul play, shows that Shakespeare has not only carefully studied the Biblical narrative, but that he has based it upon the remark in the margin against the passage (Gen. xxx. 37) in the Bishops' Bible."

This perhaps will be sufficient to warn us that there may be more in a Shakespearian Biblical allusion than meets the ordinary eye. It is well to approach the allusions with some degree of caution. It would be easy to formulate a number of questions relative to Shakespeare's Biblical proper names that a great number of those who speak superciliously of them might find it difficult to answer off hand. King Henry V.'s reference to " Assyrian slings," seeing that it rests on an obscure passage in *Judith*, is very difficult. Perhaps not everyone would be ready to say who were St. Philip's daughters alluded to by the Dauphin in *1 King Henry VI*. Few could answer why Launce in *The Two Gentlemen of Verona* should say that pride was Eve's legacy. How many would be prepared to explain the propriety of

Boyet's " A light for Monsieur Judas: it grows dark, he may stumble " ? Yet all know of Judas, but not all know the minutiæ of the account as in *St. John's Gospel*. In how many annotated editions of *Twelfth Night* is the humour in Ague-cheek's application to Malvolio of " Fie on him, Jezabel " satisfactorily pointed out ?   How many have been bewildered by " The base Judean " in the Folio edition of *Othello ?* As to this, the editions of *Othello* tell their own tale.   Shy-lock's allusion to Daniel was evidently beyond the knowledge of the editors of the Supplementary Volume of the Oxford Dictionary, for they failed to give its correct reference.

CHAPTER IX

LIST OF BIBLICAL PROPER NAMES

Abel. The second son of Adam was a keeper of sheep and his sacrifices were acceptable to God (Gen. iv. 4); slain by Cain (*ibid.* 8), his blood cried from the ground (*ibid.* 10). In Heb. xii. 24 Abel's blood is spoken of as, unlike Christ's, calling for retribution. Tradition has it that his grave is at Abila, near Damascus.

See *1 K. Hen. VI.*, I. iii. 39-40; *K. Rich. II.*, I. i. 104-6.

Abraham. Changed from Abram (Gen. xvii. 5); the original possessor of God's promise as related in Gen. xv.; after the Parable of Dives and Lazarus (Luke xvi. 19-31) the souls of the blest were said to repose in his bosom.

Abram as ancestor of Jacob mentioned by Shylock (*Merch. of Ven.*, I. iii. 73-5). For Abraham's bosom see *K. Rich. III.*, IV. iii. 38; *K. Rich. II.*, IV. i. 103-4; *K. Hen. V.*, II. iii. 9-11 (Mrs. Quickly says " Arthur's ").

Achitophel or **Ahitophel,** possibly the grandfather of Bathsheba, despite the signification of his name (" brother of foolishness ") was noted for the wisdom and oracular character of his advice. Although he was David's trusted counsellor, he was a party to Absalom's conspiracy and for this reason he is taken as the Old Testament counterpart of Judas Iscariot, a parallel that is increased by the similarity of their fates. He advised Absalom to follow up his initial success by prompt measures making for immediate security. His advice was rejected. See 2 Sam. xv-xvii. Ps. xli. 9 is said by some to refer to him.

It was to his predilection for security and his refusal to take further chances with Absalom that Falstaff alluded. Spelt Achitophel by Shakespeare as also in later editions of the Bishops'.

FALS. A whoreson A.! A rascally yea-forsooth knave, to bear a gentleman in hand, and then stand upon security (*2 K. Hen. IV.*, I. ii. 39-41).

Adam, the first man and therefore the ancestor of all men
(Gen. i. 27); created of the dust (ii. 7); set to dress the
garden of Eden (*ibid.* 15); was in a state of innocence
(*ibid.* 25); at the instigation of Eve transgressed (iii. 6);
no longer innocent, condemned to eat of the ground in
sorrow (*ibid.* 17).

See *Com. of Err.*, IV. iii. 15; *2 K. Hen. VI.*, IV. ii. 146;
Love's L. L., IV. ii. 40; V. ii. 323; *K. Rich. II.*, III. iv. 73;
1 K. Hen. IV., II. iv. 106-7; III. iii. 184-5; *K. Hen. V.*,
I. i. 29 (an allusion to the old Adam of Baptism); *Much
Ado*, I. i. 268-9; II. i. 67-8, 260-2; V. i. 185-6; *As Y. L.*,
II. i. 5; *Hamlet*, V. i. 33-4, 39-40.

Assyrians were stated in Judith ix. 7 *G* to " trust in shield,
speare, & bow, and sling." See Chapter IV., page 66.

KING. *Enforced from the old A. slings (*K. Hen. V.*,
IV. vii. 66).

In Isa. x. 6, 13 *B*, the Assyrians were definitely associated with robbery and pillage and hence possibly the
significance of Falstaff's *" O base Assyrian knight " to
Pistol (*2 K. Hen. IV.*, V. iii. 102).

Babylon. See Rev. xvii. 5: " great Babylon, the mother of
whoredome and abominations of the earth." In the
Apocalypse, Babylon is taken to signify imperial Rome
while new Jerusalem represents the Christian Church.
In verse 4 the Genevan margin stated: " this woman is
the Antichrist, that is, the Pope."

MRS. Q. . . . and talk'd of the whore of Babylon (*K.
Hen. V.* II. iii. 40-1).

It should be noted that Babylon occurs in *Merry Wives*,
III. i. 24, as " Pabylon " by Sir Hugh Evans in a snatch
of Whittingham's metrical version of Ps. cxxxvii. Also
in *Twelfth Night* by Sir Toby Belch in a snatch of a
popular song.

Barrabas or **Barabas** or **Barabbas,** referred to in Matt.
xxvii. 16 as " a notable prisoner "; in Mark xv. 7 and
Luke xxiii. 19 as an insurgent who had committed
murder; in John xviii. 40 as a robber; and by St. Peter
in Acts iii. 14 as a murderer, was preferred by the
Jews to Christ for release. The name is spelt Barrabas
by Shakespeare and thus also in the Prayer Book, as

well as in all printed Bibles before the Whittingham,
Genevan, Bishops' and Rheims.

SHY. Would any of the stock of B. Had been her husband,
rather than a Christian ! (*Merch. of Ven.*, IV. i. 297-8).

Basan or **Bashan,** as well as for its rich grain-growing land,
its giants and its splendid oaks, was noted for its hill and
for its magnificent breed of wild cattle, and it is in respect
of its hill and cattle that it is mentioned in Shakespeare
and definitely in connection with two Psalms. Ps.
xxii. 12: " fat bulls of Basan close me in on every side."
Ps. lxviii. 15: " As the hill of Basan, so is God's hill:
even an high hill, as the hill of Basan."

Spelt " Basan " by Shakespeare and 'in the Prayer
Book; both as " Basan " and " Bashan " in the Bishops'
and as " Bashan " in the Genevan.

ANT. O, that I were Upon the hill of B., to outroar The
horned herd ! (*Ant. and Cleop.*, III. xi. 126-8).

Bel, the god of earth, became identified with Merodach,
the younger Bel, the city god of Babylon. His priests,
as related in *Bel and the Dragon* (Vulgate, Dan. xiv.),
pretended that he ate the food set before him.

His priests alluded to by Borachio (*Much Ado*,
III. iii. 142-3).

Belzebub or **Beelzebub,** is in the New Testament treated
as the prince of devils (Matt. xii. 24). Spelt by Shakespeare as " Belzebub " but in Bibles as " Beelzebub."

See *K. Hen. V.*, IV. vii. 144-5; *Twelfth Night*, V. i. 294-5,
and *Macbeth*, II. iii. 4-5.

Bible is only mentioned once and that as " Pible " by Caius
in angry mimicry of Sir Hugh Evans.

CAIUS. he has pray his P. well, dat he is no come (*Merry
Wives*, II. iii. 7-8).

Elsewhere as " God's Book " (2 *K. Hen. VI.*
II. iii. 4); " Holy Writ " (*K. Rich. III.*, I. iii. 337;
All's Well, II. i. 141; *Othello*, III. iii. 325); " Scripture "
(*K. Rich. III.*, I. iii. 334; *Merch. of Ven.*, I. iii. 99;
Hamlet, V. i. 39; *Cymbeline*, III. iv. 83); " Sacred
Writ " (2 *K. Hen. VI.*, I. iii. 61).

Cain, the first born man (Gen. iv. 1), slew his brother Abel (*ibid.* 8), declared cursed from the earth (*ibid.* 11), banished (*ibid.* 12-4), marked (*ibid.* 15).

See *1 K. Hen. VI.,* I. iii. 39; *K. John,* III. iv. 79; *Love's L. L.,* IV. ii. 36; *K. Rich. II.,* V. vi. 43; *2 K. Hen. IV.,* I. i. 157; *Hamlet,* V. i. 81-2. See also *Merry Wives,* I. iv. 23-4: " Simple—' a little yellow beard, a Cain-colour'd beard.' " Cain is said to have been presented in religious plays with a yellow beard.

Christ is alluded to by name as follows: *1 K. Hen. VI.,* I. ii. 106; *2 K. Hen. VI.,* V. i. 214; *K. Rich. III.,* I. iv. 199; *K. Rich. II.,* IV. i. 93, 99, 170; *1 K. Hen. IV.,* I. i. 19 and III. ii. 111; *K. Hen. V.,* IV. i. 65. Otherwise referred to as " My Redeemer " (*K. Rich. III.,* II. i. 4); " Our dear Redeemer " (*K. Rich. III.,* II. i. 124); " Blessed Mary's Son " (*K. Rich. II.,* II. i. 56); " our Saviour " (*Hamlet,* I. i. 159); " the Best " (*Winter's Tale,* I. ii. 419). See also Jesu.

Damascus, according to popular belief, is not only the oldest city of the world still inhabited, but also its site was said to have been the scene of Abel's murder by Cain.

BEAUF. This be D., be thou cursed Cain, To slay thy brother Abel, if thou wilt (*1 K. Hen. VI.,* I. iii. 39-40).

Daniel, although a young child, displayed great wisdom in confounding the two accusers of Susanna by examining them separately. See *The Story of Susanna* (Vulgate, Dan. xiii). 45: " the Lorde raised vp the spirite of a young childe, whose name was Daniel "; 64: " From that day forth was Daniel had in great reputation in the sight of the people." See also *The History of Bel* (Vulgate, Dan. xiv). It was Portia's apparently extreme youth that evoked Shylock's comparison with the Daniel of *Susanna.*

SHY. A D. come to judgment ! yea, a D.! O wise young judge, how I do honour thee ! (*Merch. of Ven.,* IV. i. 223-4). GRAT. A second D., a D., Jew ! (*ibid.* 334).

Debora or **Deborah** (Judg. iv., v), the wife of Lapidoth, a prophetess and judge of Israel, was the inspiring spirit in the revolt against Jabin, King of Canaan. She accompanied Barak, her general, in his campaign against Sisera, the captain of Jabin's hosts. Like Joan of Arc, she united all classes against the foreign invader ; even men of letters as well as princes joined her standard (Judg. v. 14), a fact emphasized in the margins of both the Genevan and the Bishops'. Like Joan of Arc she kindled national enthusiasm and the frontiers of her country were secured. The allusion to her sword may be taken as being to her invincibility since even the forces of nature fought on her side.

DAUPH. Thou art an Amazon And fightest with the sword of D. (*1 K. Hen. VI.*, I. ii. 104-5).

Dives, of the Parable of Dives and Lazarus (Luke xvi. 19-31), often referred to as the Glutton, because he fared " very delitiously " every day (*ibid.* 19), and was usually represented pictorially as feasting. He was clothed in purple (*ibid.* 19), he was tormented by the flames of hell (*ibid.* 23-4) and desired that his tongue should be cooled (*ibid.* 24).

See *1 K. Hen. IV.*, III. iii. 35-7, and *2 K. Hen. IV.* I. ii. 38-9.

Eden, the garden inhabited by Adam and Eve in their innocence (Gen. ii. 10, iii. 23), referred to in Gen. xiii. 10 and Ezek. xxxi. 8-9 as " Garden of the Lorde " or " the garden of God." In the Greek Bible (the Septuagint) the word " Paradise " was applied to it and hence it came to signify a land of exceeding fruitfulness. It was in this sense applied to England by John of Gaunt.

See *Com. of Err.*, IV. iii. 15, and *K. Rich. II.*, II. i. 42.

Egypt suffered ten plagues because Pharaoh refused to let the Israelites depart (Exod. vii-xii). The land was enveloped in darkness (*ibid.* x. 21-3), the ninth plague. The tenth and final plague was the slaying of all the first-born in the land (*ibid.* xii. 29).

JAQ. *I'll rail against all the first-born of E. (*As Y. L.*, II. v. 60-1).

As Jaques's " first-born of Egypt " has aroused some comment, it should be observed that it occurs in Exod. xii. 12 *B*: " and will smite all the first borne of Egypt, from man to beast " (*G*, " first borne in the land of Egypt ").

CLOWN.   . . . thou art more puzzl'd than the Egyptians in their fog (*Twelfth Night*, IV. ii. 48-9).

Eve, the first woman (Gen. ii. 22) and mother of all living (*ibid.* iii. 20), tempted by the serpent (iii. 1-5), tempted Adam (*ibid.* 6).

SPEED. " Item, she is proud." LAUNCE. Out with that too: it was E.'s legacy, and cannot be ta'en from her (*Two Gent. of Ver.*, III. i. 344-6).

The point of Launce's remark lies in Ecclus. x. 14: " For pride is the original of all sinne." Since Eve was the original sinner, and since it was her pride, as according to Ecclus. x. 14, that caused her to sin, therefore pride is part and parcel of female human nature.   It is a good example of an allusion to a well-known Biblical character, which yet would be beyond the knowledge of most.

See also *Love's L. L.*, I. i. 263-4; V. ii. 323; *K. Rich. II.*, III. iv. 75-6; *Merry Wives*, IV. ii. 24; *Twelfth Night*, I. v. 29-30.

God. In 1605 an Act was passed forbidding on the stage the jesting or profane use of the Name of God, or of Jesus Christ, or of the Holy Ghost or the Holy Trinity.   It is often very evident in the plays that " Heaven " has been substituted for " God " and in *1* and *2 K. Hen. IV.*, where we have quartos as well as the Folio for the text, we have direct evidence of such substitution in the Folio.   Sometimes we have the absurdity of such a character as Malvolio asserting his reliance on Jove.

There are seven plays in which the Name of the Christian Deity does not occur: *Two Gent. of Ver.*, *Julius Cæsar*, *Meas. for Meas.*, *Timon of A.*, *Cymbeline*, *Winter's Tale* and *Tempest*, all published in the Folio for the first time.   In two of them (*Two Gent. of Ver.* and *Tempest*) the term " Lord " as applied to God is found.

In addition to " heaven " and " heavens," the following equivalents are found: " King of Heaven " (*K. Rich. III.*, I. ii. 106); " King of kings " (*1 K. Hen. VI.*, I. i. 28; *K. Rich. III.*, I. iv. 204; *K. Rich. III.*, II. i. 13), see Rev. xix. 16; " High All Seer " (*K. Rich. III.*,

V. i. 20); "Lord of Hosts" (*1 K. Hen. VI.*, I. i. 31),
see Isa. xiii. 4, etc.; "Th' Eternal" (*Two Gent. of Ver.*,
V. iv. 81); "The Highest"* (*All's Well*, IV. ii. 24),
see Ecclus. xli. 4 *B*; "The Everlasting" (*Hamlet*,
I. ii. 131), see *Baruch*, iv. 14, 20 *G*, v. 2 *G*.

Golgotha, the scene of the Crucifixion. See Chapter IV.,
pages 61-2.

BP. CAR. . . . *and this land be call'd The field of
G. and dead men's skulls (*K. Rich. II.*, IV. i. 143-4).
SERG. Or memorize another G. (*Macbeth*, I. ii. 41).

Goliath, a giant of Gath serving with the Philistine army
opposing Saul (1 Sam. xvii). His height was said to
be "sixe cubites and an hand breath long" (*ibid.* 4),
which height the *B* margin said was "a cubite and a
handbreath more then a wonder"; "the shaft of his
speare was like a weauers beame" (*ibid.* 7).

ALEN. For none but Samsons and Goliasses It sendeth
forth to skirmish (*1 K. Hen. VI.*, I. ii. 33-4). FALS. I
fear not G. with a weaver's beam (*Merry Wives*, V. i. 23-4).

Hagar, an Egyptian woman, handmaid (or slave) of Sarai,
given by her to Abram as concubine (Gen. xvi. 1-3);
when Hagar conceived "her mistresse was despised in
her eyes" (*ibid.* 4); she fled from Sarai's harsh treatment
(*ibid.* 6); she returned and gave birth to Ishmael.
After the birth of Isaac, Sara, as she now was called,
according to xxi. 9, saw "the sonne of Hagar the
Egyptian, which she had borne vnto Abraham, (to
be) a mocker." *B* margin stated: "Ismael mocked
Gods promise made to Isahac."

SHY. What says that fool of Hagar's offspring? (*Merch.
of Ven.*, II. v. 44).

Herod the Great, King of Judæa, promised the Wise Men
to worship the infant Christ (Matt. ii. 8); on perceiving
that he had been mocked by the Wise Men, he caused
all the male infants of two years and less in and round
about Bethlehem to be slain (*ibid.* 16). His son, Herod
the Tetrarch, to please Herodias's daughter had John
the Baptist's head brought in on a charger (Matt.
xiv. 6-11). Herod the Great figured in the mystery
plays as a bloodthirsty raging tyrant.

KING. As did the wives of Jewry At H.'s bloody-hunting slaughtermen (*K. Hen. V.*, III. iii. 40-1). MRS. PAGE. What a H. of Jewry is this ! (*Merry Wives*, II. i. 20). HAM. It out-herods H. (*Hamlet*, III. ii. 16).

In all probability an allusion to the raging tyrant of the religious plays.

CHARM. Let me have a child at fifty, to whom H. of Jewry may do homage ! (*Ant. and Cleop.*, I. ii. 29-30).

In allusion to H.'s promise to the Wise Men to worship the infant Christ (Matt. ii. 8).

ALEX. H. of Jewry dare not look upon you But when you are well pleas'd. CLEOP. That H.'s head I'll have. But how, when Antony is gone Through whom I might command it ? (*ibid.* III. iii. 3-6).

In probable allusion to the incident of John the Baptist's head. It did not matter that that H. was the son of Cleopatra's contemporary, whom she had tried to fascinate; the important point was to interest the audience by a familiar allusion.

Israel, the name bestowed on Jacob and consequently the name by which the Hebrews called themselves (*Hamlet*, II. ii. 431).

Jacob, although the younger son of Isaac, was the third possessor of God's promise to Abraham, first by purchase from Esau, Gen. xxv. 33: " and sold his byrthright vnto Iacob "; and secondly, by stratagem and his mother's direction, *ibid.* xxvii. 13: " And his mother said vnto him, Vpon mee be the curse, my sonne: onely heare my voyce, & goe & fetch me them." *Ibid.* xxviii. 4: " And giue the blessing of Abraham vnto thee, and to thy seede with thee, that thou maiest receiue to inherite the land." To avoid the wrath of Esau, he fled to his maternal Uncle Laban and grazed his herds. According to *ibid.* xxx. 37 *et seq.*, by means of an artifice he obtained possession of a large portion of Laban's flocks but, according to the account he gave his wives (to which a marginal note in the Bishops' draws attention), it was an issue decided by an angel of God (xxxi. 11-13). Jacob throve and was prosperous, *ibid.* xxx. 43: " And the man increased exceedingly, and had much cattell, and mayde seruants, and men seruants, and Camels, and Asses."

In Gen. xxxii. 10 it is related that Jacob with his staff passed over Jordan. Jacob's staff is also alluded to in Heb. xi. 21 G, that, as he was dying, he blessed both of Joseph's sons and, leaning on his staff, he worshipped God. But it was the staff with which he passed over Jordan which was in all probability in Shakespeare's mind, for he evidently had been reading the whole narrative in *Genesis*. Besides, allusion to that staff would be more appropriate to Shylock. For the account of Jacob's deal with Laban as narrated in *Genesis*, see Chapter IV., pages 59-61.

Shakespeare has in this story followed *Genesis* like in other instances he did Holinshed and North. The transaction between Laban and Jacob was not free from complications but Shakespeare has it accurately. Shakespeare spells it " Iacob " and so *B*, but *G* spells the name " Iaakob " or " Iakob."

Merch. of Ven., I. iii. 72 *et seq.*

SHY. *When Jacob graz'd his Uncle Laban's sheep—
This Jacob from our holy Abram was,
As his wise mother wrought in his behalf,
The third possessor. Ay, he was the third.
ANT. And what of him ? Did he take interest ?
SHY. No: not take interest: not, as you would say,
Directly interest. Mark what Jacob did.
When Laban and himself were compromis'd
That all the eanlings which were streak'd and pied
Should fall as Jacob's hire, the ewes, being rank,
In th'end of Autumn turned to the rams,
And, when the work of generation was
Between these woolly breeders in the act,
The skilful shepherd peel'd me certain wands
And, in the doing of the deed of kind,
He stuck them up before the fulsome ewes,
Who then conceiving did in eaning time
Fall parti-colour'd lambs, and those were Jacob's.
This was a way to thrive, and he was blest:
And thrift is blessing if men steal it not.
ANT. This was a venture, sir, that Jacob serv'd for,
A thing not in his power to bring to pass,
But sway'd and fashion'd by the hand of heaven.

Shylock had tried to justify craft by asserting that Jacob was blest as a result of his stratagem. This Antonio denied on the strength of Gen. xxxi. 11-2.

SHY. By Jacob's staff I swear (*ibid.* II. v. 36).

Japhet or **Japheth,** the third son of Noah and from Gen. x. 5 regarded as the ancestor of the Europeans. *The Golden Legend:* " Cham affryke, Iaphet all Europe." It is in the sense of the father of Europeans he is mentioned by Prince Henry.

PRIN. HEN. Nay, they will be kin to us, or they will fetch it from J. (*2 K. Hen. IV.*, II. ii. 129-30).

Jephah or **Jephthah,** Judge of Israel, went against the Ammonites to deliver Israel from them. Judg. xi. 31 relates that he vowed that if he had the victory " Then that thing that commeth out of the doores of my house against me, when I come in peace from the children of Ammon, shalbe the Lords, & I wil offer it vp for a whole burnt offring." *G* substantially agrees. His daughter, his only child, on his victorious return came dancing out of the door of his house to greet him and verse 39 relates that he " did with her according to his vowe which he had vowed." The name is spelt by Shakespeare as in the passages given, " Iephthah " in *B*, Iphtah in *G*. See Chapter V.

CLAR. To keep that oath were more impiety Than Jephah, when he sacrific'd his daughter (*3 K. Hen. VI.*, V. i. 90-1).

In *Hamlet*, II. ii. 431-40, allusion is made to a ballad called " Jepha Judge of Israel."

Jerusalem in *Revelation* symbolizes the Heavenly Kingdom. See Rev. xxi. 2: " And I Iohn saw the holy citie newe Hierusalem, come downe from God out of heauen, prepared as a bride garnished for her husband." 10: " And hee carried mee away in the spirite to a great and high mountaine, and hee shewed me the great citie holy Hierusalem, descending out of heauen from God." The page heading, both *G* and *B*, is " The heauenly Hierusalem " (in roman letter). It is in this last sense Q. Margaret refers to " sweet Jerusalem." As the abode of the blest " Jerusalem " was common.

Q. MAR. So part we sadly in this troublous world, To meet with joy in sweet J. (*3 K. Hen. VI.*, V. v. 7-8).

Jesu was a form of Jesus that occurred occasionally in the Bishops' Bible and in the Elizabethan Liturgy—*e.g.*, in the *Nicene Creed* : " and in one Lorde Iesu Christ." In this form it is found in *2 K. Hen. VI.*, V. i. 214 and *K. Rich. II.*, IV. i. 93, in both cases in conjunction with Christ. Shakespeare otherwise uses both Jesu and Jesus, but only in invocations and exclamations.

Jewry* was the form of Judæa as in the Liturgy and in all the Bibles except the Genevan. Thus, *L, Gospel* (Matt. ii.) for *Epiphany Sunday* : " When Iesus was borne in Bethlehem a city of Iury, in the tyme of Herode the kyng."
Shakespeare so used it, see *K. Rich. II.*, II. i. 55, "stubborn Jury"; *K. Hen. V.*, III. iii. 40, "wives of Jewry"; *Merry Wives*, II. i. 20, "Herod of Jurie." In *Ant. and Cleop.* "Jewry" is derived from North, the source for the play.

Jezabel or **Jezebel,** Ahab's queen, was remembered for her promotion of the worship of Baal and her persecution of the prophets of the Lord, and thus she came to figure in *Revelation* as the teacher of idolatry. See Rev. ii. 20: " that woman Iezabel, which called her selfe a prophetisse, to teach, and to deceiue my seruants, to make them commit fornication, and to eate meate sacrificed vnto idols." According to a Bezan note in the Tomson Testament, " By fornication, is oftentimes in the scripture Idolatrie meant." As Puritans accused the Latin Church of idolatry, " Jezebel " appears to have been a term applied to the Church of Rome by extremists.
Aguecheek might be supposed to have heard fanatics use the term in invective and his misapplication would cause amusement, especially as it was directed at Malvolio, himself suspected of being a kind of Puritan.
AGUE. Fie on him, J. ! (*Twelfth Night*, II. v. 47).

Job was slandered by Satan (Job i. 9-11, ii. 4-5), he was reduced to absolute poverty (i. 21), he was urged by his wife to curse God and die (ii. 9), but as in all his sufferings he did not sin with his lips, his patience became a proverb.
FALS. I am as poor as J., my lord, but not so patient (*2 K. Hen. IV.*, I. ii. 145-6). FORD. And one that is as

slanderous as Sathan ?   PAGE. And as poor as J.?   FORD.
And as wicked as his wife ? (*Merry Wives*, V. v. 167-9.)

This summary of the prologue of the Book of *Job* has
often excited comment. Satan the adversary occurs
in *Job* as the slanderous accuser and also elsewhere,
but the immediate reference to Job by Page would
indicate that it was Satan of the Book of *Job* that was
in Shakespeare's mind. The marginal note to Job ii. 9
in the Bishops' of 1568 and 1572 (the note was displaced
by a Genevan note in the 1585 edition) is: " A cruel
temptation of an euyl and vngodly wife."

Joshua, the successor of Moses, and a great soldier, mentioned
in *Love's L. L.*, V. i. 137-8, as one of the Nine Worthies,
three of whom, Joshua, David and Judas Maccabæus,
were Hebrews.

Judas Iscariot, the betrayer of Christ, was represented in
painting and tapestry as having red hair. Legend also
stated that he hanged himself on an elder. See also
Judean.

RICH. To say the truth, so J. kiss'd his Master, *And
cried " All Hail," when as he meant " All Harm "
(*3 K. Hen. VI.*, V. vii. 33-4).

Matt. xxvi. 49: " And forthwith when he came to
Iesus, he said, Haile master: & kissed him " (so also *R*
and *L*, *Gospel Sunday before Easter* ; *G*, " God saue thee,
Master ").   Mark xiv. 45 *T*: " Haile Master " (this is
the only version to give this rendering here).

BOYET. To make J. hang himself. HOL. Begin, sir, you
are my elder. BER. Well followed: J. was hanged on
an elder (*Love's L. L.*, V. ii. 605-7). BOYET. A light
for Monsieur J.! it grows dark, he may stumble (*ibid.*
630).

In allusion to its being night when Judas went out
to betray Christ. See John xiii. 30: " As soone then as
he had receiued the sop, hee went immediatly out: and
it was night."   Also xviii. 3: " Iudas then, after he had
receiued a band of men, & officers of the high priests
and Pharisees, commeth thither with lanternes, and
torches, and weapons."

See also *Love's L. L.*,* V. ii. 340-1, and V. ii. 597-603;
K. Rich. II., III. ii. 132; *As Y. L.*, III. iv. 7-9.

RICH. *Did they not sometime cry, "All Hail!" to me? So J. did to Christ: but he, in twelve, Found truth in all but one (*K. Rich. II.*, IV. i. 169-71).

For this emphasis on the truth of all but one *cf.* John xiii. 10: "ye are cleane, but not all," and *ibid.* 18: "I speake not of you all, I know whom I haue chosen: but that the scripture may be fulfilled, He that eateth bread with mee, hath lift vp his heele against me."

POLIX. O then, my best blood turn To an infected jelly, and my name Be yok'd with his, that did betray the Best (*Winter's Tale*, I. ii. 417-9). In allusion to Iscariot.

Judas Maccabæus, the heroic leader of the Jews against the power of Antiochus Epiphanes. Mentioned as one of the Nine Worthies in *Love's L. L.*, V. i. 138, V. ii. 596, etc.

Judean means a man of Judæa, which generally is taken to apply to the country formerly known as the Kingdom of Judah. In *Othello* Judas Iscariot is so called because he was the Judæan disciple, unlike the others, who were Galileans. See the note to Iscariot in the Tomson Testament at Matt. x. 4: "A man of Kerioth. Nowe Kerioth was in the tribe of Iudah, Iosh. 15. 25."

OTH. ... *of one whose hand, Like the base Judean, threw a pearl away Richer than all his tribe. ... I kiss'd thee, ere I kill'd thee (*Othello*, V. ii. 345-7, 357).

The kiss of Judas as a token of undoing was frequent (see Judas and *3 K. Hen. VI.*, *Love's L. L.*, and *As Y. L.*). See Chapter V., pages 90-2.

Laban, grandson of Nahor, Abraham's brother, and Jacob's maternal uncle, for whom Jacob grazed cattle and sheep. Is alluded to by Shylock with reference to the transaction to settle Jacob's remuneration. See Jacob.

Lazarus, the beggar in the Parable of Dives and Lazarus (Luke xvi. 19-31). He lived at the gate of Dives, full of sores which the dogs licked (*ibid.* 20-1). See *1 K. Hen. IV.*, IV. ii. 27-9.

Legion, the name professed by the unclean spirit in Mark v. 9: "for we are many." Hence applied to the hosts of fiends.

See *K. Rich. III.*, I. iv. 58-60; *K. Hen. V.*, II. ii. 124; *Twelfth Night*, III. iv. 96-8; *Tempest*, III. iii. 102-3.

Leviathan, a monster in the water identified in the Genevan and Bishops' as the whale, though treated in ordinary speech as a proper noun was not so in the Bible.   There are four references in the Bible to Leviathan: Job xli. 1, and Ps. civ. 26, and also in Ps. lxxiv. 15 and Isa. xxvii. 1. The most famous is Job xli. 1-4: " Canst thou drawe out Leuiathan with an hooke? . . . Will he make many faire words with thee, or flatter thee?   Will he make a couenant with thee? or wilt thou take him for a seruant for euer?"   The most popular is Ps. civ. 26: " There go the ships, and there is that Leviathan: whom thou hast made to take his pastime therein."

Since the Leviathan of Job xli. 1 appears to be a river monster, Shakespeare's allusions would be more appropriate to Ps. civ. 26, where it is definitely associated with the sea, but as in all cases contemporary Bibles treated the creature as a whale this may be discounted.   In *K. Hen. V.* its intractable character is emphasized in the spirit of Job xli.

PROT. Make tigers tame, and huge l's. Forsake unsounded deeps to dance on sands (*Two Gent. of Ver.*, III. ii. 80-1). OBER. . . . . and be thou here again Ere the L. can swim a league (*Midsummer-N. D.*, II. i. 173-4). K. HEN. As send precepts to the L. To come ashore (*K. Hen. V.*, III. iii. 26-7).

Lucifer, the morning star Venus, when it appears above the Eastern horizon before sunrise, is applied to the Babylonian Empire in Isa. xiv. 12.   See Chapter VI., page 100.

St. Jerome was no doubt assisted in his mistaken exegesis by Rev. ix. 1: " I sawe a starre fall from heauen vnto the earth: and to him was giuen the key of the bottomlesse pit."   On which Beza commented as in the Tomson: " By the bottomlesse pit, hee meaneth the deepest darkenesse of hell."

MALC. Angels are bright still, though the brightest fell (*Macbeth*, IV. iii. 22). WOLS. And when he falls, he falls like L., Never to hope again (*K. Hen. VIII.*, III. ii. 372-3).

See also *K. John*, IV. iii. 122; *1 K. Hen. IV.*, II. iv. 376; *2 K. Hen. IV.*, II. iv. 365-7; *K. Hen. V.*, IV. vii. 144-5; *Merry Wives*, I. iii. 81-2.

Mary, the Blessed Virgin, Mother of Christ. Alluded to by Gaunt (*K. Rich. II.*, II. i. 56): " Of the world's ransom blessed Mary's Son." Otherwise alluded to in *K. Hen. VIII.*, V. i. 154: " God's blest mother!" and by Joan of Arc in *1 K. Hen. VI.*, as " our Lady gracious " (I. ii. 74); as " God's mother " (*ibid.* 78); as " Christ's mother " (*ibid.* 106). In Act V. iv. 49-51 she compares herself with Our Lady.

> Joan of Arc hath been
> A virgin from her tender infancy,
> Chaste and immaculate in very thought.

Nabuchadnezar, King of Babylon, is said, according to Dan. iv. 33, to have been driven from men and to have eaten grass like oxen. This is the way Shakespeare spelt the name. " Nebuchadnezzar " in the *G* in *Daniel*. *B* in that book has " Nabuchodonosor."

CLOWN. I am no great N., sir, I have not much skill in grace (*All's Well*, IV. v. 21-2).

> The Clown is punning on " grass." *Cf.* " herb of grace " (l. 18). The pronunciation of " grace " and " grass " was almost identical.

Nazarite was the name given to a votary who separated himself for the service of God and he was supposed to act as stated in Num. vi. 2 *et seq.* Samson and John the Baptist were Nazarites. In the sense that these were Nazarites, Christ was not a Nazarite. The question then is, Did Shakespeare make a mistake in placing " Nazarite " in Shylock's mouth when he meant " man of Nazareth "? The answer is, No. All Tudor versions from Tindale to Rheims translated Matt. ii. 23 as: " He shall be called a Nazarite." The Authorised was the first to make a distinction and translate " Nazarene " for " man of Nazareth." Shylock used the only term that Bibles of the day gave for Christ in Matt. ii. 23. Shylock also was correct from his religious point of view in describing Christ as " Prophet."

SHY. . . . your Prophet the N. (*Merch. of Ven.*, I. iii. 35).

Noah, the Patriarch, whose experiences of the Flood are related in Gen. vii. and viii., was a very popular figure in religious plays.

See *Com. of Err.*, III. ii. 109-10; *Twelfth Night*, III. ii. 18-9.

Numbers, the fourth book of the Pentateuch, is the only Biblical book specifically mentioned, and then only in quotation from Holinshed.

CANT. For in the Book of N. is it writ (*K. Hen. V.*, I. ii. 98).

Persian. See *K. Lear*, III. vi. 84-6 and page 31.

Peter, the Apostle, to whom were given the keys of Heaven (Matt. xvi. 19) and who therefore is regarded as its gate-keeper.

BEAT. . . . and away to St. Peter for the heavens: he shows me where the bachelors sit (*Much Ado*, II. i. 50-2).

OTH. You mistress, That have the office opposite to Saint Peter And keep the gate of hell ! (*Othello*, IV. ii. 89-91).

For the " office opposite to St. Peter," see Rev. ix. 1-2.

Pharaoh, title of the Kings of Egypt. In Gen. xli. 3-4, it is related that Pharaoh dreamt that seven lean kine devoured seven fat kine, which Joseph divined to mean that the fat kine were good years and the lean kine bad years. A later Pharaoh that knew not Joseph (Exod. i. 8), in pursuing after the departing Israelites, was drowned in the midst of the Red Sea with all his soldiers (Exod. xiv. 9, 28).

FALS. If to be fat be to be hated, then P.'s lean kine are to be loved (*1 K. Hen. IV.*, II. iv. 526-8). BORACH. Sometime fashioning them like P.'s soldiers in the reechy painting (*Much Ado*, III. iii. 141-2).

Philip, the Evangelist, was one of the seven (who included St. Stephen) appointed to superintend the fair distribution of alms as between the Grecian and Hebrew disciples. About 18 or 19 years later he was the host of St. Paul and his companions at Cæsarea as related in Acts xxi. 8-9: " and we entred into the house of Philip the Euangelist (which was one of the seuen) and abode with him. And the same man had foure daughters, virgins, which did prophecie."

DAUPH. Nor yet St. Ph.'s daughters were like thee (*1 K. Hen. VI.*, I. ii. 143).

Pilate, Pontius Pilate, the fifth Roman Procurator of Judaea, washed his hands in assertion of his innocence of Christ's blood (Matt. xxvii. 24). Notwithstanding this, after he had scourged Jesus, he delivered him to be crucified (*ibid.* 26), and this dereliction of duty is emphasized by Richard as inexpiable in his indictment of his own judges.

2ND MURD. How fain, like P., would I wash my hands Of this most grievous guilty murder done ! (*K. Rich. III.* I. iv. 282-3). RICH. Though some of you with P. wash your hands Showing an outward pity, yet you P.s. Have here deliver'd me to my sour cross, And water cannot wash away your sin (*K. Rich. II.*, IV. i. 239-42). Also *K. Rich. II.*, III. i. 5-6.

Prodigal. The Parable of the Prodigal Son (Luke xv. 11-32) is the most frequently mentioned Parable of the Gospels in the plays. From the mention of " husks " (*1 K. Hen. IV.* and *As Y. L.*), instead of " cods " as in *B*, we may presume that Shakespeare was familiar with the story as related in the Genevan, although the Rheims also reads " husks."

GRAT. How like a younger or a Prodigal
The scarfed bark puts from her native bay,
Hugg'd and embraced by the strumpet wind !
How like the Prodigal doth she return
With overweather'd ribs and ragged sails,
Lean, rent, and beggar'd by the strumpet wind !
        (*Merch. of Ven.*, II. vi. 14-19.)

Note.—The alternative title for the " Prodigal " was the " younger," as the alternative for the good brother was the "elder." (See Luke xv. 12-3, 25.) [In this connection note Falstaff's " What ? will you make a younker of me ?" (*1 K. Hen. IV.*, III. iii. 90-1).] The Prodigal spent his living on harlots, hence the emphasis on " strumpet." Compare the paraphrase of the

19

Parable of the Builder (*2 K. Hen. IV.*, I. iii. 41-62)
and that of the Talents (*Meas. for Meas.*, I. i. 29-40).

For other references to the Prodigal see *Com. of Err.*,
IV. iii. 18; *Two Gent. of Ver.*, II. iii. 3-4; *1 K. Hen. IV.*,
IV. ii. 36-8*; *2 K. Hen. IV.*, II. i. 160-1; *As. Y. L.*,
I. i. 40-2*; *Merry Wives*, IV. v. 7-9; *Winter's Tale*,
IV. ii. 103-4.

Saba or **Sheba.** The Queen of Sheba, on account of her
journey to prove the wisdom of Solomon (1 Kings
x. 1-10), came to symbolize a delight in wisdom. Hence
the comparison of the infant Elizabeth with Sheba.

The name is spelt "Saba" in *B* and whilst in the
text of *G* it is spelt "Sheba" yet the Latin form occurs
in the page and chapter headings. *Cf.* also Ps. lxxii. 10:
"the kings of Arabia and Saba shall bring gifts."

CRAN. Saba was never More covetous of wisdom and fair
virtue Than this pure soul shall be (*K. Hen. VIII.*,
V. v. 24-6).

Salomon or **Solomon,** noted not only for his profound
wisdom and songs but also for the number of his wives,
to please whom he took to idolatry. See Ecclus. xlvii. 17:
"All landes marueyled at thy songs, prouerbes, simili-
tudes, and at thy interpretations." *Ibid.* 19: "Thou
wast moued in inordinate loue towarde women, and
wast ouercome in affection." 1 Kings iv. 32: "And
Solomon spake three thousande prouerbes: and his
songes were a thousand and fiue."

Spelt "Salomon" by Shakespeare as also in *G* and *L*;
B, "Solomon."

ARMAD. . . . yet was S. so seduced, and he had a very
good wit (*Love's L. L.*, I. ii. 183-4). BER. And profound
S. to tune a jig (*ibid.* IV. iii. 168). In reference to Solomon
as a maker of songs.

Samson, a Nazarite and famous for his physical strength;
his exploits are related Judg. xiii.-xvi. He carried off
the gates of Gaza, Judg. xvi. 3: "And Samson toke his
rest til midnight, and arose at midnight, & toke the dores
of the gate of the citie, & the two postes, and rent them
off, with the barre and all, and put them vpon his
shoulders, and caried them vp to the top of an hill."

He fell in love with Delilah (*ibid.* 4), who tried to worm his secret out of him and eventually succeeded.

MOTH. S., Master, he was a man of good carriage; great carriage; for he carried the town-gates on his back like a porter: and he was in love.

ARMAD. O well-knit S.! strong-jointed S.! I do excel thee in my rapier as much as thou didst me in carrying gates. I am in love too. Who was S.'s love, my dear Moth?

MOTH. A woman, Master.

ARMAD. Of what complexion?

MOTH. Of all the four, or the three, or the two, or one of the four.

ARMAD. Tell me precisely of what complexion?

MOTH. Of the sea-water green, sir.

ARMAD. Is that one of the four complexions?

MOTH. As I have read, sir, and the best of them too.

ARMAD. Green, indeed, is the colour of lovers: but to have a love of that colour, methinks S. had small reason for it. He surely affected her for her wit.

MOTH.* It was so, sir, for she had a green wit.

(*Love's L. L.*, I. ii. 75 *et seq.*)

Moth here plays on the green " with " with which S. was bound by Delilah. Judg. xvi. 8: " And then the lords of the Philistines brought her seuen withs that were yet greene, and neuer dried, and she bound him therewith " (*G* " cordes ").

ARMAD. There is no evil angel but Love, yet was S. so tempted, and he had an excellent strength (*ibid.* 181-3.)

MAN. I am not S., nor Sir Guy, nor Colbrand, To mow 'em down before me (*K. Hen. VIII.*, V. iv. 23-4).

In allusion to Samson's slaughter of 1,000 Philistines with the jaw-bone of an ass (Judg. xv. 15).

Sathan or **Satan,** the title of the Evil One as adversary or accuser. Thus Satan is he who slanders God to man or man to God with the object of setting them at variance. For this reason the reference in *Merry Wives* " as slanderous as S." is the most interesting of Shakespeare's references to Satan (see Job i. 9).

Shakespeare spells the name as " Sathan." The statement that thus it was spelt in no contemporary version of Scripture requires some modification in view

of the fact that " Sathan " is the spelling in Matt. iv.
in the *Gospel for the First Sunday in Lent* both in the First
Prayer Book of Edward VI. and the First of Elizabeth:
" Auoide Sathan." [1]

Satan is alluded to in the course of the plays not only
as Belzebub and Lucifer (q.v.) but also as the " Prince
of this world " (*All's Well*) and " Prince of darkness "
(*All's Well*).   Macbeth alludes to him as " adversary "
as " the common enemy of man."

ANT. SYR. *S., avoid ! I charge thee, tempt me not (*Com.
of Err.*, IV. iii. 47).

   L, Gospel, 1st Sunday in Lent, Matt. iv. 10: " Auoide
Sathan " (*G*, " Auoyde Sathan," as also *B*1; *B*2 reads
" Get thee hence behinde me, Satan "); *R*, " Auant
Satan ").   Compare *2 K. Hen. VI.*, I. iv. 43: " False
fiend, avoid !" also *Cymbeline*, I. i. 125: " Thou basest
thing, avoid ! hence, from my sight !"

PINCH. I charge thee, S., hous'd within this man (*Com.
of Err.*, IV. iv. 56).   Also see *1 K. Hen. IV.*, II. iv. 516;
Twelfth Night, III. iv. 131-2; IV. ii. 36-9; *Merry Wives*,
V. v. 167; *All's Well*, V. iii. 263-4.

[1] Note.   In the 1596 Genevan black letter quarto (the text
followed in this book) 'Sathan' occurs in Matt. iv. 10.
The normal Genevan spelling was Satan and the spelling
'Sathan' in Matt. iv. in the 1596 quarto is probably almost
unique.   The normal Genevan reading agrees with B1.

APPENDIX

INDEX OF BIBLICAL BOOKS AND CHAPTERS

VULGATE Titles of books where difficulty in identification might arise are given in brackets. The Vulgate numbering of Psalms differs from the Psalter's as from the 9th to the 148th. Where a chapter contains a relevant Prayer Book Gospel or Epistle, the fact is indicated by brackets wherein are stated the opening and concluding verses of such Gospel or Epistle.

*Sunday Morning Proper Lesson; ** Sunday Evening Proper Lesson; (Christmas Day and Good Friday reckoned as Sundays). In the same way † and †† denote Proper Lessons for Holy Days, and ‡ a chapter not appointed to be read at any time.

Lessons are noted as in Calendar in Bishops' 1572 Folio.

In this Index the following abbreviations for the names of plays are made:

Err	= Comedy of Errors.	Ado	= Much Ado About Nothing.
1H6	= 1 King Henry VI.		ing.
Jn	= King John.	Cæs	= Julius Cæsar.
Shr	= Taming of the Shrew.	As	= As You Like It.
2H6	= 2 King Henry VI.	Alls	= All's Well that Ends Well.
3H6	= 3 King Henry VI.	Ham	= Hamlet.
R3	= King Richard III.	TN	= Twelfth Night.
Titus	= Titus Andronicus.	Troil	= Troilus and Cressida.
TG	= Two Gentlemen of Verona.	Oth	= Othello.
		Meas	= Measure for Measure.
LLL	= Love's Labour's Lost.	Lear	= King Lear.
Rom	= Romeo and Juliet.	Mac	= Macbeth.
R2	= King Richard II.	Tim	= Timon of Athens.
MND	= A Midsummer-Night's Dream.	Ant	= Antony and Cleopatra.
		Cor	= Coriolanus.
Merch	= Merchant of Venice.	Cym	= Cymbeline.
1H4	= 1 King Henry IV.	Wint	= Winter's Tale.
2H4	= 2 King Henry IV.	Temp	= Tempest.
Wives	= Merry Wives of Windsor.	H8	= King Henry VIII.
H5	= King Henry V.		

The Acts are given in roman notation and scenes in arabic.
Thus 2H6, iii. 2 means *2 King Henry VI.*, Act III., Sc. 2.

GENESIS.

Chapter.	Plays.	Pages.
*i.	Err, ii. 1. Temp, i. 2. H8, iii. 2	107, 249, 257, 262
**ii.	Err, iv. 3. 2H6, iv. 2. LLL, iv. 2. R2, ii. 1; iii. 4. Ado, ii. 1. Ham, v. 1	144, 188, 262, 265, 266
*iii.	LLL, v. 2. 1H4, iii. 3. Ado, ii. 1; v. i. As, ii. 1. Oth, iv. 2	189, 219, 262, 266
iv.	1H6, i. 3; v. 4. Jn, iii. 4. R3, i. 2. Titus, iii. 1. LLL, iv. 2. R2, i. 1; v. 6. 2H4, i. 1. Ham, v. 1. H8, ii. 1	130, 139, 253, 261, 264
vii.	Err, iii. 2. Cæs, i. 2. As, v. 4. TN, iii. 2	23, 66, 191, 194 276
*ix.	Jn, iii. 4. R3, i. 3. Mac, iii. 4. Tim, iii. 5	117, 132, 236, 238
‡x.	2H4, ii. 2	104, 161, 270
xv.	Merch, i. 3	261
*xix.	R2, i. 2. Ado, ii. 1. As, v. 3. Alls, i. 3	151
xx.	H8, v. 3	256
xxi.	Merch, ii. 5	267
*xxvii.	1H6, i. 2. Merch, i, 3	109, 268
**xxviii.	Merch, i. 3	268
xxx.	1H6, v. 4. Merch, i. 3	59, 60, 113, 268
xxxi.	Merch, i. 3	60, 61, 268, 270
xxxii.	Merch, i. 3	269
xxxvii.	As, ii. 3. Cym, iii. 4	192, 245
xli.	1H4, ii. 4	276
**xlii.	2H6, ii. 3. TG, iii. 1	123, 141
xlvii.	1H6, ii. 5. R2, ii. 1. MND, i. 1. As, iii. 2, Oth, i. 3. Meas, ii. 1	111, 160, 199
xlix.	Jn, iii. 3. Oth, v. 2. Wint, i. 2	116, 220, 248

EXODUS.

*iii.	1H4, iii. 3	173
**x.	TN, iv. 2	265
*xii.	As, ii. 5	265
**xiv.	Ado, iii. 3. Alls, ii. 1	198, 276
xvi.	Merch, v. 1	169
xvii.	Alls, ii. 1	198
xx.	Jn. ii. 1. Shr, iii. 2. R3, i. 4. Merch, iii. 5. Meas, i. 2. Lear, iii. 4	86, 114, 119, 133, 166, 228

HOSEA.

Chapter.	Plays.	Pages.
vi.	2H4, iv. 4	35, 180
x.	Cor, iii. 1	241
xiii.	Titus, iv. 1	140

JOEL.

*ii.	Ham, iii. 4	205
(12-17)		
iii.	Jn, v. 2	117

AMOS.

ix.	2H6, v. 2. H5, iv. 1	127, 185

MICAH.

iv.	H8, v. 5	257
vii.	R3, v. 4. Lear, i. 2	138, 229

NAHUM.

iii.	Mac, iv. 3	235

HABBAKUK.

*ii.	Jn, ii. 4. Wint, v. 3	117, 248

ZECHARIAH.

i.	R2, ii. 2	62, 153
vii.	MND, i. 1	160
xiii.	2H6, ii. 2	123

1 ESDRAS (3 ESDRAS).

iv.	Troil, iv. 2. Meas, v. 1	216, 228

2 ESDRAS (4 ESDRAS).

vii.	Ham, v. 2	209

TOBIT.

v.	Merch, ii. 2	73, 164
viii.	H5, iii. 2	75, 185
x.	R2, iii. 2. Merch, ii. 2	63, 73, 154, 164

PHILIPPIANS.

Chapter.	Plays.	Pages.
i. (3-11)	H5, ii. 4; iv. 1	75, 88, 184, 186
ii.	2H4, iv. 2; iv. 5. Ado, ii. 3	179, 180, 189

COLOSSIANS.

iii. (1-7) (12-17)	LLL, i. 1. Oth, i. 2. Cym, ii. 3	143, 216, 244
iv.	1H4, i. 2	74, 171

1 THESSALONIANS.

iv. (1-8)	Oth, iv. 2	220
v.	R3, i. 3. TG, ii. 2	132, 141

2 THESSALONIANS.

iii.	2H6, iv. 2. 1H4, i. 2	125, 170

1 TIMOTHY.

ii.	R2, ii. 1. Lear, iii. 4	153, 230
iii.	H8, i. 3	253
vi.	R3, ii. 2. Ham, v. 2. Meas, iii. 1	135, 208, 227

2 TIMOTHY.

iv. (5-15)	R2, v. 1	157

TITUS.

ii.	Alls, i. 3	197

PHILEMON.

	H5, ii. 4	184

HEBREWS.

i. (1-11)	1H4, iii. 3. Ham, i. 4	173, 202
ii.	R2, iv. 1. H5, ii. 2. Cæs, ii. 2. Lear, iii. 4	156, 190, 230

Chapter.	Plays.	Pages.
‡xii. (7-12)	Mac, iii. 1	234
‡xiv. (1-5)	Ado, ii. 1	188
‡xvii.	H5, ii. 3	262
††xix.	1H6, i. 1. 2H6, v. 1. R3, i. 4; ii. 1. Ham, iv. 3	126, 206, 266
‡xx.	Err, iv. 3 Titus, v. 1	9, 108, 140
‡xxi.	3H6, v. 5. Meas, iii. 1. Ant, i. 1	228, 238, 270

GENERAL INDEX

DATE DUE

01 DE '78			
16 NO '79			
09 MY 80			
19 NU 82			
OC 2 1 '88			